Exploring Woodworking
Fundamentals of Technology

by

Fred W. Zimmerman
Professor Emeritus, Industrial Education and Technology
Western Illinois University

Larry J. McWard
Professor, Industrial Education and Technology
Western Illinois University

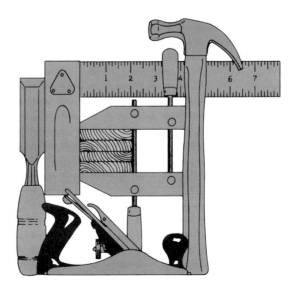

Publisher

The Goodheart-Willcox Company, Inc.

Tinley Park, Illinois

ABOUT THE AUTHORS

Fred W. Zimmerman is a Professor Emeritus from Western Illinois University in Macomb, Illinois. Fred has earned several degrees, including a Bachelor of Science degree from Southern Illinois University, a Master of Science degree from Kent State University, and a Doctorate in Industrial Education from Bradley University in Peoria, Illinois. He has had extensive experience as both an instructor and woodworker, and has been active in the Illinois Vocational Industrial Clubs of America as a judge in the cabinetmaking and millwork contest. Fred is a member of the Illinois Woodworking Teachers Association and is a Life Member of the International Industrial Education Association. In addition to *Exploring Woodworking*, Fred is also the author of *Upholstery Methods* published by Goodheart-Willcox.

Larry J. McWard is a professor in the Industrial Education and Technology department at Western Illinois University. He has earned several degrees, including a Bachelor of Science degree in Industrial Education and Vocational Education, and a Master of Science degree in Instructional Technology (Media) from Southern Illinois University. He has also earned a Doctorate in Vocational-Technical Education from The Ohio State University. Larry's work experience includes 20 years of teaching experience at the junior high, high school, and university levels. Courses taught include vocational building trades and cabinetmaking. Larry also has 12 years of work experience as a carpenter, cabinetmaker, and general contractor. Larry is actively involved in the National Association of Industrial and Technical Teachers Educators, American Vocational Association, and is past-president of the Illinois Woodworking Teachers Association.

SAFETY NOTICE

Operating procedures and shop practices described in this book are effective methods of performing given operations. Use tools and equipment as recommended; carefully follow all safety warnings and cautions.

Copyright 1999

by

THE GOODHEART-WILLCOX CO., INC.

Previous Editions Copyright 1993, 1991, 1981, 1979, 1976, 1972

Library of Congress Catalog Number 98-23072
International Standard Book Number 1-56637-484-7

4 5 6 7 8 9 10   99   02

Library of Congress Cataloging-in-Publication Data

Zimmerman, Fred W.
Exploring woodworking: fundamentals of technology / by Fred W. Zimmerman, Larry J. McWard.

p. cm.
Includes index.
ISBN 1-56637-484-7
1. Woodwork (Manual training) I. McWard, Larry J. II. Title.
TT180.Z54 1999
684'.08—dc21   98-23072
                                                       CIP

INTRODUCTION

EXPLORING WOODWORKING is designed to assist you in learning the fundamentals of working safely and efficiently with hand tools and power tools. In addition, the book acquaints you with the different types of woods and their uses. It also introduces you to the industrial woodworking environment, and describes the technology in use today.

Information included in EXPLORING WOODWORKING is presented in an easy-to-understand format. New terms are capitalized and then are immediately defined. This allows you to be introduced to a new term in context, resulting in the best understanding of the material being presented. Safety is highlighted using a predominant second color. This enables you to easily locate important information regarding the care and safe operation of tools and equipment.

Color is used throughout the book to clarify details and highlight important parts of drawings. Color photographs are used to show you the natural colors of various woods, and to enhance the appearance of new tools and equipment.

The contents of this book are presented in an orderly and organized manner. Information regarding the characteristics of wood, product planning, and safety are first presented. Layout tools are then described, followed by sawing, drilling, and planing tools. Information about manual and machine operations for sawing tools and planing tools is presented in separate chapters. This allows the information to be presented thoroughly, without omitting important details. Chapters presenting information on automated manufacturing, entrepreneurship, and careers are also included in this book. Many operations that occur in an industrial setting are different than those that occur in a woods laboratory. However, the theory and principles of operation remain the same.

The final chapter of EXPLORING WOODWORKING provides construction details of carefully selected products. Alternative designs and design variations are also shown to allow you to customize your products.

EXPLORING WOODWORKING emphasizes the important role that wood and wood by-products play in our everyday lives. Wood is also a vital part of our future. Improved technology, conservation, and recycling will be critical in ensuring an adequate supply of wood for the future.

Fred W. Zimmerman
Larry J. McWard

CONTENTS

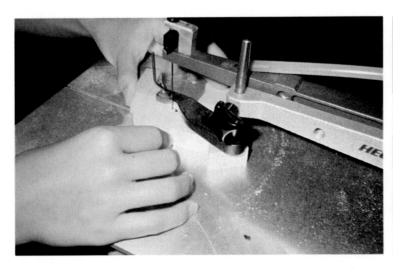 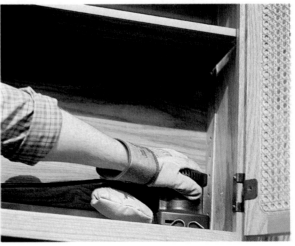

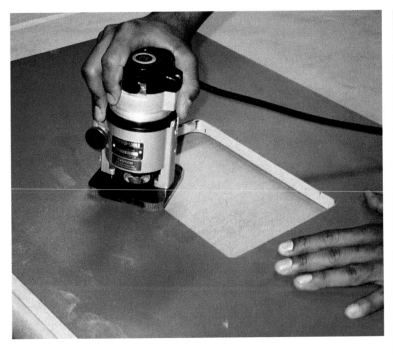

ACKNOWLEDGEMENTS

The authors would like to thank the following companies for their contributions in the form of photographs and other technical information.

Accu-Router, Inc.
Advanced Machinery Imports, LTD.
American Plywood Association
Bekenmar Church Furniture
Black and Decker
Capital Machines International Corp.
Michael J. Cognetti
Delta International Machinery Corp.
DeVilbiss
Fisher Hill Studios Inc.
Frank Paxton Lumber Company
Georgia-Pacific
Hoge Lumber Company
James Machinery, Inc.
LeHigh-Leopold Furniture Co.
Light Machines Corporation
Mannhardt Refinishing

John and Ellen Melton
Miller Falls Company
George W. Mount, Inc.
National Forest Products Association
Plants, Gifts, Etc.
Porter-Cable Corporation
Powermatic-Houdaille, Inc.
Skil Corporation
Southern Forest Product Association
Stanley Tools
Vega Enterprises, Inc.
John Walker
Warrensburg Cabinet Shop
Western Wood Plywood Association
Weyerhauser
Woodworker's Supply of New Mexico

Unit 1

WOODS

This unit discusses the development of the forest industry. After studying this unit, you will be able to identify the basic parts of a tree, and how these parts function together to form usable wood. You will understand the basic classifications of wood and be able to identify common defects. In addition, you will be able to list and recognize different kinds of sheet stock manufactured from wood and wood products.

As a result of continuing lumber industry research, conservation, and a rapidly changing woods technology, the lumber industry is able to provide a larger quantity and a greater variety of wood species. Today, our lumber industry grows more wood every year than is used in both the construction and the furniture-making industries. This is only possible through planned forestry techniques. Even though a large amount of wood is lost through fire, disease, and insects, more wood is being produced than used. This overproduction allows for affordable lumber in the United States. In addition, a large quantity of logs and lumber are exported to other countries.

Good lumber production techniques have not always been used. The process of replanting small seedling trees as the mature trees are harvested, or REFORESTATION, is a slow process. Most trees require 20 or more years of growth before harvesting. Hardwoods require even more time to grow, often 50 to 75 years. In the past, many lumber companies only harvested the trees and did not consider the damage to the environment and ecology. This technique resulted in erosion, the rapid depletion of forests, and the loss of an acceptable setting for many species of animals and plants. Today,

studies are made to determine the ecological effects before any major harvesting occurs. Methods that result in minimal damage to soils, plants, and animals have been developed and are now commonly used.

STRUCTURE AND GROWTH OF WOOD

Wood is composed of many very small cellulose fiber units called CELLS. These cells are held together with a natural adhesive made by the tree itself called LIGNIN. A typical wood sample is composed of 70% cellulose, 12 to 28% lignin, and up to 1% ash-producing materials. This make-up, while causing wood to be HYGROSCOPIC (expanding as it absorbs moisture and shrinking as it dries), is also responsible for its decay and its strength. In addition, the grain pattern and all other properties of the wood are determined by the way these cells are formed and grouped together.

Tree growth is unique because all new wood is formed from the perimeter of the tree outward and from last year's growth upward. New wood cells are formed in the CAMBIUM LAYER which is near the bark. The inside of this layer forms new wood cells and the outside forms new bark cells. In the spring when the year's growth begins, the wood fibers are larger with thin walls, large open centers, and light colored. This early growth is called SPRINGWOOD. Fibers that grow later in the season are smaller and stronger. They have thicker cell walls, smaller openings, and are darker colored. This later growth is called SUMMERWOOD. The summerwood forms on the outer side of the springwood. Each band of springwood and summerwood results in one year's growth called an ANNUAL RING. The age of a tree may be determined by counting the annual rings, Fig. 1-1. An exception to this concept is in the tropics, where growth is almost continuous. Annual rings are much less apparent or do not appear.

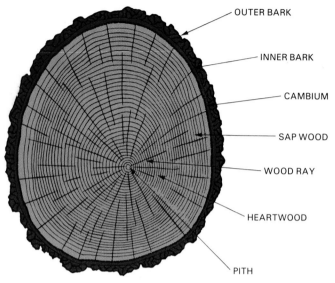

Fig. 1-1. Cross section of a tree trunk.
(Frank Paxton Lumber Co.)

OUTER BARK
INNER BARK
CAMBIUM
SAP WOOD
WOOD RAY
HEARTWOOD
PITH

The wood nearest the bark of a tree, or SAPWOOD, contains living cells. As the sapwood becomes inactive it gradually changes into heartwood. HEARTWOOD is usually darker in color because of the presence of gums and resins. MEDULLARY RAYS are rows of cells that run perpendicular (at right angles) to the annual rings toward the PITH (center of the tree). The medullary rays carry sap to the center of the tree. These rays are large in oak, beech, and sycamore and small in most other woods.

While a tree is growing upward and outward it is also growing downward. The downward growth of a tree is its root system. The ROOT SYSTEM provides the necessary support that prevents a tree from falling over. The root system also provides a means of transporting water and other nutrients from the ground to the leaves.

CLASSIFICATION AND IDENTIFICATION OF WOOD

There are several hundred species of trees in the United States. Most of the lumber used in construction and furniture making comes from about 35 species. The other species do not have the qualities necessary for commercial purposes.

Trees and lumber can be divided into two main classes, softwood and hardwood. SOFTWOODS come from cone-bearing trees. Softwood trees also have needles, and are frequently referred to as evergreens. Another name for evergreen trees is CONIFERS meaning "cone bearing." Examples of conifers are pine, fir,

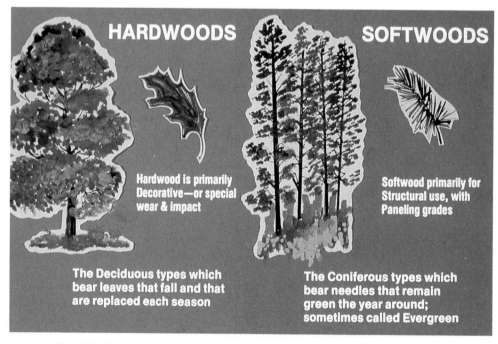

HARDWOODS

Hardwood is primarily Decorative—or special wear & impact

The Deciduous types which bear leaves that fall and that are replaced each season

SOFTWOODS

Softwood primarily for Structural use, with Paneling grades

The Coniferous types which bear needles that remain green the year around; sometimes called Evergreen

Fig. 1-2. Trees and woods can be classified as hardwoods or softwoods.
(National Forest Products Association)

spruce, cedar, redwood, and cypress. HARD-WOODS come from broad-leaf trees that shed or lose their leaves every year. See Fig. 1-2. DECIDUOUS is a term given to hardwood trees. Oak, walnut, birch, maple, hickory, ash, and poplar are examples of deciduous trees. The terms "softwood" and "hardwood" do not refer to the actual hardness or softness of the wood.

Softwoods and hardwoods can also be divided into the general classifications of OPEN-GRAINED (porous) or CLOSE-GRAINED (nonporous) woods. When lumber is cut at the mill, the cells that come into contact with the saw or planer are cut or sliced, leaving small openings at the surface called PORES. Lumber with large cells form open-grained woods. Lumber with small cells form close-grained woods. Most broad-leaf trees produce open-grained lumber, but not all. Examples of open-grained lumber are oak, walnut, and mahogany. Close-grained woods include pine, birch, gum, maple, basswood, and fir. Determining whether the wood is open grained or close-grained is easy. Open-grained wood is porous; the pores are easy to see using a magnifying glass. In close-grained wood, the pores are not as readily seen.

LUMBERING AND REFORESTATION

The lumber industry is an important contributor to our nation's economy. There are currently about 7000 active saw mills, 5000 wholesalers, and over 28,000 retail lumber yards in the United States. Nearly 750,000 people are employed in all aspects of the lumber industry.

The lumber industry uses two distinct methods of harvesting trees for lumber production-clear cutting and selective cutting. In the CLEAR CUTTING process, all the trees in a given area are harvested at one time. When this area has been harvested, seedling trees are then planted. These seedlings are then cared for until they are mature and ready for harvesting. This method is primarily used for softwoods due to their rapid growth and the method of milling being used.

SELECTIVE CUTTING is commonly used for furniture-grade lumber. It generally includes hardwoods and certain softwoods, such as redwood and Ponderosa pine. The reforestation procedure for selective harvesting is quite different from clear cutting. Fewer seedlings are planted when selective cutting, and the planting is not in "rows" as with the clear cutting process. Selective cutting increases the risk to surrounding trees that may not be ready for harvesting. In addition, it is more expensive to FELL (cut standing trees) trees when selective cutting. A benefit of selective cutting, however, is that it is less disruptive to the ecology.

Scientific forest management includes proper cutting, planting, and forest fire prevention, as well as disease and pest control. Millions of hardy seedlings are grown in tree farm nurseries where they reach a good start before they are transplanted into forest areas, Fig. 1-3. Currently, forestry practice replants small nursery trees shortly after the last log is removed from an area. The sound forest management now being practiced will ensure a continuous supply of wood for generations to come.

Fig. 1-3. Tree farm nursery. (Weyerhauser)

LUMBER MANUFACTURING PROCESS

When logs arrive at the sawmill they are stored in large piles or in ponds until they are ready to be cut into lumber. Storing the logs in water prevents end checking, washes off dirt, and allows easy sorting into sizes and qualities. Logs are usually pulled lengthwise into the mill by a chain device called a JACK-LADDER (bull-chain). Jets of water are used to remove any remaining mud and grit as the log is moved into position.

Fig. 1-4. The bark must be removed before the tree is sawed into lumber. (Southern Forest Products Association)

The bark is removed after the log is pulled inside the sawmill, Fig. 1-4. The logs are then placed onto a carriage that moves past a stationary saw blade. See Fig. 1-5. The operator of this carriage/saw machine is called a SAWYER. The sawyer quickly looks at the log to determine the cuts needed to receive the most usable lumber with the least amount of waste in the shortest period of time. Today, automation has been integrated into even the smallest sawmills. This allows the sawyer to "saw" more logs into lumber more efficiently than ever. When the most efficient cuts have been determined, the HEAD-SAW cuts a slab from a log. The slab is rapidly transported to the TRIMMER SAWS where several saws cut the slice into desired lengths. Each of these trimmer saws may be raised or lowered independently so that boards can be trimmed to the exact lengths required, Fig. 1-6. Other saws are then used to cut the boards to desired widths.

The manner in which the headsaw cuts through the log determines much of the appearance and strength of the resulting lumber. There are various methods of cutting logs into lumber. The most common method is PLAIN, or FLAT SAWING, where the saw blade cuts tangent (at an angle) to the annual rings. This method is the

Fig. 1-5. The head sawyer cutting a log into huge slabs. (Western Wood Plywood Association)

Fig. 1-6. Trimmer saws cut the slab into desired lengths. Each trimmer saw can be raised and lowered as needed.

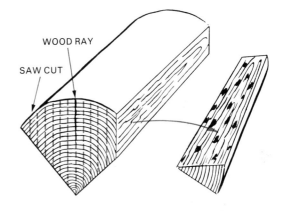

QUARTERSAWED

Fig. 1-8. Quartersawed lumber has a better grain pattern than flat sawed lumber.

Freshly sawed lumber is referred to as ROUGH because it has not been planed or surfaced to the final thickness. Rough hardwood lumber is carried from the mill to a sorting shed where it is graded and sorted. Rough softwood lumber is sorted, but it is not graded until after it has been planed and dried, Fig. 1-9. In order for lumber to be usable for construction or furniture making, it must first be SEASONED. This means the excess moisture in the wood cells must be removed.

most economical because of its low waste and speed. See Fig. 1-7. Another method of cutting logs into lumber is QUARTER SAWING. This sawing process cuts parallel to the wood rays. It is more wasteful and time-consuming, but the resulting lumber warps and checks less. Quarter-sawn lumber is desirable for furniture making because of the exposed FIGURE (grain pattern). See Fig. 1-8.

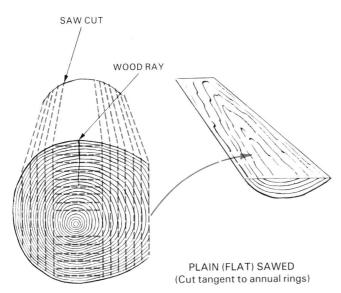

SAW CUT

WOOD RAY

PLAIN (FLAT) SAWED
(Cut tangent to annual rings)

Fig. 1-7. Plain or flat sawed lumber produces less waste.

Fig. 1-9. Rough softwood lumber is planed and dried before it is sorted.

MOISTURE CONTENT, SHRINKING, SWELLING

Wood, like most fibrous materials, shrinks as it loses moisture and swells as it absorbs moisture. This characteristic is called hygroscopic. Excess moisture must be removed from GREENWOOD (freshly cut unseasoned wood) by drying or seasoning it.

The moisture content (M.C.) of lumber is expressed as a percentage. It represents a comparison of the amount of moisture in a wood sample to that of a totally dry sample. Before lumber is seasoned, it may contain a M.C. ranging from 30% to as high as 200% or more. Moisture is found in two forms within a board. First, moisture is contained *in* the cell cavities or pores. This moisture is called FREE WATER. The other form, ABSORBED WATER, is the moisture found in the cell walls or fibers. See Fig. 1-10. The FIBER SATURATION POINT is when the cell walls have absorbed their maximum amount of water. Any additional moisture would be stored *in* the cell cavities as free water.

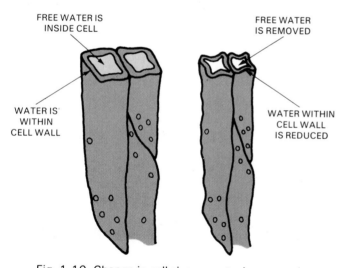

FREE WATER IS INSIDE CELL

FREE WATER IS REMOVED

WATER IS WITHIN CELL WALL

WATER WITHIN CELL WALL IS REDUCED

Fig. 1-10. Change in cell size as water is removed.

The fiber saturation point is critical to wood's hygroscopic characteristic. No substantial size change occurs until the water in the cell walls (fiber) is reduced. It is easy to begin understanding the basic expansion and contraction properties of wood by considering the structure of a typical wood cell with the hygroscopic effect. This expansion and contraction directly influences design, joinery, adhesives, and the application of finishes.

Expansion and contraction of a board is from 0% M.C. to the fiber saturation point, typically 30% M.C. Wood changes size about 3.3% (1/30) of the maximum possible expansion for each percentage point of moisture change. A slight change in M.C. can cause sticking drawers or doors, and splits in wood with an inadequate finish or that have been improperly glued or fastened.

Hardwoods are typically used in furniture making. They are dried to a M.C. ranging from 6 to 12 percent. Softwoods used in home construction are dried to only about 19% M.C. It has been found that decay resistance can be achieved at 20% M.C. or less and that best conditions for decay occur at 25% or higher M.C.

Seasoning may be done naturally, allowing moisture to evaporate. The lumber is stacked with small strips of wood between each new piece of lumber, allowing the air to pass around it. This is called AIR-DRYING. Air-drying is done outdoors where the sun and wind slowly reduce the moisture content to about 18 to 20 percent. Often air-dried lumber is stored in a well-ventilated shed.

Air-drying is inexpensive, but time consuming. Lumber resulting from air-drying is less desirable because the moisture removal was uncontrolled. Warping and twisting occur more often. The amount of moisture from one piece of lumber to another varies. In addition, the M.C. from one end of a board to the other also varies. Gluing and finishing air-dried lumber also present problems.

KILN-DRYING is another method used for seasoning lumber. This process uses controlled heat to remove excess moisture. The rate of moisture removal is monitored. The lumber resulting from kiln-drying meets predetermined requirements. Kiln-drying is done by placing the lumber in a large oven called a KILN at temperatures usually ranging from 110 to 180 degrees Fahrenheit (F), Fig. 1-11. Humidity, air circulation, and air temperature are carefully controlled. Kiln-dried lumber has less moisture content than air-dried lumber. Lumber is often dried to 6% or less M.C. using the kiln. During the drying process, shrinking begins to occur when the free water is removed. Since there is little or no change in the size of a board until it reaches an M.C.

Fig. 1-11. Kiln-drying provides better humidity, air circulation, and temperature control. (Hoge Lumber Company)

of about 30%, lumber is often air dried to this point. After reaching 30% M.C., the lumber is then moved into the kiln when heat and air flow are carefully monitored. When the desired M.C. is achieved, the wood is removed.

All woods have a tendency to reach a balance in moisture content with the surrounding air after drying. This is called the EQUILIBRIUM MOISTURE CONTENT. The equilibrium moisture content varies from 6 to 12 percent M.C. Wood actually gets larger as it absorbs moisture and smaller as it loses moisture. Most size change takes place across the grain of the wood. A board may vary 4 percent or more in dimension across the grain. There is less change in thickness than in width, and almost no change in length. Kiln-dried lumber usually has less change in its dimensions resulting from differences in the moisture content. This is one reason for using kiln-dried lumber for furniture and cabinetmaking.

DEFECTS

Defects in wood may be roughly classified into two large groups—those occurring naturally during the growth of the tree, and those occurring after felling. Natural defects include physical damage such as abrasions, fire damage,

insect and animal damage, and growth defects. Growth defects includes common defects, such as knots, shakes, and pitch pockets, Fig. 1-12. Embedded branches and limbs result in KNOTS that weaken the strength of a board. Knots are usually considered to be undesirable. A SHAKE is a grain separation that runs parallel to the annual rings of a board or log. Shakes seldom develop after the tree is cut. The PITCH POCKET is also a grain separation that occurs along the

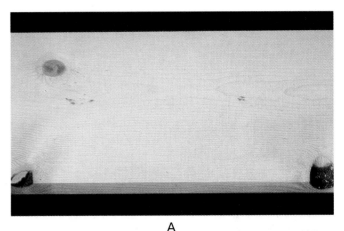

A

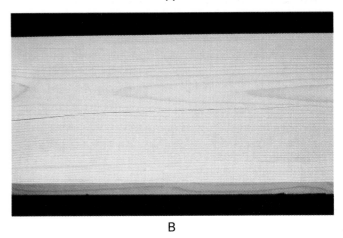

B

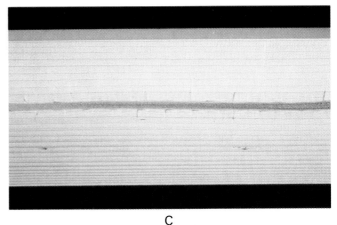

C

Fig. 1-12. Natural defects in lumber. A–Knots. B–Shakes. C–Pitch pockets.

annual rings. It may contain solid or liquid resin. Pitch pockets are commonly found in softwoods, such as Douglas fir and pines.

Some of the defects that occur after a tree is felled are the result of the log losing its high moisture content. Others are a direct result of the failure to properly control the wood. Wood that is dried too fast or improperly stored often warps or develops other defects. WARPING is considered to be the change in a board from a true surface. See Fig. 1-13. Warping includes CUP (curved across the grain), BOW (surface curved lengthwise), CROOK (edge curved lengthwise), and TWIST or WIND (both surfaces and edges curved lengthwise). Small cracks or separations in the end grain of a board that are at right angles to the annual rings are called CHECKS, as shown in Fig. 1-14. Those that are along or parallel to the annual rings are called SHAKES. CRACKS or SPLITS are separations at the end of a board.

GRADING

LUMBER GRADING is the term applied to evaluating the quality and usability of a board. The following features are taken into account when

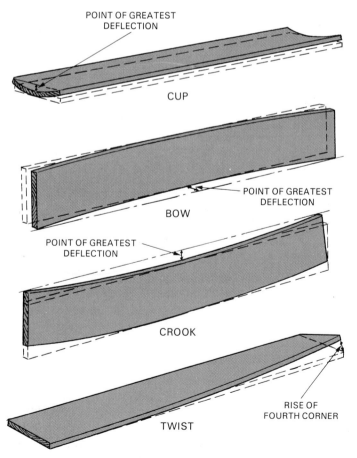

Fig. 1-13. Types of warp.

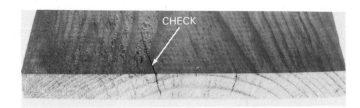

Fig. 1-14. Checks in a flat-grain board.

judging the quality of a board: size and number of defects; number and size of clear pieces remaining after the defects have been removed; and overall width and length of the board.

Grading rules, called STANDARDS, vary for hardwoods and softwoods. Softwoods are graded by looking at the best face of a board after surfacing. The grade is then stamped on the face. Hardwoods are graded by looking at the poorer face of a rough board prior to surfacing. The grade is then marked on the edge.

SOFTWOOD GRADING

Softwoods can be divided into three forms: method of manufacture, species, and grade. Softwood lumber is broadly classified as rough, surfaced, or worked. ROUGH LUMBER is sawn, trimmed to length, and edged. The faces show the saw marks. SURFACED LUMBER has been smoothed. Surfaced lumber is further broken down by the number of surfaces that have been smoothed. Surfaced lumber that has been matched according to grain pattern is WORKED LUMBER.

Softwoods can also be classified as shop and factory lumber or yard lumber. SHOP AND FACTORY LUMBER is milled for special applications such as molding. YARD LUMBER is classified as boards, dimensional, and timbers. BOARDS are pieces less than 2 inches in nominal thickness and are usually 4 to 12 inches in width. DIMENSIONAL LUMBER is from 2 to 5 inches thick and commonly 4 to 12 inches in width. TIMBERS have a width and thickness exceeding 5 inches.

Yard lumber is commonly available in retail lumber yards. It is divided into select (finish) grades, common (utility) grades, and dimensional grades. SELECT GRADES range from A through D, with the best grades being B and better. Select grades are used for siding, partitions, and finish flooring. COMMON GRADES range from #1 through #5. They are used for general building such as sheathing and subflooring. DIMENSIONAL GRADES are used for framing and applications where additional strength is required.

Softwoods are usually surfaced on four sides to finished dimensions (S4S). They are available in a variety of standard finished dimensions, Fig. 1-15. Standard lengths for softwoods range from 6 to 20 feet in 2-foot intervals.

STANDARD THICKNESS AND WIDTH OF SOFTWOOD LUMBER (Dimensions in Inches)			
Rough (Nominal)	S4S (Dry)	Rough (Nominal)	S4S (Dry)
1 x 2	3/4 x 1 1/2	2 x 2	1 1/2 x 1 1/2
1 x 4	3/4 x 3 1/2	2 x 4	1 1/2 x 3 1/2
1 x 6	3/4 x 5 1/2	2 x 6	1 1/2 x 5 1/2
1 x 8	3/4 x 7 1/4	2 x 8	1 1/2 x 7 1/4
1 x 10	3/4 x 9 1/4	2 x 10	1 1/2 x 9 1/4
1 x 12	3/4 x 11 1/4	4 x 4	3 1/2 x 3 1/2

Fig. 1-15. Standard thickness and widths of softwood lumber.

HARDWOOD GRADING

Hardwoods are graded according to minimum sizes and the percentage of clear surface cuttings that can be made. FIRSTS AND SECONDS (FAS) is the best grade of hardwoods. They must yield about 85 percent clear cuttings. Minimum board size for FAS lumber is 6 inches and wider by 8 feet and longer. NUMBER 1 COMMON is the lowest grade of hardwoods. This grade permits smaller board size with about 65 percent clear cuttings.

Standard dimensions for hardwood are given in thickness only. See Fig. 1-16. Hardwoods are sold in random widths and lengths (RW&L). Hardwoods are used for furniture and cabinetmaking, where maximum yield of material can be obtained using a variety of widths and lengths. In addition, hardwoods may be purchased ROUGH (RGH) or SURFACED

ON BOTH SIDES (S2S). Although hardwoods are normally sold as rough, some retailers may surface and edge trim hardwood stock.

VENEER AND PLYWOOD

More and more products are being produced using veneers. Many products have a core that is composed of wood byproducts. These products are then covered with veneer to give them an appearance of "solid wood."

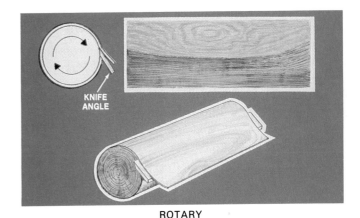

ROTARY

FLAT SLICED

STANDARD THICKNESS OF SURFACED HARDWOOD LUMBER (Dimensions in Inches)			
Rough	S2S	Rough	S2S
3/8	3/16	1 1/2	1 5/16
1/2	5/16	2	1 3/4
5/8	7/16	2 1/2	2 1/4
3/4	9/16	3	2 3/4
1	25/32	3 1/2	3 1/4
1 1/4	1 1/16	4	3 3/4

Fig. 1-16. Standard thickness of surfaced hardwood lumber.

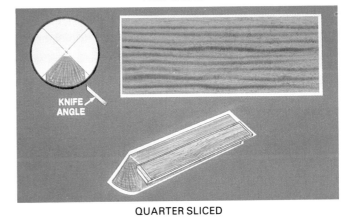

QUARTER SLICED

Fig. 1-17. Methods of producing veneer. (National Forest Products Association)

VENEER

VENEER is a thin sheet of wood that is peeled or sliced from a log with a knife-like device rather than with a saw. The thickness of veneer ranges from 1/100 to 1/4 inch. Veneer is made by ROTARY CUTTING, FLAT SLICING, or QUARTER SLICING, Fig. 1-17.

Veneer produced using rotary cutting has a rippled or marble-like grain pattern. The grain pattern tends to be spread out. A more even and tighter grain pattern is preferred for furniture making. Fig. 1-18 shows a continuous sheet of veneer being produced using rotary slicing. Flat slicing is commonly used for hardwoods. The grain pattern is more even than that produced by rotary cutting. Quarter slicing produces a striped grain pattern. The grain lines may be straight or slightly wavy.

Veneers with grain designs for a variety of uses may be obtained by using the right kind of wood and the correct method of cutting. Decorative and exotic grain designs are found in some woods by cutting veneer from the tree crotch, burl, and stump, Fig. 1-19.

PLYWOOD

PLYWOOD is a wood product made of veneers bonded to a core of crossbanded veneers,

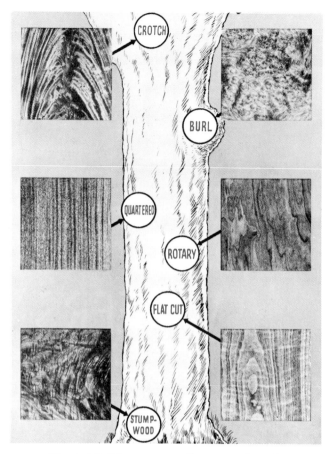

Fig. 1-19. Where veneer figures are found.

solid lumber, or composite materials, Fig. 1-20. The grain of the outside veneers (face and back) run the same direction. When the core consists of crossbanded veneers, it is called PLYCORE.

Fig. 1-18. Rotary cutting a continuous sheet of veneer.

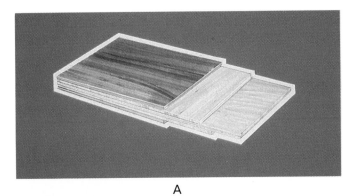

A

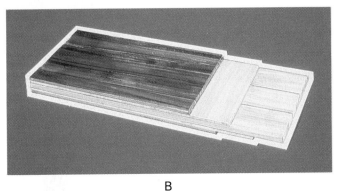

B

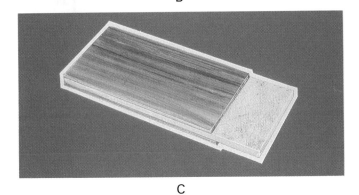

C

Fig. 1-20. Plywood cores are made of various materials. A–Plycore. B–Lumber core. C–Composition core. (National Forest Products Association)

In plycore plywood, an odd number (3, 5, 7, etc.) of layers, or PLIES, of veneer are used. The plies of the crossbanded veneers are at right angles to each other. When solid boards are laid side-by-side to make up the core, it is called LUMBER CORE. A crossbanded veneer is placed on each side of the lumber core and a face and back veneer are attached. When the core is made up of composite materials, such as scrap wood chips or pressed paper, it is called COMPOSITION CORE or MINERAL CORE.

Plywood is generally available in standard-size sheets measuring 4 feet wide and 8 feet long. Plywood may be classified several ways depending upon its use. SOFTWOOD PLYWOOD is

primarily used in construction for sheathing or subflooring. It complies with established standards, U.S. Product Standard PS1-83, for appearance, strength, dimensions, type of adhesive used, and classification of wood species. The two factors a consumer is normally concerned with are glue type and grade designation. Adhesives (glues) used to bond the plies together are either exterior (waterproof) or interior (moisture resistant). See Fig. 1-21.

Fig. 1-21. Unloading plywood panels from the gluing press. (American Plywood Association)

There are five grades of veneers used in construction plywood–A, B, C, D, and N. The A grade has the best appearance and D grade has the poorest appearance. The N grade is applied only to special-order plywood. Typically, the grade will be stamped on the poorer of the two faces using two letters. The first letter represents the best face and the second letter represents the poorer face.

Fir plywood is the most common type of construction plywood. It is available in standard thicknesses of 1/4, 3/8, 1/2, 5/8, and 3/4 inch. These sizes are nominal–actual thickness is 1/32 inch less. The plywood may be sanded on both sides. Plywood used for sheathing or subflooring is not normally sanded.

HARDWOOD PLYWOOD, frequently referred to as decorative plywood, does not comply with the U.S. Product Standard. It is mill stamped on the edge, not the face. Grade and glue requirements are not universally applicable as each mill sets its own standards. Generally, 1/28-inch veneer is adhered to both faces of a variety of cores. Currently, a composition core that looks much like compressed paper is very popular among cabinet shops.

MANUFACTURED PANELS

Manufactured panels, such as hardboard and particleboard, have gained wide acceptance in the furniture and cabinetmaking industries. This allows the industry to use large panels without edge gluing several smaller pieces of stock. Manufactured panels are DIMENSIONALLY STABLE, meaning that changes in humidity have little effect on their size. Typically, the initial cost of a manufactured panel is less than the cost of individual pieces glued together. One of the best reasons for using manufactured panels is that scrap and waste stock is used to manufacture the panels. This helps to conserve the raw materials and energy used to produce solid stock.

HARDBOARD

HARDBOARD is made by breaking wood chips into individual fibers, arranging them into a mat, and compressing this mat with heavy rollers. Lengths of mat (wetlap) are fed into multiple presses where heat and pressure form the fibers into a hard, thin, dry sheet. The fibers are held together with wood's natural adhesive called lignin. When hardboard is saturated with oils and resins, it is called TEMPERED HARDBOARD. Tempered hardboard is more dense and water repellent than standard hardboard. This is because the fibers are packed more closely together. Hardboard is widely used for underlayment. It is also used for paneling after a thin layer of wood-like material has been added to the surface.

PARTICLEBOARD

Particleboard production begins with planer shavings, wood chips, and logs. Milling equipment produces wood chips that are separated into desired sizes. Dryers then remove the excess moisture from the chips, and resins and binders are combined with them. Forming machines deposit the wood chips on belts forming them into mats. These mats are cured with heat and

pressure, trimmed, and sanded into desired panel sizes. Particleboard is used extensively as core stock for wood veneers and plastic laminates. It is also used for siding, underlayment, sheathing, and other construction and industrial purposes. See Fig. 1-22.

Common woodworking tools may be used to cut and form hardboard and particleboard. However, it is necessary to slightly vary traditional methods due to the material characteristics. An example would be when using screws or applying a finish. Carbide-tipped tools should be utilized in order to give smoother, more accurate cuts, and to extend cutter life.

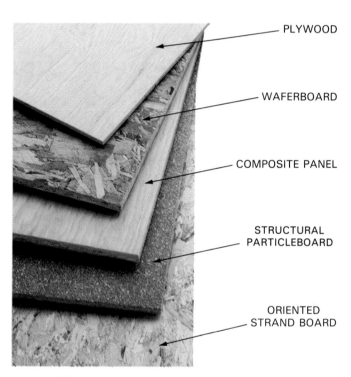

Fig. 1-22. Manufactured panels have gained wide acceptance in the furniture and cabinetmaking industries. (Georgia-Pacific)

WOOD IDENTIFICATION

A key element in the woodworking field is the proper identification of the wood. Fig. 1-23 shows a variety of wood species. Notice how the color and grain characteristics distinguish each of the species from the other.

Fig. 1-23. The wood species on the following pages are commonly used in the woodworking field. Study the color and grain characteristics of each species.

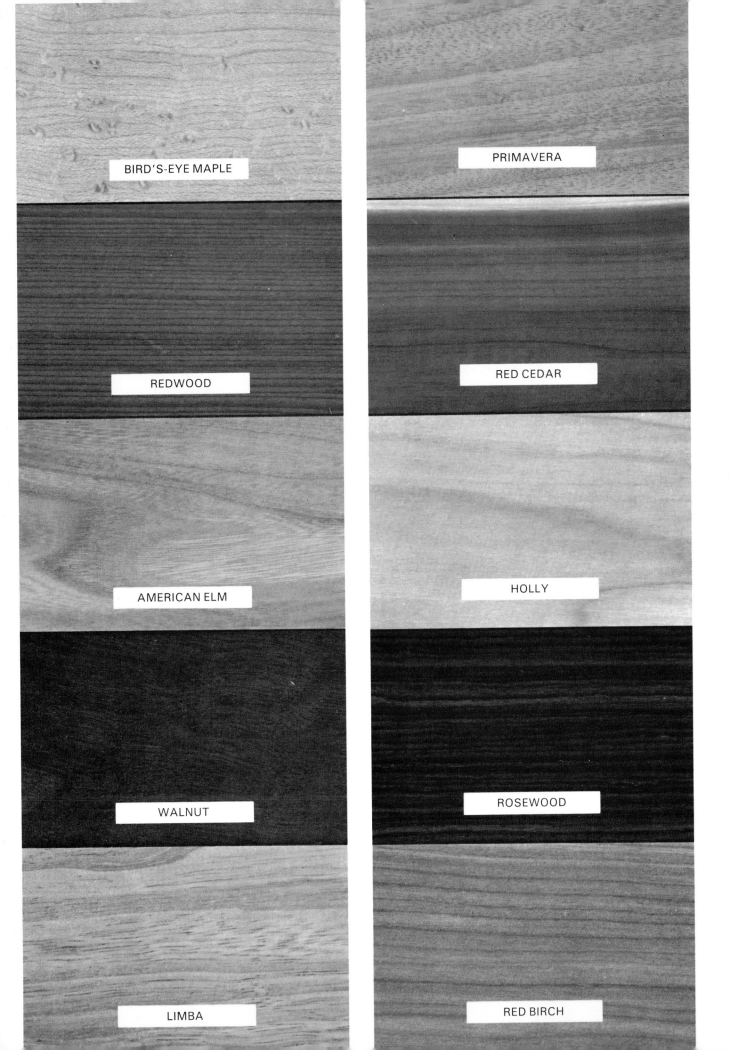

BIRD'S-EYE MAPLE

PRIMAVERA

REDWOOD

RED CEDAR

AMERICAN ELM

HOLLY

WALNUT

ROSEWOOD

LIMBA

RED BIRCH

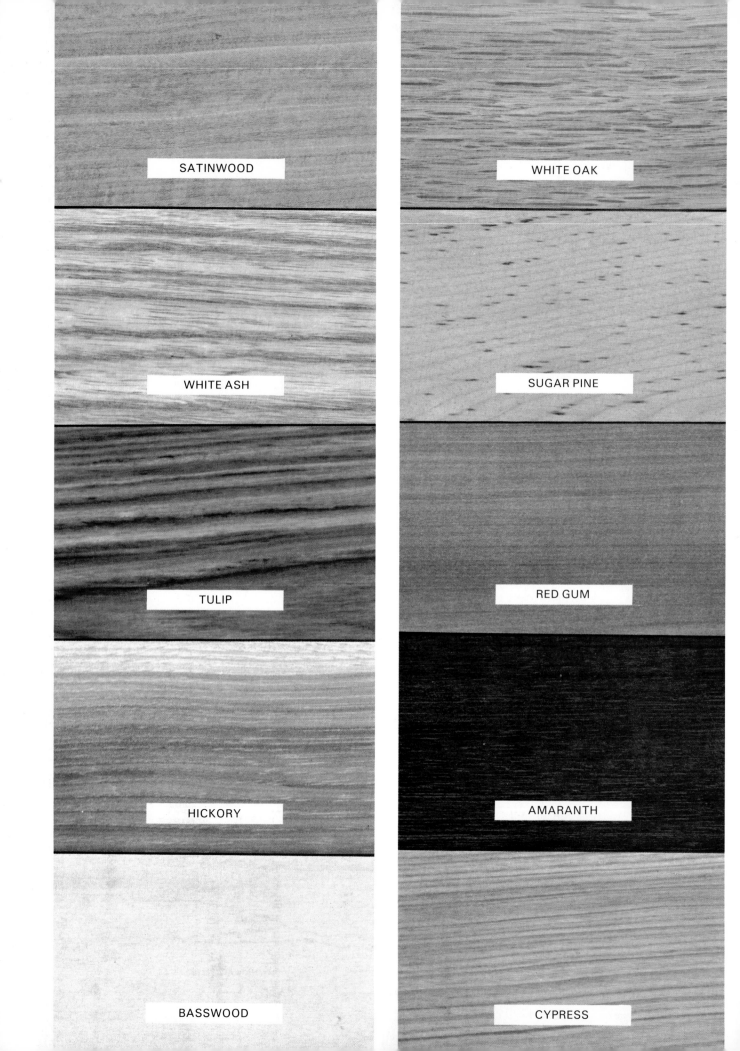

SATINWOOD

WHITE OAK

WHITE ASH

SUGAR PINE

TULIP

RED GUM

HICKORY

AMARANTH

BASSWOOD

CYPRESS

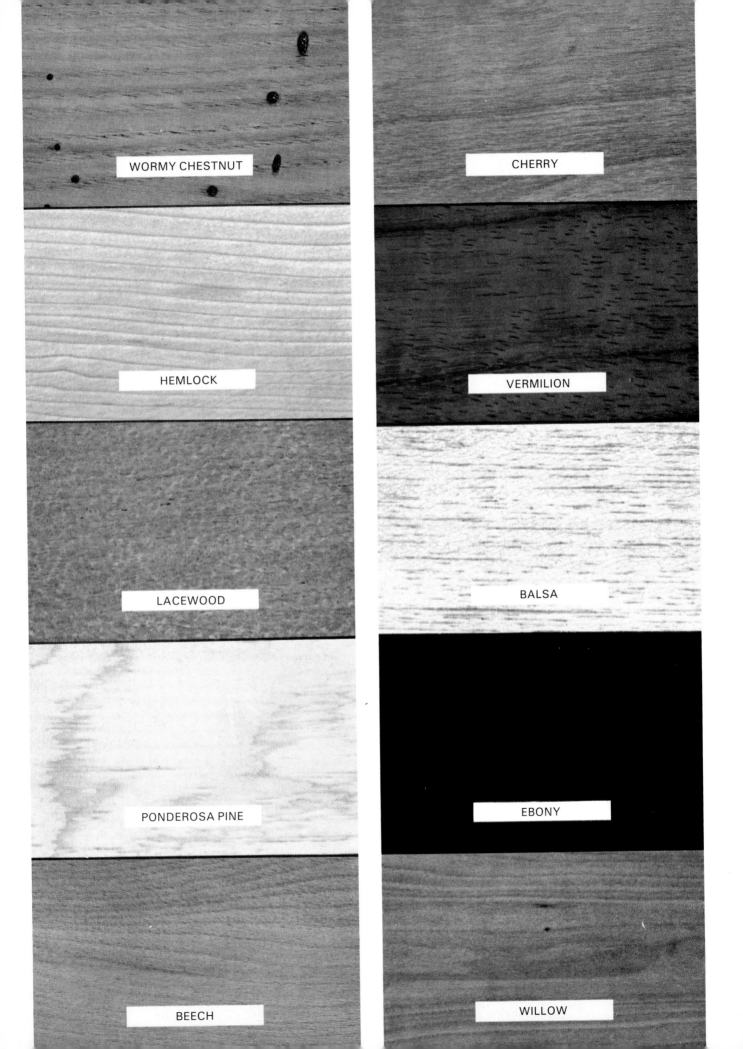

WORMY CHESTNUT

CHERRY

HEMLOCK

VERMILION

LACEWOOD

BALSA

PONDEROSA PINE

EBONY

BEECH

WILLOW

SYCAMORE

DOUGLAS FIR

AFRICAN MAHOGANY

TEAK

BUTTERNUT

SPRUCE

ZEBRAWOOD

ORIENTAL WOOD

HARD MAPLE

POPLAR

TEST YOUR KNOWLEDGE, Unit 1

Please do not write in this text. Place your answers on a separate sheet of paper.

1. Wood is composed of fiber units held together with a natural adhesive called _____.
2. New wood cells are formed in the _____ layer near the bark.
3. The age of a tree can be determined by counting the _____ rings.
4. Wood nearest the bark of a tree is called _____.
5. Medullary rays running perpendicular to the annual rings toward the pith carry _____ to the center of the tree.
6. Lumber can be divided into two main classifications–_____ and _____.
7. Softwoods are generally products of _____ bearing trees.
8. Hardwoods are mostly products of _____ leaf trees.
9. Three examples of open-grained wood are _____, _____, and _____.
10. Most lumber is plain or flat sawed (cut) tangent to the annual rings. True or False?
11. Some freshly cut lumber is placed in large ovens for _____ drying.
12. Wood _____ as it loses moisture, and _____ as it absorbs moisture.
13. Wood has a tendency to reach a balance in moisture content with surrounding air. This is called the _____ moisture content.
14. Warping is a change in a board from a true surface. In a cup, the board is curved _____ the grain. In a bow, the board surface is curved _____.
15. An even number of layers, or plies, are used when making plywood. True or False?
16. Define the term "hygroscopic."
17. What are two functions of a root system of a tree?
18. The terms "hardwood" and "softwood" refer to the hardness or softness of the wood. True or False?
19. How does clear cutting differ from selective cutting of trees?
20. The grain pattern that is exposed when logs are cut into lumber is called _____.
21. Lumber before it is seasoned may have a moisture content ranging from _____ to _____ percent.
22. Lumber that is stacked outside or in well-ventilated sheds to dry is called _____.
23. Construction-grade plywood is identified by the face veneer and back veneer grading letters. What are these letters?
24. Manufactured panels are said to be _____ _____ because changes in humidity have very little effect on their size.
25. Hardboard that is saturated with oils and resins is called _____ _____.
26. Carbide-tipped tools should be used when working with particleboard in order to provide smoother and more accurate cuts. True or False?
27. Veneers are very thin pieces of wood cut with a saw. True or False?
28. The thickness of veneer may range from _____ to _____ inch.
29. Grading rules used for evaluating the quality and usability of a board are called _____.
30. Veneers may be cut using one of three methods. What are these methods?

ACTIVITIES

1. Trace the growth cycle of trees using in-class resources and the library. Why do redwood trees usually live longer than other trees?
2. Select at least four small samples of different kinds of wood. On the back of each sample, write the name of the wood and list some of its characteristics.
3. Visit a local lumber yard to see how they store and care for wood.
4. Reforestation plays a major role in having plenty of trees available for future use. List things that you can do to support conservation of our natural resources.
5. Prepare an outline for a short report about the history and development of hardboard or particleboard.

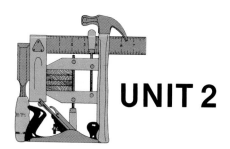

UNIT 2
PLANNING

Efficient planning helps us to solve problems, avoid mistakes, and use correct techniques. After studying this unit, you will be able to identify basic product design considerations. In addition, you will be able to clearly define the design problem. You will also be able to prepare a sketch, a bill of materials, and a plan of procedure.

DESIGN CONSIDERATIONS

Several factors play a role in the design of a product. These factors include: function or usefulness of the product, kind of wood that is to be used, size and proportion of the product, expected durability of the product, and cost.

FUNCTION OR USEFULNESS

You should ask yourself several questions about the function or usefulness of a product when designing it. Is the product needed or is it something that you just want to make? Will the product perform well for the purpose for which it is intended? For example, products intended for use outdoors should be made from a wood that is weather resistant, such as redwood. A bookshelf should be designed to hold books of the desired size and quantity.

KIND OF WOOD

The kind of wood to be used for a product is largely dependent on the use, function, and finish of the product. If an opaque finish is planned, an inexpensive wood could probably be used. It could have a poor grain pattern as long as it could hold paint well. Basswood, pine, spruce, and poplar are good woods to use if an opaque finish is planned. If a natural or transparent stained finish is to be used, a wood with a desirable color and grain pattern should be chosen. Birch, oak, walnut, maple, and cherry are a few of the fine woods that are enriched by finishing. Refer to Fig. 1-21 in the previous chapter to see the color and grain pattern of these woods.

SIZE

A product should be constructed to the proper size for its intended purpose. Furniture and cabinets are generally constructed to standard dimensions. A coffee table is usually 16-18 inches high. A chair is usually 18 inches from the floor to its seat. A bathroom vanity is often 31 inches high and a kitchen base cabinet is 36 inches high. Furniture catalogs and brochures will detail standard sizes of furniture and cabinets.

PROPORTION

Proportion is the ratio of the dimensions of a product. An odd ratio, such as 1/3 or 2/5 is generally more pleasing than an even ratio, such as 1/4 and 1/2. To determine the ratio, place the shorter dimension over the longer dimension and reduce to lowest terms. For example, a coffee table measuring 18 inches wide and 42 inches long has a size ratio of 18/42 or 3/7.

DURABILITY

A product is usually only made strong enough to fulfill its purpose to avoid giving it a heavy and awkward appearance. A box for light storage purposes, for example, could be built with 1/4 inch stock. The following questions should be asked:

- Is the product designed to fit its surroundings?
- Can it be built with a minimum of time and effort?

- Is it durable enough to withstand any forces that will be placed upon it?
- Are the most appropriate materials being used?

OTHER CONSIDERATIONS

Economy, balance, and harmony are other factors that should be considered when designing a product. Will the product be worth the necessary time and effort? Do the parts blend well together? Does it have eye appeal?

BALANCE is very important in determining how people perceive a design. Two types of balance can be used when designing a product–formal balance and informal balance. See Fig. 2-1. FORMAL BALANCE is obtained when all of the elements on one side of a design are "mirror images" of the elements on the other side. Formal balance gives a design an even appearance. INFORMAL BALANCE is achieved when the elements of a design are different on each side. This creates an uneven appearance.

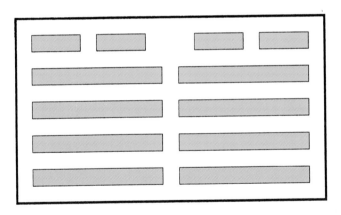

FORMAL BALANCE

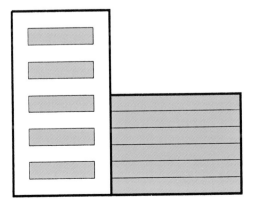

INFORMAL BALANCE

Fig. 2-1. Two types of balance.

HARMONY is the organization of all design elements so that the product is viewed as one piece. All elements must fit together properly to give the product a feeling of unity.

FURNITURE STYLES

Some of the best designers and artists of their time have developed furniture styles that are known by the period during which the furniture was created. Furniture styles created in Europe, particularly during the 18th and 19th centuries, are sometimes known as Traditional and French Provincial. Queen Anne and Louis XIV furniture styles are named for the rulers who ordered the furniture built. Sheraton and Chippendale styles are named for the designers who originated the furniture. Other popular styles of period furniture are Colonial and Early American. Contemporary (modern) furniture reflects the thinking of our present day designers. Contemporary furniture is simple furniture consisting of smooth, trim lines.

STEPS IN PLANNING A PRODUCT

Many steps are involved in the design and construction of a product. Each of the steps depends on decisions that were made in the previous step or steps. Do not overlook any of the steps, or make a quick decision in any of the steps. The more thought and time that is put into each one of these steps will reduce the number of errors or problems that may occur. The steps in designing a product follow:

1. Identify the problem.
2. Sketch the product in its simplest form.
3. Determine the resources that you have available.
4. Determine what tools and equipment will be required to build the product.
5. Prepare a working drawing.
6. Construct the product.
7. Determine the overall success of your product.

IDENTIFY THE PROBLEM

The identification of the problem is one of the most difficult steps in the overall design of a product. State the problem in its simplest terms. The problem may be as simple as choosing a product design from several books or catalogs, or as complex as designing a storage/work unit for a computer. Do not choose a product that is too difficult to construct. A well-made simple product is better than a complex product that results in nothing more than a pile of lumber.

Unit 22 provides several product ideas and information to aid in selecting and planning worthwhile products. Products with varying degrees of difficulty are included. Products should be selected that can be made with a minimum of effort and can be completed in the allotted time. Select products that match your own interests. Use your imagination when designing products. Developing more than one design for a product will allow you to compare designs and make improvements. You will feel a keen sense of satisfaction when a design is developed that is different and pleasing. Design suggestions may also be obtained by visiting shops and stores that specialize in wood products such as furniture, gift items, and novelties. There are also many excellent books and magazines that provide product plans, techniques, and other information for the beginning or skilled woodworker.

SKETCH THE PRODUCT

When the product has been determined, the next step is to sketch the product in its simplest form using a pencil. A pencil allows you to make changes in the design. Pictorial (three-dimensional) sketches should first be sketched to give you an idea of how the parts of the product fit together.

When drawing a pictorial sketch, first draw the front of the product and then draw the top and sides of it. Fig. 2-2 shows a pictorial sketch of a jewelry box. Sketch the object lines freehand, and then darken them with a pencil and straightedge. Do not be concerned with the details at this time unless a particular problem, such as a joint detail, must be kept in mind throughout the design process. This step is frequently omitted only to find out later the design was not in it simplest form.

DETERMINE THE AVAILABLE RESOURCES

The third step in the design process is to determine resources. Resources are defined as anything available for use in making the product,

Fig. 2-2. Pictorial sketch of a jewelry box.

including personal skill, available tools and materials (their condition and accessories), and finishing capabilities. If the product is to be used for resale, packaging, marketing, inventory control, product storage, and cash flow should also be considered.

Personal skill usually improves with experience, and can be evaluated after review of previously completed work. Nothing is more frustrating than to have purchased materials and supplies, only to find basic knowledge is lacking or to find someone else doing the same product faster and better.

Available materials should not be a problem if a product is designed properly. The list of woods, veneers, adhesives, hardware, etc., available is almost endless. However, hard-to-find materials and supplies may cost more than you had expected. If the desired item must be ordered, allow enough lead time for delivery.

DETERMINE AVAILABLE TOOLS AND EQUIPMENT

The fourth factor to consider when designing a product is available tools and equipment. Review and list the equipment that will be required to build the product. Compare this list to the tools and equipment available in the shop. If the tools or equipment required to build the product are not available, determine whether different tools can be used. For example, rough-sawn 4/4 lumber generally should not be purchased if a planer is not available to smooth the surfaces. However, you may be able to use a hand plane to smooth the stock. A less obvious

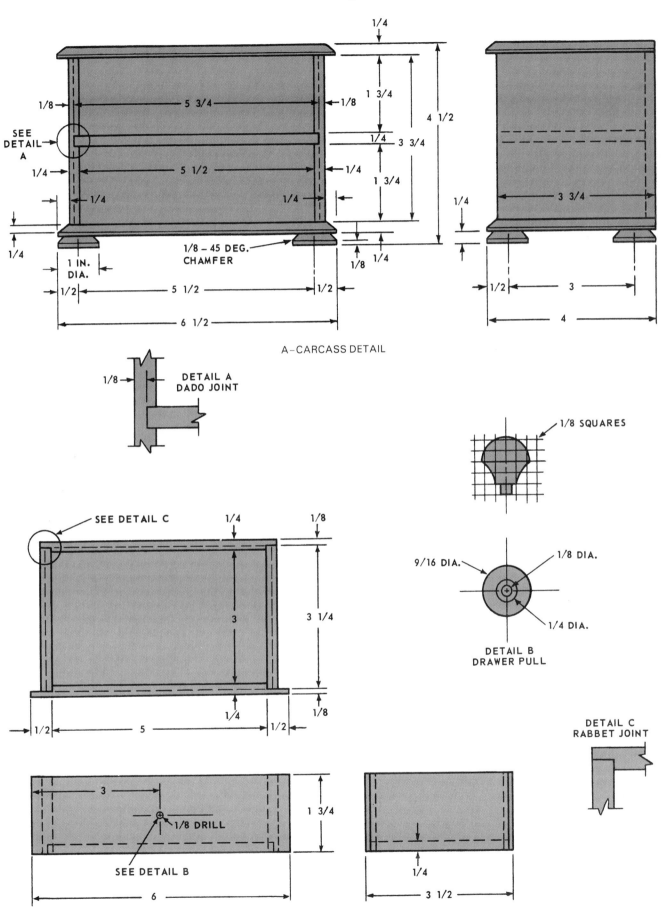

Fig. 2-3. Working drawing for a jewelry box. A–Carcass detail. B–Drawer and pull detail.

tool consideration is in designing joints. Do not plan on a locking miter joint if a shaper or router with the proper cutters is not available.

The last element to consider in this step is finishing capabilities. There are many options for a good-quality finish. Some finishes only require a rag or a disposable brush, while others require a moisture-controlled spray area with filtration and high-tech spray equipment. Some finishes may explode under certain conditions (such as when a light switch is turned on), while others are totally safe in all conditions.

PREPARE A WORKING DRAWING

When you have established what resources you have available, revise the sketch to include the overall size, joints, drawers, and other details. Fig. 2-3 shows a working drawing for a jewelry box. Prepare a WORKING DRAWING that indicates the exact size and other details necessary to construct the product. Select a scale for the working drawing that will show the necessary detail. Full-size plans may be required for some products.

A final working drawing may be drawn to scale using grid paper. This usually consists of

two or more views. Detailed views (often enlarged) are used to show types of joints and shapes of special or irregular parts.

Figs. 2-4 and 2-5 show the completed jewelry box and provide alternate designs for the jewelry box. Many other designs are possible.

Fig. 2-4. Completed jewelry box.

Fig. 2-5. Alternate styles of jewelry boxes.

A BILL OF MATERIALS should then be developed from the working drawings. This should include every item required to complete the product, including all hardware and finishing materials. Both the rough and finish sizes of all stock should be clearly indicated. A sketch of the uncut stock with cutting plans for the finished pieces is commonly used to reduce waste or to avoid an improper cut.

Computing Lumber Measure

Lumber dimensions are listed in the order of thickness (T), width (W), and length (L). The THICKNESS is the distance that is perpendicular to both the width and length. The WIDTH is the distance across the grain of the wood. The LENGTH is the distance along the grain of the wood.

The BOARD FOOT is the basic unit of measure for all lumber. A board foot is equal to a piece of lumber measuring 1-inch or less in thickness, 12-inches wide, and 12-inches (1 foot) long. Nominal (rough-sawn) sizes are used in computing board feet. Lumber that is 1-inch thick or less is considered to be 1 inch. For example, a board that is 1/4-inch thick is considered to be 1-inch thick when computing board feet. Lumber that is thicker than 1 inch is rounded up to the next quarter inch. For example, a board that is 1 1/8-inches thick is figured to be 1 1/4-inches thick, and a board that measures 1 3/8-inches thick is figured as a 1 1/2-inches thick.

A formula for computing board feet for small pieces of lumber is Board feet (Bd. ft.) equals the number of pieces times the thickness (in inches), times the width (in inches), times the length (in inches) divided by 144. The number 144 is the number of square inches in a square foot. If there is more than one piece of lumber, multiply the number of board feet by the number of pieces. The board foot formula is usually shown as:

$$\text{Bd. ft.} = \frac{\text{no. of pcs.} \times T'' \times W'' \times L''}{144}$$

EXAMPLE: Compute the board foot measure of 3 pieces of wood measuring 1/2" x 6" x 9".

Substituting in the above formula:

$$\text{Bd. ft.} = \frac{3 \text{ pcs.} \times 1'' \times 6'' \times 9''}{144}$$

$$\text{Bd. ft.} = 1.125$$

Large pieces of wood are computed as follows:
Board feet equals the number of pieces times the thickness (in inches) times the width (in inches) times the length (in feet) divided by 12. The board foot formula is usually shown as:

$$\text{Bd. ft.} = \frac{\text{no. of pcs.} \times T'' \times W'' \times L'}{12}$$

EXAMPLE: Compute the board foot measure of 2 pieces of wood measuring 1 1/4-inches thick by 4-inches wide by 4-feet long.

Substituting in the previous formula:

$$\text{Bd. ft.} = \frac{2 \text{ pcs.} \times 1.25'' \times 4'' \times 4'}{12}$$

$$\text{Bd. ft.} = 3.33$$

Note: It may be easier to figure board feet as square feet first, and then multiply by the thickness of the board. Remember to multiply feet by feet and inches by inches.

EXAMPLE: Compute the board foot measure of 1 piece of white pine that measures 3/4" thick by 4-inches wide by 3-feet long.

Substituting in the formula to compute square feet:
$$4/12 \times 3' = 1 \text{ sq. ft.}$$

Substituting in the formula to compute board feet:
$$1 \text{ pc.} \times 1 \text{ sq. ft.} \times 1'' (T) = 1 \text{ Bd. ft.}$$

Another method used to measure and sell wood products is SQUARE FEET. Square foot measure is usually applied to sheet stock, such as plywood and paneling. It can also apply to milled lumber, such as tongue and groove flooring.

The area, or square feet, of a piece of stock is calculated by multiplying the length by the width. The length and width must be measured in feet, not length in feet and width in inches.

EXAMPLE: Compute the number of square feet in a sheet of paneling measuring 4' x 4'.

Substituting in the formula to compute square feet:
$$4' \times 4' = 16 \text{ sq. ft.}$$

The final method of measurement used in woodworking is RUNNING FEET, or LINEAL FEET. This measurement is nothing more than the actual length of the material given in feet. Most milled lumber, such as molding, is measured and sold by running feet.

Preparing the Bill of Materials

The working drawing is used to determine the dimensions of the stock to prepare a bill of materials. Rough and finish dimensions are given in the bill of materials. Fig. 2-6 shows a bill of materials for the jewelry box. Board foot measure and costs are computed based on the rough size dimensions. Rough size dimensions allow for extra stock to be removed in trimming and smoothing the parts to the finished sizes. The following guidelines should be followed when figuring rough size dimensions:

Add 1/16-1/8 inch to the finish size thickness.
Add 1/4 inch to the finish size width.
Add 1/2 inch to the finish size length.

Making a Stock Cutting List

A STOCK CUTTING LIST is made by grouping similar rough sizes of stock given in the bill of materials. The dimensions listed in the stock cutting list are rough sizes only, Fig. 2-7. The stock cutting list allows you to conserve both time and materials.

CONSTRUCT THE PRODUCT

The next step in the process is to construct the product. Planning does not stop here; continue to think through the entire product. List the steps needed to build the product using a plan of procedure. This will allow for a smoother flow of the tasks at hand. Good planning will allow many tasks to be performed at one time. For example, shaping activities may proceed while another part of the product is being glued. If you have a tight budget or a cash flow problem, it may be necessary to purchase certain parts of the product as needed. This can only be accomplished by thorough planning.

BILL OF MATERIALS

NAME CHARLES E. HARPER   PLANNING DATE MARCH 15   COMPLETION DATE APRIL 22

PROJECT JEWELRY BOX   TOOLS NEEDED: TRY SQUARE, MARKING GAUGE

HAND SAWS, HAND PLANES, HAND DRILL & BIT, CHISELS, CLAW HAMMER & CLAMPS

STOCK LIST:

No. of Pcs.	Name of Part	Size in Inches (Rough)	Size in Inches (Finish)	Kind of Wood	Bd. Ft.	Bd. Ft. Cost	Cost
2	TOP & BOTTOM (CARCASS)	3/8 × 4 1/4 × 7	1/4 × 4 × 6 1/2	WALNUT	.41	$3.15	$1.29
2	ENDS (CARCASS)	3/8 × 4 1/4 × 4 1/4	1/4 × 3 3/4 × 3 3/4	"	.25	3.15	.79
1	SHELF (CARCASS)	3/8 × 3 3/4 × 6 1/4	1/4 × 3 1/2 × 5 3/4	"	.16	3.15	.50
1	BACK (CARCASS)	1/4 × 4 × 6 1/4	1/4 × 3 3/4 × 5 3/4	WAL. PLY G1S	.17 SQ.FT.	1.72	.29
4	FEET (CARCASS)	3/4 × 1 1/4 × 1 1/4	1/4 × 1 DIA.	WALNUT	.04	3.15	.13
2	FRONTS (DRAWER)	3/8 × 2 × 6 1/2	1/4 × 1 3/4 × 6	"	.17	3.15	.54
2	BACKS (DRAWER)	3/8 × 2 × 6	1/4 × 1 3/4 × 5 1/2	"	.16	3.15	.50
4	SIDES (DRAWER)	3/8 × 2 × 3 3/4	1/4 × 1 3/4 × 3 1/4	"	.21	3.15	.66
2	BOTTOMS (DRAWER)	1/4 × 3 3/4 × 5 1/2	1/4 × 3 × 5	WAL. PLY G1S	.25 SQ.FT.	1.72 SQ.FT.	.33
2	PULLS (DRAWER)	3/4 × 3/4 × 1 1/4	9/16 DIA. × 5/8	WALNUT	.013	1.6 1.70	.04
						TOTAL STOCK COST	5.17

HARDWARE AND OTHER MATERIALS:

No. of Pcs.	Description	Size	Unit	Unit Cost	Cost
4	FLAT HEAD SCREWS	NO. 4 × 1/2"	EACH	$.02	.08
36	WIRE BRADS	GAUGE NO. 18 × 3/4"	EACH		.15
	LIQUID WHITE GLUE				.25
	SAND PAPER	60, 100, AND 150 GRITS			1.50
	FINISH				1.50

TOTAL HARDWARE & MISC. $3.48
TOTAL PROJECT COST $8.65

Fig. 2-6. Bill of materials for a jewelry box.

PCS.	NAMES OF PARTS	SIZE	MATERIAL
1	Top, bottom, ends and shelf (carcass)	3/8'' x 4 1/4'' x 30''	Walnut
1	Fronts, backs and sides (drawer)	3/8'' x 4'' x 20''	Walnut
1	Back (carcass) and bottoms (drawer)	1/4'' x 4'' x 18''	Walnut Plywood GIS
1	Feet (carcass)	3/4'' x 1 1/4'' x 5 1/4''	Walnut
1	Pulls (carcass)	3/4'' x 3/4'' x 3''	Walnut

Fig. 2-7. Stock cutting list for a jewelry box.

Preparing a Plan of Procedure

A PLAN OF PROCEDURE enables you to "think through" the processes needed to construct a product before you actually start working. This enables work to be organized so time and material can be saved, and also to detect minor errors in the drawing, bill of materials, or stock cutting list. Mistakes are much easier to change on paper than with materials. In addition, ways to improve a product design or construction can also be found. A plan of procedure should be made in outline form with enough information to indicate procedures involved.

Plan of Procedure for the Jewelry Box

1. Check your working drawing, bill of materials, and stock cutting list carefully.
2. Select and cut stock given in your stock cutting list. Try to find already-cut stock near the correct sizes.
3. Make carcass parts.
   a. Plane the stock to finish thickness.
   b. Saw parts to rough sizes.
   c. Plane and saw parts to finish sizes.
   d. Saw and chisel dados in ends to receive the shelf.
   e. Chamfer edges on the top and bottom.
4. Make carcass feet.
5. Assemble carcass with glue and wire brads or clamps. Attach the feet with screws.
6. Make drawer fronts, backs and sides.
   a. Plane stock to finish thickness.
   b. Saw parts to rough sizes.
   c. Plane and saw parts to finish sizes.
   d. Cut rabbet joints at each end of the fronts and backs to receive the sides. Then cut rabbet joints along the bottom edges to receive the bottoms.
   e. Drill 1/8 in. hole in each drawer front to receive the pulls.
7. Make the drawer pulls.
8. Cut plywood to finish sizes to fit the drawer bottoms and carcass back.
9. Assemble drawers with glue and wire brads or clamps. Install the drawer pulls.
10. Smooth surfaces and edges with 60, 100, and 150 grit sandpaper.
11. Apply finish.
    a. Raise grain, let dry, then smooth again with 150 grit sandpaper.
    b. Apply paste wood filler, let dry until it begins to turn dull then remove excess filler by rubbing ACROSS the grain and let dry.
    c. Sand filler coat lightly with 220 grit sandpaper, then apply a coat of sealer and allow to dry.
    d. Sand sealer coat lightly with 220 grit sandpaper, then apply two coats of topcoat finish.
    e. Rub final topcoat with rubbing oil and rottenstone or pumice.
    f. Wax.
12. Attach the carcass back with glue and wire brads or clamps.

DETERMINE YOUR SUCCESS

This last step is frequently overlooked, but it is essential if you want to continually grow and develop skills in woodworking. Consider the obvious–does product fulfill the needs of the original problem identified? If yes, then there is success, but it is necessary to evaluate other factors to determine the degree of success. What is the overall appearance? Is the finish adequate? Are the joints tight? Was the cost and effort reasonable? This kind of evaluation allows for modification of future products and personal growth as a woodworker.

Tool Selection

Tools must be shared and properly cared for so that everyone receives the greatest benefit from their use. Always return tools to the storage center after use. Fig. 2-8 shows a typical storage cabinet for tools.

Fig. 2-8. Typical tool storage cabinet.

TEST YOUR KNOWLEDGE, Unit 2

Please do not write in this text. Place your answers on a separate sheet of paper.

1. List three important factors that should be considered when designing products to be constructed in the shop.
2. Queen Anne and Louis XIV furniture is named for the _____ who first ordered that type of furniture to be built.
3. _____ furniture reflects the thinking of present day designers.
4. Planning in the school laboratory involves selecting a product and developing and refining its _____.
5. A working drawing provides shapes and _____ of a product.
6. List the three units of measure for lumber and sheet stock.
7. Calculate the total board foot measure for 3 pieces of stock measuring 1/2″ x 6″ x 24″.
8. Lumber less than 1-inch thick is figured the same as if it were _____ inch thick.
9. Calculate the number of square feet in a sheet of plywood measuring 1/2″ x 4′ x 8′.
10. _____ size dimensions allow for extra stock to be removed in smoothing parts to finish sizes.
11. The processes used to construct a product are listed in the _____.
12. The _____ size of materials is listed in the stock cutting list.

ACTIVITIES

1. Prepare a short report on a famous furniture designer.
2. How do we decide whether something has good or bad design? Make a chart showing characteristics of good and bad design.
3. Choose a product that you would like to make. Make several pencil sketches of the product, along with alternate design suggestions.
4. Select several small pieces of wood and compute the board foot measure in each piece. Compute the cost of each piece based on current prices.

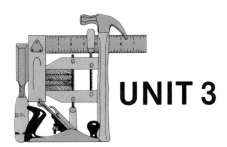

UNIT 3

GENERAL SAFETY

This unit deals with general safety precautions that should be taken in the woods laboratory. After studying this unit, you will have a basic foundation of safe practices to be followed when using tools, equipment, and machines. In addition, you will begin "thinking safety" before beginning any hand or power tool operation.

GENERAL SAFETY PRACTICES

Safety should be an important part of every job. Safe work habits acquired now will be useful in years to come.

1. Always think "safety first" before performing an operation.

2. Wear safety glasses, goggles, or a face shield in danger zones or other designated areas. See Fig. 3-1.
3. Report even the slightest injury. Small cuts or other minor injuries may become serious if left unattended.
4. Notify your instructor of any unsafe conditions observed. This may include such things as dull tools and frayed electrical cords.
5. Keep the floor clear of scraps of material and wood shavings.
6. When stacking lumber, make sure it will not shift or fall.
7. Place clamped stock so it will not fall. Make sure the clamps do not extend into the pathway.

Fig. 3-1. Drill press safety. The stock is securely clamped in place. The operator is wearing a face shield.

33

8. Place all used rags in a metal fireproof container.
9. Keep the air as clean as possible. Use the dust collection system (if available in your laboratory) or wear a dust mask, if dusty conditions prevail. The dust mask should be approved by the National Institute for Occupational Safety and Health (NIOSH).
10. Respect the rights of others and their property.
11. Keep the lids on finish containers when not in use. Many finishes emit vapors that may be harmful if the area is not properly ventilated. Use a NIOSH-approved respirator with an organic filter if harmful vapors are present.

The Occupational Safety and Health Administration (OSHA) has added several items to their hazardous materials list. One of these items is wood dust. In the past, wood dust was always considered a nuisance, not a hazard. Studies have shown that prolonged exposure to high concentrations of wood dust to be a health hazard. The dust that presents the largest hazard is not normally visible by the naked eye, and is therefore overlooked. The majority of this dust results from sanding operations. The use of dust masks and properly operating dust collection equipment is necessary.

WORKING SAFELY WITH TOOLS AND EQUIPMENT

Tools and equipment are one of the primary sources of injury in the woods laboratory. Your instructor should explain or demonstrate the safe operation of any tool or piece of equipment prior to its use.

1. Make sure tools and accessories are properly assembled and adjusted prior to use.
2. Do not use a file that does not have a handle securely in place.
3. Make sure all cutting tools are sharp. A dull tool is more dangerous than a sharp tool.
4. Carry sharp tools with their cutting edges down. Do not carry tools in your pockets. See Fig. 3-2.
5. Be sure all stock is securely held in place before beginning any cutting operation using hand or power tools.
6. Always cut away from your body when

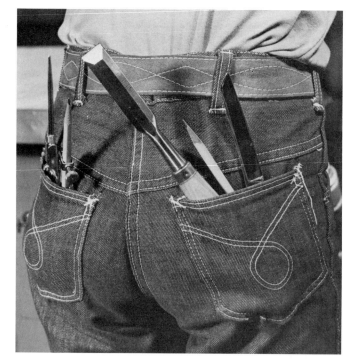

Fig. 3-2. Do not carry tools in your pockets—especially sharp-pointed tools.

using edge tools, Fig. 3-3. This rule has few exceptions.
7. Report all broken tools to the instructor immediately. Do not use a broken tool.
8. Always store tools in their proper manner.

Fig. 3-3. Always cut away from your body when using edge tools.

34

Tools are damaged frequently, or an injury may needlessly occur, because a tool was improperly stored.

9. When cleaning, avoid blowing or brushing sawdust into your eyes or your classmates eyes. Do not rub your eyes if sawdust or any other foreign object gets in them. Get immediate assistance. Avoid creating excessive amounts of dust while sanding or during clean-up. Use a NIOSH-approved dust mask.

10. Close vise handles so they do not protrude into the aisles. However, do not tighten them.

WORKING SAFELY WITH AND AROUND MACHINES

Power equipment and machines allow you to perform tasks easier and in less time than using hand tools. However, they can be more dangerous than hand tools if not used properly. Your instructor should explain or demonstrate the safe operation of any machine or piece of power equipment prior to you using it.

1. Ask your instructor for permission before using any machine.
2. Have the instructor check the setup before using any machine.
3. Use machine guards. Get permission first, if a special set-up requires temporary removal of a guard. Do not leave the machine unattended without the guard. Carefully think the total process through before beginning. Ask for assistance in the operation if it is needed.
4. Be sure everyone is out of the danger zone around a machine before beginning an operation.
5. Stay alert! Keep your mind on the operation of the machine at all times. Do not talk to anyone while operating a machine. Do not operate any power equipment if you do not feel well or are taking certain medications.
6. Be sure to work only within the capacity of the machine. Do not attempt operations beyond its limits.
7. Turn off the machine before making any adjustments.
8. Remove the plug from the receptacle, or turn off the disconnect switch, before making any changes to the setup.

9. As a machine operator, you are in full charge of the machine.
10. Ask for assistance prior to beginning a cut on long or heavy pieces.
11. Wear safe clothing. Make sure you button your shirt. If you are wearing a long-sleeve shirt, roll up the sleeves. Shoes or sneakers should be worn. Do not go barefoot or wear just sandals. Remove any loose fitting clothing such as vests or sweaters. Do not wear ties or dangling jewelry. If you have long hair, tie it back.
12. Use a push stick to cut short or narrow stock.
13. Make sure all cutting edges of blades or bits are sharp.
14. Turn off the equipment you are using after each use.
15. Inspect stock prior to beginning a cut. Look for loose knots and twists that might bind the tools.
16. Wear ear protection when operating tools with high noise levels.

In addition to the previously mentioned safety guidelines, you should also periodically check the wiring, cords, switches, etc., for physical damage, wear, and deterioration. Occasionally, people remove the grounding pin from a grounded (three-prong) plug even though this practice is extremely hazardous. See Fig. 3-4.

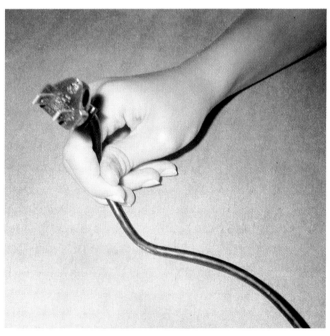

Fig. 3-4. The grounding pin should not be removed from a grounding (three-prong) plug.

This allows for a shorting condition that transfers the positive (hot) conductor to the housing of the tool and then to the operator. This results in a serious electrical shock that could easily lead to electrocution.

A hazard that is not as obvious as a missing grounding pin is when a conductor (wire) is exposed through the insulation. A volt-ohm meter may be used to determine if an electrical problem exists. It can also be used to isolate the problem.

Another electrical hazard that may exist is the overload of a circuit. When the number of plugs exceeds the design capacity of the receptacle an overload condition may occur. Overloads often occur when a number of extension cords have been connected together. This reduces the current-carrying capacity of the extension cord. If a power tool that exceeds this new current-carrying capacity is operated, the cord may overheat or the power tool will operate with less power than required. This may result in the tool overheating. The overheating of a power tool will result in a loss of efficiency, damage to the tool if operated for any length of time, or possible injury to the operator. This condition frequently does not become apparent until the extension cord becomes hot or the power tool does not have its full power.

The National Electrical Code requires all new wiring in basements, garages, bathrooms, and outdoor locations to have a ground fault protection. A ground fault circuit interrupter (GFCI) is designed to sense when an undesired ground exists and immediately breaks the circuit. This protects the operator from electrical shock.

Many machines and pieces of power equipment are powered through the use of drive belts. The operator is usually protected from these belts with guards. Since the belts are generally not seen when the equipment is in motion, they are commonly overlooked as a potential hazard. Belts crack and split with age, and must be replaced. Fig. 3-5 shows a belt that has split and must be replaced.

FIRE PROTECTION

Every woods laboratory has a fire hazard due to the sawdust, cleaning solvents, finishes, thinners, and electrical equipment. Since each lab has a variety of fire hazards, they should be equipped with an ABC-rated fire extinguisher. An ABC-rated extinguisher allows for use with an electrical fire as well as other kinds of fires. The fire extinguisher should be prominently displayed and accessible to everyone working in the lab.

It is much easier to prevent a fire than to put out a fire. Always store flammables away from open flames, heat sources, and in approved containers. Remove used rags containing oil, solvents, finishes, and thinners from the building

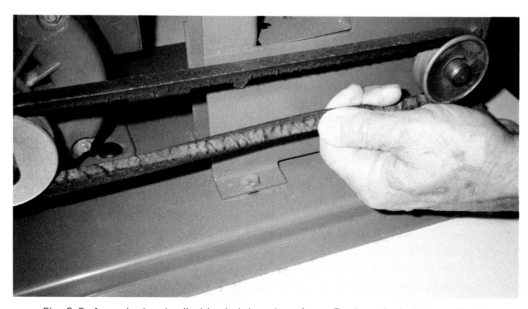

Fig. 3-5. A cracked and split drive belt is a sign of age. Replace the belt immediately.

daily, and place in a metal fireproof can with a tight-fitting lid. Used rags must also be stored in a covered metal container when not in use.

Examine dust collectors, beneath table saws and shapers, portable shop vacuums, and anywhere else sawdust might accumulate on a regular basis. These areas must be kept clean to prevent the build up of dust and potential of fire.

TEST YOUR KNOWLEDGE, Unit 3

Please do not write in this text. Place your answers on a separate sheet of paper.

1. Safety glasses must be worn anytime power tools are being used either by you or by someone else in your work area. True or False?
2. Ear protection should be worn when operating tools with high noise levels. True or False?
3. Loose clothing should be worn around power tools. True or False?
4. Pants pockets are designed to carry sharp tools to prevent damage to the cutting edge. True or False?
5. The dust collection system is a large vacuum that should only be operated at clean-up time. True or False?
6. Certain glues and most finishes are toxic. Prolonged exposure to their fumes should be avoided. True or False?
7. Used rags should be placed in a metal container except when in use. True or False?
8. Tools should be returned to their storage location after use. True or False?
9. When debris accumulates on the floor, it should be put into the trash container. True or False?
10. Minor cuts and splinters need not be reported to the instructor. True or False?

ACTIVITIES

1. Make a safety poster that would be effective in your laboratory.
2. Tour your laboratory to determine if there are any potential safety hazards. If you find any hazards, determine what should be done to correct the situation.
3. Research the various types of fire extinguishers–A, B, C, and ABC. Create a chart that lists the types and purpose of each type of extinguisher.

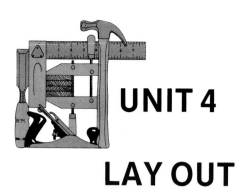

UNIT 4

LAY OUT

In this unit, the use of rules, squares, marking gauges, dividers, bevels, awls and templates is discussed. After studying this unit you will be able to identify the basic tools. In addition, you will be able to use the layout tools correctly when laying out products.

When laying out woodworking products, it is important to arrange the design carefully to avoid wasting material. You should consider the grain direction in order to allow for expansion and contraction, strength, and product attractiveness.

RULES

A RULE is a general term used to describe a lineal measuring device. Many types of rules are available.

- Tape measure.
- Folding rule.
- Bench rule.

TAPE MEASURES are commonly used for measuring longer lengths of stock, Fig. 4-1A. They are available in various lengths. This tool is handy, because when it is closed it will clip onto a belt. Some models even have nail or screw charts printed on the back of the tape. When using a tape measure, be sure that grit, such as sand, does not get inside the housing. It will wear off the finish and numbers on the tape, and may cause the tape measure to jam.

FOLDING RULES are commonly used by carpenters and other professionals, Fig. 4-1B. These rules are also used for measuring long stock. They offer the advantage of being rigid,

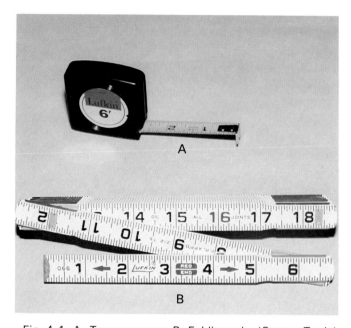

Fig. 4-1. A–Tape measure. B–Folding rule. (Copper Tools)

allowing you to measure long distances without being supported. Be sure the joints (hinges) of folding rules are lubricated to prevent breakage.

Another rule commonly used in the woods laboratory is the BENCH RULE. The bench rule may be made of either wood or steel. They are usually available in 12-inch, 24-inch, and 36-inch lengths. In addition to being used for measuring, they may also be used as a straightedge. See Fig. 4-2.

SQUARES

SQUARES are one of the most important basic layout tools. They are used for making accurate joints, squaring boards, and general layout work. All squares must be treated as precise tools and greatly respected. Laying boards, tools, or other items on top of them will reduce

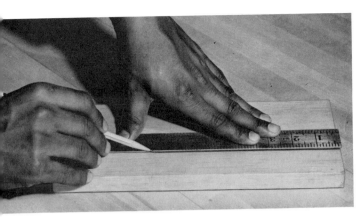

Fig. 4-2. Using a steel rule as a straightedge.

Fig. 4-4. Use a carpenter's square and pencil to lay out
large pieces of wood.

their accuracy. Care should be taken not to drop them. Sometimes a square that is "knocked-out" of adjustment can be readjusted–other times it cannot.

When using a square, make sure that the handle is held firmly against the edge or surface of the wood as shown in Fig. 4-3. Accurate, 90-degree angles cannot be formed unless this is done. There are three kinds of squares normally found in a woods laboratory.

- Steel square.
- Try square.
- Combination square.

The STEEL SQUARE is used to layout or square large pieces of stock, Fig. 4-4. The steel square, is also called a RAFTER SQUARE or CARPENTER'S SQUARE. It has many useful scales engraved in its tongue and blade, in addition to an accurate rule. The proper use of this

square will allow you to perform complex operations, such as laying out rafter lengths and cuts, stair steps, and multisided cuts.

The TRY SQUARE is used to lay out and square smaller pieces of stock. A try square has a rule engraved on the blade. Some try squares have a 45-degree miter formed in the handle for accurate layout of miter cuts. In general, try squares are very easy to use to make accurate layouts. See Fig. 4-5.

The COMBINATION SQUARE can perform more functions than the other types of squares.

Fig. 4-5. Laying out hole center with a try square and pencil.

Fig. 4-3. Squaring end of a board with a try square. Make sure the handle is held firmly against the edge of the board.

It is called a combination square because it can do a number of operations very accurately. Refer to Fig. 4-6. First, it has a blade that slides in a handle. This sliding feature allows it to be used like a marking gauge. The blade is also a one-foot rule. The handle allows for 45- and 90-degree angle layouts. Many combination squares have a small level in the handle. This allows you to level table tops and other items that should be parallel to the floor. In addition, some combination squares have a scribe in the end of the handle. If you do not have a pencil handy for marking your wood, you may be able to use the scribe.

SLIDING T-BEVEL

The SLIDING T-BEVEL, also called a BEVEL or a SET SQUARE, is similar to a square in its use. However, the angle may be varied and set as desired. This tool is needed when laying out an angle other than 45 or 90 degrees. It can also be used as a guide when performing operations such as boring holes, Fig. 4-7. It is usually set using a protractor, or by measuring an angle that has already been cut. The handle must be held firmly against the stock in order for you to get an accurate angle.

ANGLE DIVIDER

The ANGLE DIVIDER is another useful layout tool. It allows you to quickly bisect (divide in half) any angle. In addition, the angle divider allows you to accurately lay out 4-, 5-, 6-, 8-, and 10-sided objects.

AWLS, SLOYD KNIVES, AND PENCILS

An AWL is used to lay out the center point of a hole before drilling it. See Fig. 4-8. This is done so that the drill bit does not slide across the surface of the wood. Awls may also be used to align parts or temporarily hold parts together.

A SLOYD KNIFE is a knife used to accurately cut a small mark or groove into the surface of a board. Any sharp knife will perform this operation. This tends to be more accurate than a pencil mark. However, the mark or groove cannot be erased; it must be sanded or planed out.

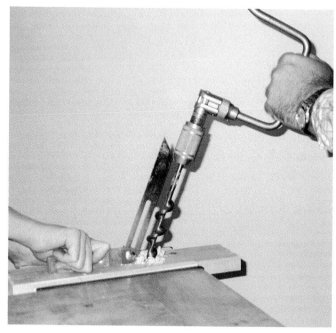

Fig. 4-7. Determining an angle for boring with a sliding T-bevel.

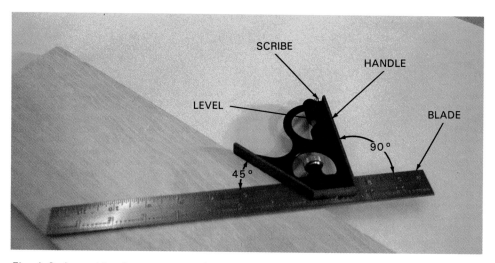

Fig. 4-6. A combination square, as the name implies, is used for a combination of tasks. (John Walker)

Fig. 4-8. Marking hole centers with an awl.

Fig. 4-9. Marking lines parallel to an edge with a marking gauge. Make sure the head of the gauge is held firmly against the edge of the stock.

Fig. 4-10. Scribing a circle with pencil dividers.

Fig. 4-11. Scribing a large arc with trammel points.

The most common marking tool found in the woods laboratory is the PENCIL. They should be kept sharp to avoid a thick line when marking on wood. The pencil can be used to lay out straight lines with a straightedge, curved lines with a compass, or trace a template.

A technique should be developed that allows you to identify the exact point that you are laying out. One technique is to mark your layout line with an "X". Another technique is to draw an arrow on the waste side of the line. In either case, the exact point should be easy to identify.

MARKING GAUGE

The marking gauge is very useful for laying out chamfers, rabbets, and other lines that run parallel to a straight edge, Fig. 4-9. The head of the marking gauge must be held firmly against the edge to ensure a uniform layout.

DIVIDERS, COMPASS, AND TRAMMEL POINTS

The DIVIDERS or COMPASS are commonly used to scribe arcs and circles. Fig. 4-10 shows an example of scribing a circle with pencil dividers. In addition, they are also used to lay out distances and find centers. TRAMMEL POINTS are generally used to lay out large arcs and circles. See Fig. 4-11.

CALIPERS

CALIPERS are used to make precision inside and outside measurements, such as inside and outside diameters. Three types of calipers are available: inside, outside, and hermaphrodite. Inside and outside calipers are shown in Fig. 4-12. Hermaphrodite calipers can be used for inside or outside measurements. In most cases, the measurement taken with the calipers must be read by a separate rule.

TEMPLATES

A TEMPLATE is a device that allows you to lay out the same pattern time after time. They are normally made from available materials such as tempered hardboard, plywood, cardboard, or posterboard. A template is made by laying out the design on the material exactly as it is to appear. The pattern is cut out and transferred to the wood stock using a pencil or other marking device as shown in Fig. 4-13. It is also possible to use the template as a guide for drilling holes directly into a product.

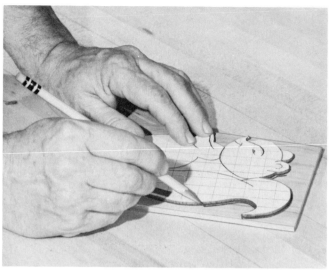

Fig. 4-13. Transferring a template design to wood.

TEST YOUR KNOWLEDGE, Unit 4

Please do not write in this text. Place your answers on a separate sheet of paper.

1. A general term used to describe a measuring device is a _____.

A

B

Fig. 4-12. Calipers are used to make precision measurements. A—Inside caliper. B—Outside caliper.

2. List three kinds of squares normally found in a woods laboratory.
3. A sliding T-bevel allows for accurate layout of angles other than 45 and 90 degrees. The angle is normally set using a _____.
4. An _____ is used to mark the center point before drilling a hole.
5. The marking gauge is very useful for laying out _____ and _____.
6. _____ _____ may be used for making large arcs and circles.
7. The measurement taken by a caliper normally must be read by a separate rule. True or False?
8. The _____ allows you to lay out the same pattern time after time.
9. A device that quickly allows you to bisect (divide in half) an angle is called the _____ _____.
10. In order to accurately lay out a line with a pencil, the pencil must be sharp. True or False?
11. A combination square can perform a number of different functions. Name three.
12. A compass is really a set of dividers with a pencil attached. True or False?
13. A sloyd knife actually cuts a small groove in the surface of the wood. This groove may be easily erased using a pencil eraser. True or False?

14. Calipers look very similar to dividers. Name two different kinds of calipers.
15. List three different materials that may be used to make a template.

ACTIVITIES

1. Obtain catalogs and magazines that contain photographs or drawings and descriptions of many types of rules. Prepare a bulletin board display of these rules and discuss the differences between them.
2. Prepare a short report on using a steel square to lay out a common rafter. You may need to reference a carpentry book to obtain information about this procedure.
3. Create a safety poster for your woods laboratory describing the safe use of pointed layout tools. Make sure that you include layout tools such as awls, sloyd knives, dividers, and pencils.
4. Using cardboard or posterboard, make a template that could be used to lay out an irregular shape.
5. On a board or long piece of paper, lay out the following lengths using at least two different kinds of rules: 3/8″, 1 1/8″, 2 1/4″, 11 15/16″, 25″, 16.5″, 14.25″, and 18.875″.

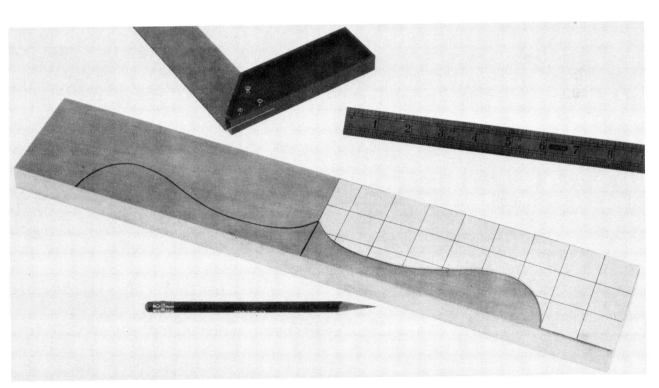

A design can be drawn on posterboard, and then cut out and used as a template. In this case, the design is symmetrical (equal on both sides), so the same template is used for both sides. (John Walker)

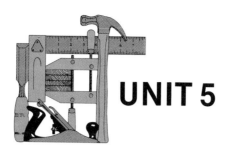

UNIT 5

HAND SAWING

After the correct dimensions have been laid out, you will need to saw the wood. After reading this unit, you will be able to identify saws for cutting curves, ripping, and crosscutting wood. In addition, you will be able to make cuts using the proper saw and sawing technique.

When using woodworking tools, it is important that the tools are used properly and safely. All saws should be kept sharp and set. When working with saws, be sure to select the proper saw for the job. Saws are designed to remove very small portions of the stock with a cutting action. If the saw is not sharp, the saw tears or pulls the wood fibers, rather than cutting them. The use of a dull saw results in a poor cut that may not be square, and that will require more preparation for gluing or finishing.

HAND SAWS

Three basic types of hand saws (other than coping saws) are commonly used to cut wood. They are the:

• Crosscut saw.
• Ripsaw.
• Back or miter saw.

These saws are very similar. All of them cut on the push stroke. All of them have set in their teeth, and all have a wooden handle attached to a steel blade.

CROSSCUT SAW

The CROSSCUT SAW is designed to cut across the grain of the wood. Most crosscut saws have 8, 10 or 12 points (teeth) per inch. The front

faces of the teeth have a 15 degree angle, Fig. 5-1. The back sides of the teeth have a 45 degree angle. The edges of the teeth are beveled about 24 degrees to give them the appearance and cutting action of a series of knives. The teeth are SET (bent to alternate sides). This makes the KERF (cut) wider than the thickness of the blade to prevent binding. The tips of the crosscut teeth score the wood, and the edges of the teeth form a groove and clear the sawdust from the kerf.

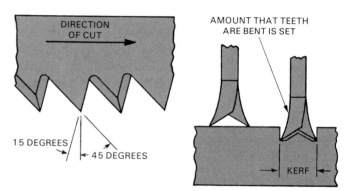

Fig. 5-1. Left. Crosscut saw teeth. Right. Cross section of teeth.

When crosscutting stock, first draw a line across the end of the board using a try square and pencil. Hold the board firmly against a sawhorse or clamp it in a vise. In order to saw a straight and square edge, you must properly grip the handle of the saw. Start by pointing your index finger. The index finger does not wrap around the saw handle, but remains along side of the handle and points toward the line being cut. Insert your other fingers into the saw handle and wrap your thumb around the outside of the handle.

Start the cut with a series of short backward strokes. Make sure the saw teeth are on the waste side of the line. Guide the saw by placing your

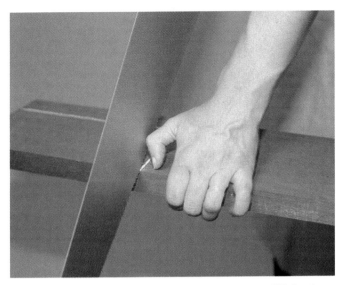

Fig. 5-2. Sawing with a crosscut saw. (John Walker)

thumb above the teeth. When the saw begins to cut, move your thumb away from the blade and make longer forward strokes with the saw. Hold the saw at an angle of about 45 degrees, as shown in Fig. 5-2. Gradually lengthen the strokes using light, uniform pressure. Normally, you should not exceed 30 complete strokes per minute. If this speed is exceeded the saw could be damaged, the operator will tire and the accuracy of the cut will be reduced. If the saw moves away from the line, twist the handle slightly while continuing to saw. When nearing the end of the cut, slow down and lighten the strokes to prevent splitting.

RIPSAW

The RIPSAW is designed to cut with the grain of the stock. The front faces of the teeth have an 8 degree angle. The back sides of the teeth have a 52 degree angle. The ripsaw teeth are filed straight across as shown in Fig. 5-3. This gives them the appearance and cutting action similar to a series of vertical chisels. The saw teeth are set evenly to about one-third the thickness of the blade to

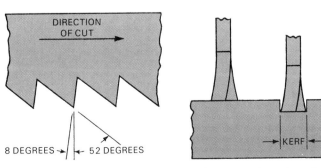

Fig. 5-3. Left. Ripsaw teeth. Right. Cross section of teeth.

give the saw blade clearance in the kerf. Ripsaws normally have 5 1/2 points (teeth) per inch.

When ripping a board, first lay out a straight line along the grain of the board with a square, marking guage, or straightedge. Hold the board firmly against a sawhorse or clamp it in a vise. Hold the ripsaw at an angle of about 60 degrees and saw as with crosscutting, Fig. 5-4, and using the same gripping procedure as recommended for crosscutting.

Fig. 5-4. Sawing with a ripsaw.

BACKSAW

A BACKSAW is used to make fine, accurate cuts. Backsaws are normally 12-, 14-, or 16-inches long. They are generally used for making wood joints and finish cuts. A backsaw has small teeth, usually twelve or more points per inch. The blade is thin for making a narrow kerf. This is the reason that a backsaw has a thick steel "back" and hence the name backsaw. The teeth of a backsaw are cut and set like a crosscut saw. In reality, the backsaw is a crosscut saw.

When using a backsaw, first mark a layout line using a square and a pencil, Fig. 5-5. Clamp a straight board along the layout line to be used as a guide. Use a scrap board beneath the stock to protect your bench top. Keep the blade against the guide as you make slow, light strokes. See Fig. 5-6.

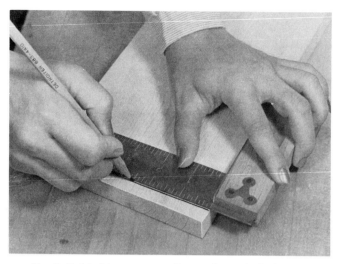

Fig. 5-5. Marking a square line at the end of a board.

Start the cut using a backsaw by aligning the saw blade with the guide clamped to the stock. Slightly raise the handle of the saw to about 30 to 45 degrees. Pull the saw back and make several short cuts. Slowly lower the handle as the cut is started until the saw teeth contact the entire face of the stock. Continue sawing, making sure that the blade is perpendicular to the face. Reduce the speed of the cut and the length of the cut as you approach the other face of the stock. This helps to avoid splintering the bottom edge of the cut.

Miter Box Saw

A MITER BOX SAW is a type of backsaw that is usually used with a miter box. A miter box saw ranges from 24 to 28 inches in length. A MITER BOX is a device that is used to guide the miter box saw. The miter box commonly has settings for cutting common angles such as 45 degrees and 90 degrees. It is very useful for jobs, such as cutting molding and picture frames, that require precise angles. See Fig. 5-7. Exact depths can also be cut on a miter box using a depth stop.

COPING SAW

The COPING SAW is commonly used to cut curves in stock that is one-inch or less in thickness. Use quick, easy strokes with only enough pressure to keep the saw cutting. Hold the saw straight to prevent binding.

Two methods are commonly used to hold stock when cutting with a coping saw. If the stock is thin (3/8-inch or less in thickness), fas-

Fig. 5-6. Making a finish saw cut with a backsaw and a fixture.

Fig. 5-7. Cutting a miter with a miter box saw.

ten a V-block to a bench with a clamp to be used as a platform, or clamp the V-block in the bench vise. When cutting stock with this method, the saw cuts best with a downward stroke. See Fig. 5-8. Therefore, the teeth of the blade point toward the handle. When cutting thicker stock (1/2-inch or more in thickness) fasten the stock in the vise, Fig. 5-9. The saw cuts best with a forward stroke when using this method. The saw teeth should point away from the handle. Occasionally the stock is hand-held, such as when back-cutting cove molding. This method should not be attempted by the beginner, nor should this method be used if a clamping device is available.

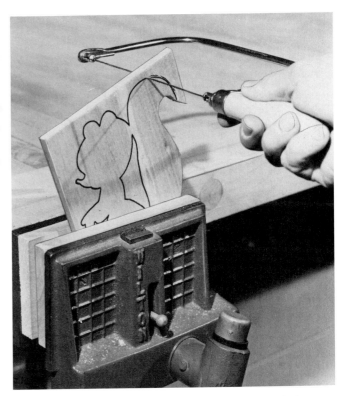

Fig. 5-9. Sawing a curve with a coping saw and vise.

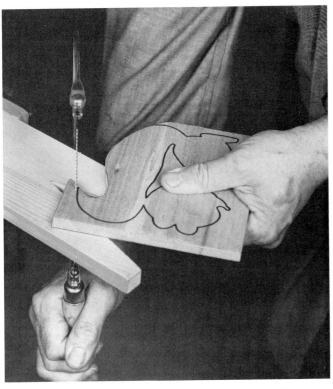

Fig. 5-8. Sawing thin stock with a coping saw and V-block.

Pin-end type or loop-end type blades are available for coping saws. In addition, the number of teeth per inch for coping saw blades vary. They typically have from 10 to 32 teeth per inch. More teeth per inch produce a finer cut.

Most coping saws provide tension to the blade through the use of the handle. The blade is changed by loosening the handle three or four turns and then pressing forward on the front of the frame. The old blade can be removed and the new blade is inserted into the slots at each end. Some frames do not have handles that screw in

and out. They rely on the spring tension of the frame to hold the blade in place. In this case, apply pressure to the front of the frame while pushing on the handle. (It may be necessary to have someone assist in inserting the blade).

In addition to making external curved cuts, coping saws are also used to make internal cuts. Several steps are needed to make an internal cut. First, drill a hole with a large enough diameter to insert the blade in a waste area of the stock. Be careful when drilling the hole so you do not splinter the backside of the stock. Then, remove the blade from the saw, insert it through the hole, and reattach the blade to the frame. The internal cut can then be made.

KEYHOLE AND COMPASS SAWS

The KEYHOLE and COMPASS SAWS are used to cut gentle curves in stock. The tapered blades allow you to cut inside radii after drilling a hole in the waste area of the stock. Manufacturers have a variety of blades that can be used for different materials and varying radii of the curves.

Keyhole and compass saws are very similar in appearance. The keyhole saw is a bit smaller than the compass saw. The keyhole saw, as the name implies, was originally used for cutting lockset openings in doors. The compass saw usually has 7 to 10 teeth per inch, while the keyhole saw has 12 to 14 teeth per inch.

TEST YOUR KNOWLEDGE, Unit 5

Please do not write in this text. Place your answers on a separate sheet of paper.

1. List three types of hand saws other than the coping saw and the keyhole saw.
2. A hand crosscut saw is designed to cut _____ the grain on the _____ stroke.
3. On a crosscut saw, the teeth are set to make a kerf _____ than the thickness of the blade.
4. A hand ripsaw is designed to cut _____ the grain.
5. Ripsaw teeth are filed _____ _____.

6. Coarseness of a saw is designated by the number of teeth per _____.
7. A backsaw is used to make finer cuts than a ripsaw. True or False?
8. The cut made by the teeth of a saw blade is called the _____.
9. A coping saw is used mostly to make _____ cuts.
10. A coping saw cuts best when used to make _____ strokes with the teeth pointed _____ the handle.

ACTIVITIES

1. Research the history of hand saws. Determine the origin of each of the types of saws.
2. Make pencil sketches showing the shapes of the teeth of crosscut and ripsaws.
3. Visit a cabinet shop to determine other types of hand saws that they use. Write a report on your visit and present it to the class.

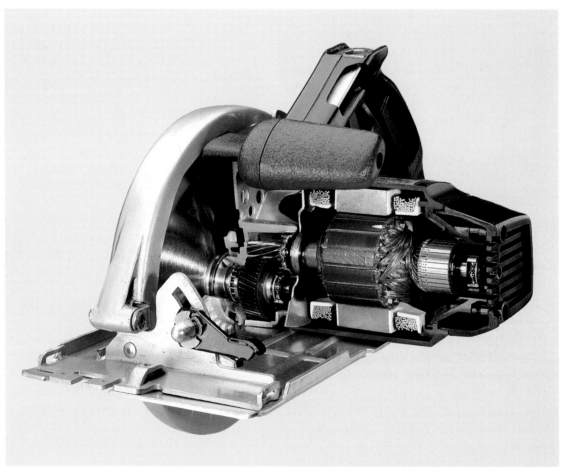

Internal construction of a portable circular saw. (Skil Corp.)

UNIT 6

POWER SAWING

Portable and stationary power can be used to cut lumber and other wood products quickly and easily. In this unit, you will study the basic portable and stationary power saws commonly found in the woods laboratory. You will be able to identify each type of saw and explain which saw is best for the different cutting operations. In addition, you will be able to list the basic safety procedures for each power saw.

In this unit, power saws–both portable and stationary–will be discussed. Certain factors must be kept in mind prior to operating any tool powered by an outside source, such as electricity. One important factor is that the cutting motion is not the result of a force exerted by the operator. With that in mind, you should realize any problem that may occur will continue until the outside force is removed. Some general safety rules must be understood before operating any type of power tool.

1. Never operate a power tool without prior permission of the instructor. Even after you have received permission to use the tool, do not operate the power tool unless the instructor is present.
2. Determine the method of starting and stopping the tool before using it to cut stock. Some saws are equipped with a brake button that must be pressed after the power switch is released. The brake button is used to stop the blade from rotating (coasting). If the tool continues to coast after the machine has been shut off, do not leave the tool unattended until the blade stops. Someone might inadvertently be injured.
3. Safety glasses (or other eye protection) must be worn by the operator of portable and stationary power tools, as well as by everyone in the area of the tool.
4. Many portable and stationary power tools produce high noise levels. Wear ear protection if the noise level is high, or if you will be exposed to the noise for a long period of time.
5. Inspect the power cord of any power tool prior to starting it. If the cord is frayed, split, or worn do not use the tool. Do not use the tool if the grounding pin is missing from a grounded plug. Refer to Fig. 3-4.
6. When changing the blade or setting up a tool for a cut, always remove the plug from the wall receptacle or switch the electrical disconnect to the OFF position.
7. Think through every step of the procedure about to be performed. Is something in the way? Is an outfeed stand needed? Is a push stick at hand? Is additional help needed to do the procedure?
8. Make sure all guards are in place. Special setup jigs and accessories should be properly positioned and secured. If the guard must be removed for a certain cutting procedure, ask the instructor for permission before removing the guard. After you have removed the guard, ask the instructor to check the setup and procedure. Finally, ask the instructor to assist you in the procedure. Instructors have experience and knowledge of the tools that are very valuable!
9. Do not attempt to operate a power tool that has a dull blade. Blades tend to overheat when dull, causing them to warp or break easily without warning. Dull blades also cause the motor to overheat, which may result in permanent damage to the tool. In addition, a dull blade burns the cut surface of the wood. This then requires more sanding, or the surface will not readily accept glue or a finish.

When classifying power saws as stationary or portable, you should consider their use in relationship to the material being cut. A power saw is considered to be "portable" if the saw is taken to the material to be cut and it is pushed through the stock. A power saw is considered to be "stationary" if the material is brought to the saw and the stock is fed into the saw. It is obvious that a 300-pound saw bolted to the floor and wired directly into a circuit box is stationary. However, this difference is pointed out because of some of the smaller "bench-top" scroll saws, table saws, and bandsaws that are now on the market. They may indeed be movable, but are not classified as "portable" because the stock is still fed into the saw.

PORTABLE POWER SAWS

The most common portable power saws used in the woods laboratory are the SABER SAW and the CIRCULAR SAW. Some models of these power saws have a switch that must be held in the ON position during use. When the switch is released, the saw should immediately stop. Blades on some older models of the circular saws coast after releasing the switch, while some saber saws have a toggle-type ON-OFF switch.

SABER SAW

The SABER SAW is a versatile power tool. It can be used to make straight cuts across or parallel to the grain, as well as curved cuts. Most saber saws have a base that allows for tilting the blade to make angled and compound cuts. Fig. 6-1 shows two different models of saber saws.

A variety of blades may be used with the saber saw. There are blades to cut hardwoods or softwoods, blades to make smooth cuts, blades to make coarse, rapid cuts, blades to cut steel, and blades to cut plastic. Make sure that you use the proper blade for the type of cut being made and the material being cut.

Before using a saber saw, clearly mark the cutting path on the stock to be cut. If a long, straight cut is to be made, consider using a straight cutting jig. Firmly support the stock being cut, making sure the cutting path does not run into the support. Place the base of the saw flat on the stock with the blade slightly away from the stock. Turn on the saw and slowly move the blade into the stock while keeping the base firmly on the stock. Continue the cut until it is complete. To avoid breaking the blade, con-

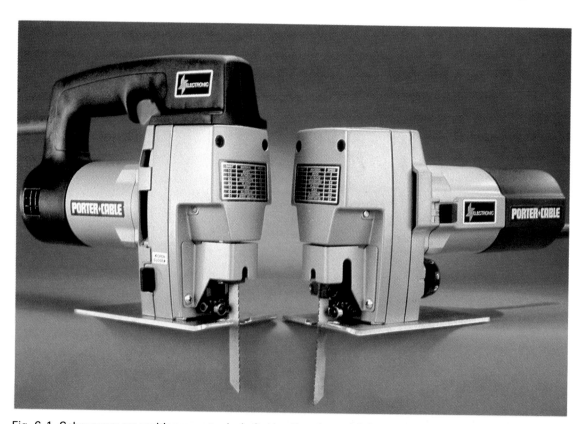

Fig. 6-1. Saber saws are multipurpose tools. Left. Handle-grip model. Right. Barrel-grip model. (Porter-Cable)

tinue running the blade for a second after the cut is complete to make sure the blade has cleared the stock.

Making Internal Cuts with a Saber Saw

Two methods can be used to make internal cuts, or cut stock when the cut does not start at the edge. The first method is similar to making an internal cut with a coping saw. A small hole, about 1/4 inch in diameter, is drilled in the waste area. The saw blade is then inserted into the hole, the saw is turned on, and then guided to the cutting line. This is generally the best method for the beginner to follow to avoid blade breakage.

The second method to make an internal cut is called a PLUNGE CUT. See Fig. 6-2. A plunge cut is made by tilting the saw at an angle and touching the front of the base on the stock to be cut directly above the cutting line. Next, align the blade with the cutting line, but hold it about 1/4 to 1/2 inch above the surface of the stock. Hold the saw firmly and turn it on. Slowly and gently lower the blade into the stock. Allow the base to move slightly toward the hole being cut with the blade while reducing the tilting angle of the base until the base is resting flat on the stock. Proceed to cut on the cutting line as previously discussed.

If it becomes necessary to remove the blade while it is still in the stock, shut the saw off and wait for the blade to stop. When the blade has stopped moving, gently lift the saw straight up to remove the blade.

PORTABLE CIRCULAR SAW

The PORTABLE CIRCULAR SAW, or POWER SAW, is a useful tool for rapid cross-cutting and ripping of large stock. It should only be used for straight cuts. This saw is available in a number of blade sizes ranging from 4 1/2 inches to special circular saws used in timber framing with 12- to 14-inch diameter blades. Newer circular saws are equipped with blade brakes that reduce coasting and a trigger-type ON-OFF switch that cannot be locked in the ON position. They also have a blade guard that automatically retracts as the cut is started and covers the blade when the saw is lifted from the stock. Fig. 6-3 shows a portable circular saw with its parts identified.

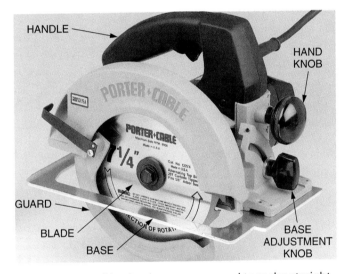

Fig. 6-3. Portable circular saws are used to make straight cuts. (Porter-Cable)

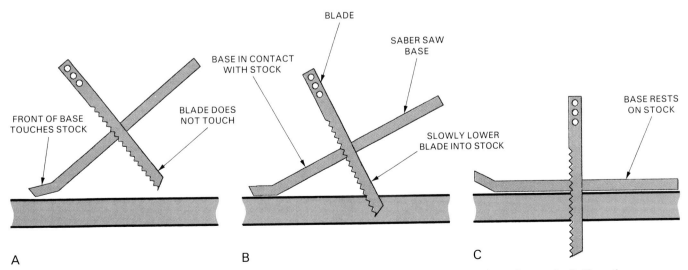

Fig. 6-2. Plunge cutting with a saber saw. A—Tilt the saw and place the front of the base on the stock. B—Turn the saw on and slowly lower the blade into the stock. C—Rest the base on the stock and proceed with cut.

Portable circular saws can have a number of attachments. The rip fence allows you to easily rip (cut to width) long stock. Other attachments, such as a dado blade or a "sawhorse-table" arrangement should not be used by the beginning woodworker. You should become familiar with the saw's basic operation before trying advanced procedures.

Making Cuts with a Portable Circular Saw

Make sure your stock is properly supported and secured into position before making a cut with a portable circular saw. Use sawhorses, clamps, or an assistant to help you support the stock. Carefully lay out the cutting line (always a straight line) on the stock. Make sure that the support is not cut by the portion of the blade that extends below the material.

Hold the stock firmly on the support with one hand. Have an assistant help you support the stock until you are familiar with the saw. Place the base of the saw on the stock with the blade about 1/2 inch away from the stock. Turn the saw on and slowly move the saw forward along the cutting line, Fig. 6-4. Be careful not to allow the saw to bind while making the cut. Binding is normally caused by not following a straight path, or by feeding the saw too quickly into the stock. Reduce the forward speed of the saw slightly near the end of the cut. Your assistant should help you hold the piece being cut off. However, make sure they do not lift up on the material causing the blade to bind.

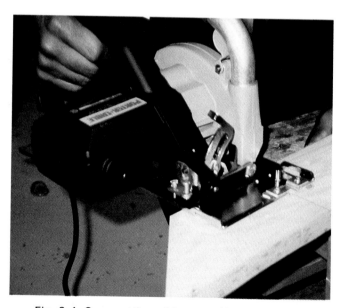

Fig. 6-4. Crosscutting with a portable circular saw.

A number of different types of blades are available, each designed for a certain purpose. Always match the blade to the type of work being done. Most woodworking can be done with a combination blade. This will work for both crosscutting and ripping stock. If a great deal of cutting is planned, a carbide-tipped blade should be used. This type of blade is similar to a standard blade, except that the teeth have carbide tips to prolong cutting life.

STATIONARY POWER SAWS

Four common and basic stationary power saws found in many wood laboratories are covered in this section. They are the:

- Scroll saw, or jigsaw.
- Bandsaw.
- Radial arm saw.
- Table saw.

Certain precautions must be followed for safe use of stationary power saws. Refer to the general safety statements at the beginning of this unit, as well as in the safety unit, before using any stationary power saws. Each of the stationary power saws also has an additional safety rule list. Every student should know the safety rules prior to the use of any of these tools.

SCROLL SAW

A SCROLL SAW, or JIGSAW, is used to cut arcs or curves in stock. The scroll saw allows you to perform the same tasks you did using the coping saw, but more quickly and with greater accuracy. These saws are fun to operate and are probably the safest of the power tools in the woods laboratory. Some woodworkers point out a difference between the scroll saws and jigsaws. However, the term "scroll saw" will be used when referring to a "scroll saw" or "jigsaw" in this book.

Scroll saws are available in three basic designs–the fixed, or rigid arm saw, the C-frame constant-tension saw, and the parallel arm constant-tension saw. See Figs. 6-5 through 6-7. Each of these saws have their own features, advantages, and benefits. The fixed, or rigid arm saw, Fig. 6-5, will cut stock up to about 1-inch thick. The maximum length of stock that can be

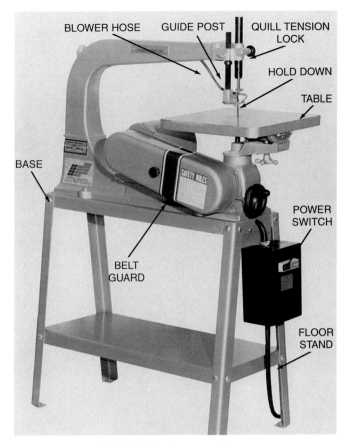

Fig. 6-5. Fixed arm scroll saw.
(Powermatic-Houdaille, Inc.)

cut is equal to the distance from the blade to the back of the arm. The blade moves up and down, cutting only on the downward stroke like any other scroll saw. The motor pulls the blade down and the tension sleeve pulls the blade up. The number of strokes (up and down cycles) per minute may be changed by either moving a belt on a cone pulley or by an adjustable pulley.

The other two types of scroll saws are CONSTANT-TENSION SAWS, meaning that the blade always has a certain amount of tension. See Figs. 6-6 and 6-7. These saws are capable of doing very detailed work in stock up to 2-inches thick. Blade breakage tends to be less of a problem with the constant-tension saws. In addition, the proper blade will allow you to actually turn around in the kerf.

There are many different blades that can be used with these saws. The type of blade to be used is determined by the kind and thickness of the stock, and the diameter of the curves being cut. Almost all blades for scroll saws are 5-inches long. The teeth of the blade must point downward toward the table when installed.

Scroll Saw–Safety and Care
1. Unplug the saw before making any adjustments.
2. Keep your fingers away from the front of the saw blade and out of the cutting path at all times.
3. Turn the saw by hand before turning on the power. This ensures that the blade is not binding.
4. Push the stock forward rather than toward the sides.
5. Always wear safety glasses when operating the scroll saw.

When using a rigid arm saw, the tension sleeve should be adjusted to prevent binding of the blade during a blade cycle (one up stroke and one down stroke). The pressure foot, or hold

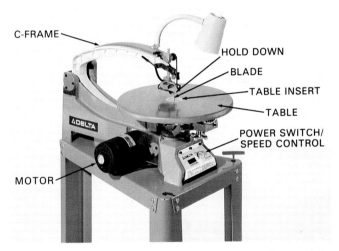

Fig. 6-6. C-frame constant-tension scroll saw. This model also offers a variable-speed option.
(Delta International Machinery Corp.)

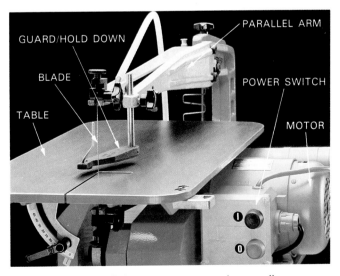

Fig. 6-7. Parallel arm constant-tension scroll saw.

down, should be placed snugly on top of the stock being cut.

When using a constant tension scroll saw, the blade is brought under tension with an adjusting knob located at the back of the saw. The thumb screw just above the blade in the front of the overarm should not be tight. However, it should be lowered just enough to prevent the upper blade clamp from popping out if a blade breaks. If this thumb screw is tightened against the upper blade clamp, blade breakage is likely to occur. The hold down is used more for guiding the blade, and for safety reasons rather than actually holding the stock being cut.

Making an Internal Cut

The procedure for making an internal cut with a scroll saw is similar to making an internal cut with a coping saw. First, make sure the scroll saw is unplugged. Drill a hole with a large enough diameter to insert the blade in the waste area of the stock near the cutting line. Loosen the guide post and hold down on the scroll saw. If you are using a fixed arm saw, turn the machine to the downward stroke by hand. Place the blade (teeth pointing downward)

through the stock to be cut and hole in the table. Insert the end in the lower blade clamp. Place the other end of the blade in the upper blade clamp and adjust the blade tension. Finally, place the hold down in position. Have your instructor check the setup before turning the saw on until you become familiar with this procedure.

When sawing, guide the work with both hands, pushing forward just fast enough to keep the saw cutting. See Fig. 6-8. Do not cut sharp bends; they may be cut out later. Avoid starting a cut in the middle of a straight or slightly curved area, rather start a cut at the endpoint. Use relief cuts whenever possible, but avoid making them too deep. RELIEF CUTS allow waste to break loose as you saw your workpiece. Each relief cut is made almost to the cutting line. Do not overcut because these marks are very difficult to sand out later.

BANDSAWS

The bandsaw has a wide variety of uses. It can be used to make straight or curved cuts, with or without a guide. It can cut wood, plastic, and metal. Fig. 6-9 shows a typical bandsaw. The

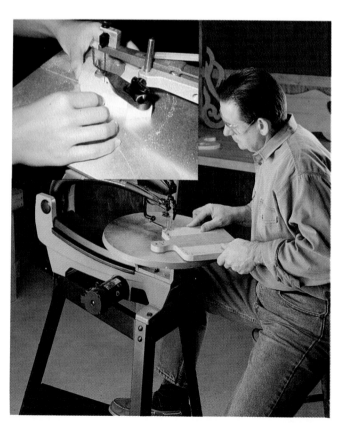

Fig. 6-8. Making detailed internal cuts. Note the hand position in the insert. (Delta International Machinery Corp.)

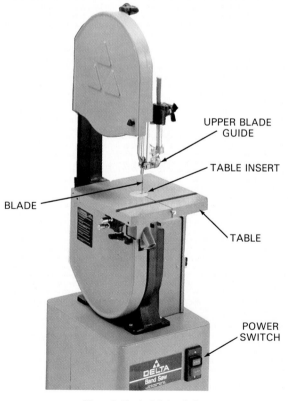

Fig. 6-9. A 14-inch bandsaw. (Delta International Machinery Corp.)

blade of a bandsaw is a continuous band that revolves on two wheels. The size of a bandsaw is determined by the distance from the blade to the back of the saw. Normally, this distance is the same as the diameters of the wheels. A 14-inch bandsaw is a popular size. The upper wheel is adjustable to tighten or loosen the blade. It can also be tilted forward and backward to adjust tracking of the blade so that it "rides" in the middle of the wheel.

Blades for the 14-inch bandsaw are available in widths from 1/8 to 1 inch. Fig. 6-10 shows the minimum radii that can be cut by a given blade width. Do not cut a radius that is smaller than the blade can handle safely. Bandsaw blades are available in a variety of tooth sizes and styles. The proper tooth style or size is determined by the type of material being cut and the coarseness of the cut you want to obtain. The total length of the blade is specified by the bandsaw manufacturer.

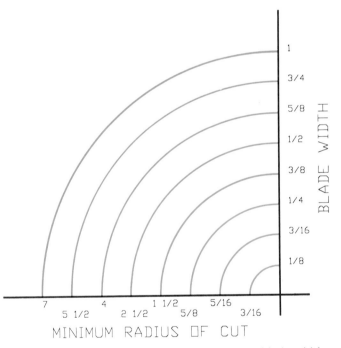

Fig. 6-10. Blade guide for selecting the proper blade width for the arc or curve radius being cut.

The upper and lower guide assemblies should be checked frequently. Always consult the instructor before making an adjustment, or if the saw is out of adjustment. The blade guides should clear the blade by about 0.003 inch (approximately the thickness of a piece of paper). The roller supports (backing bearings) should clear the back of the blade by about 1/32 inch.

Bandsaw—Safety and Care

1. Keep hands to the side of the blade, away from the path of the blade.
2. If the blade breaks, step aside and disconnect the electricity to the machine.
3. Keep your fingers at least 2 inches from the blade at all times. Use a fixture to hold small pieces.
4. Always keep the upper guide assembly 1/4 to 1/2 inch above the stock. This prevents an excess amount of the blade from being exposed.
5. Push the stock forward rather than to the side.
6. Work within the capacity of the saw. A thick piece of stock must be fed slower into the blade than a thin piece.
7. Observe the safety zone around the bandsaw. If a blade breaks, it will occasionally "climb" out to the right side of the operator.

Cutting with the Bandsaw

Lay out the cuts to be made on the stock and consider the sequence of the cuts. Short cuts should be made first so that it is not necessary to back out of a cut, Fig. 6-11. Straight cuts should be made before curved cuts for the same reason. When sharp curves are necessary, make longer curves first and then finish these cuts later. Sharp outside curves can be made by making several relief cuts perpendicular (at a 90 degree angle) to the curve, as shown in Fig. 6-12. Many pieces can be cut at one time on a bandsaw. Fasten the pieces together by placing several nails in the waste area, as shown in Fig. 6-13.

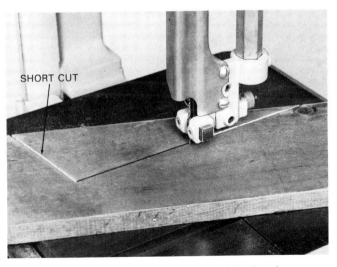

Fig. 6-11. Make the short cut first with a bandsaw.

Fig. 6-12. Make relief cuts before cutting around sharp curves with a bandsaw.

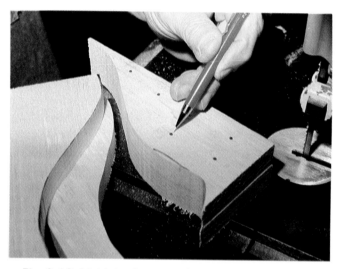

Fig. 6-13. Multiple pieces can be cut at one time on the bandsaw. Fasten pieces together by nailing in the waste area.

Before starting the cut, place the stock on the saw table and adjust the guide post so the upper guide assembly is about 1/4 inch above the work. Have the instructor check the setup before turning on the machine. When cutting, keep your hands to the sides of the cutting line, out of the direct line of the saw blade. Use only enough forward pressure to keep the blade cutting. Narrow, straight stock (less than three-inches wide) is ripped using a fence and a push stick. See Fig. 6-14.

TABLE SAW

The TABLE SAW, Fig. 6-15, is often referred to as a CIRCULAR SAW or BENCH SAW. It is

one of the most productive machines in the woods laboratory if used properly. However, it can be one of the most dangerous machines if improperly used. If you practice a few safety precautions, you can learn to use the table saw safely and efficiently.

The size of a table saw is determined by the maximum diameter of the saw blade that can be safely used on the saw. The blade revolves at

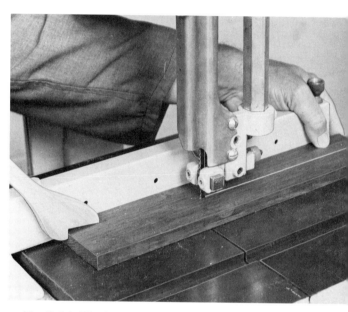

Fig. 6-14. Ripping narrow stock with a bandsaw and a push stick.

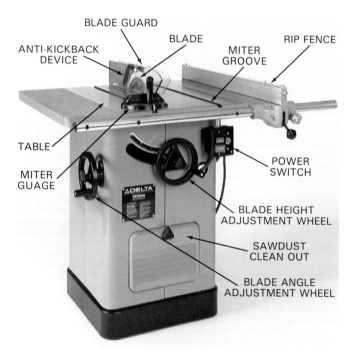

Fig. 6-15. Table saws are used to make straight cuts in stock. (Delta International Machinery Corp.)

high speed, and a GUARD is kept over the blade for protection of your fingers and hands. In addition, a guard is valuable for deflecting sawdust out of the line of sight. Most saws are equipped with small fingers called an anti-kickback device. The ANTI-KICKBACK DEVICE is designed to prevent kickbacks, or to reduce the velocity (speed) of a piece of stock if a kickback occurs.

Every table saw should be equipped with a splitter. The SPLITTER holds the saw kerf open in the ripping operation to reduce the kickback hazard. See Fig. 6-16. Splitters are commonly part of the anti-kickback device.

Fig. 6-16. Use the splitter when ripping stock.

A movable FENCE can be used for accurate ripping of stock. The fence slides along guide bars attached to the front and back of the table. Another piece of equipment used with the table saw is the miter gauge. The MITER GAUGE is used to aid in crosscutting and mitering pieces of stock. The fence and miter gauge should not be used at the same time without attaching a clearance block to the fence. See Figs. 6-17 and 6-18.

The types of blades commonly used with the table saw are the crosscut, rip, and combination blades. The CROSSCUT BLADE has teeth similar to a hand crosscut saw. They look and cut like a series of knives. The crosscut blade is usually used for cutting across the grain of the wood. The RIP BLADE has teeth similar to a hand ripsaw. The rip blade cuts like a series of

chisels, and is used for cutting along the grain of the wood. The COMBINATION BLADE has both crosscut and rip teeth. It is used for all-purpose work. Some combination blades are HOLLOW GROUND making the blade thicker near the teeth. This provides for clearance of the blade in the saw kerf, and eliminates the need for setting the teeth. A standard combination blade makes a smooth, accurate cut when crosscutting and mitering. However, when ripping stock it tends to overheat because of insufficient blade clearance.

There are many special blades for cutting plastic laminates, plywood, tempered hardboard, and similar materials. Always use the proper type of blade for the work to be performed. Today, carbide-tipped blades are available for most cutting purposes. Carbide-tipped blades offer many advantages. First, they cut cleaner and faster than standard blades. Next, they require less edge preparation before gluing, and cause less strain on the saw's motor. Some blade makers claim that a carbide-tipped blade will outlast 200 or more standard blades. Two basic problems exists with carbide-tipped blades. First, they are costly, and second, they require special sharpening equipment when they become dull.

Table Saw — Safety and Care
1. Have the instructor check the setup before turning on the saw.
2. Stand slightly to one side of the cutting path; do not stand in line with the blade. This protects you from being hit if a kickback occurs.
3. Always keep your hands and fingers 4 to 6 inches away from cutting path.
4. Make sure others are not in the safety zone around the table saw when you are using the saw.
5. Use the correct blade for the type of cutting being done. For example, do not use a rip blade to crosscut wood. Make sure the blade is sharp and the teeth have set.
6. Properly position the fence, miter gauge, outfeed stand, and other accessories before starting the saw. Do not forget the push stick for narrow stock.
7. The blade should not be raised more than 1/4 inch above the stock. The blade speed is

the same no matter how high you raise the blade.

8. Make sure the stock is properly prepared before using the table saw. Warp must be removed from the wood's surface and at least one edge must be surfaced before cutting it.

Crosscutting

Make sure your piece of stock has one true (planed smooth) edge. Layout your cutting line on the piece of stock to be cut, placing your square along the true edge. Raise the blade so it projects above the stock 1/8 to 1/4 inch. Move the fence out of the way since it will not be needed for the crosscutting operation. Lay the board on the table with the true edge against the miter gauge. Align the mark with the saw blade and place the guard in the proper position. Pull the miter gauge and stock away from the blade carefully so that you do not move the stock from side to side. Stand slightly to one side of the blade and turn on the machine. Hold the stock firmly against the miter gauge as the gauge is pushed slowly along the miter groove. Feed the stock slowly into the saw. Push the board past the saw blade and turn off the saw.

In some cases, you may need to crosscut stock to equal lengths. In these cases, you will need to clamp a clearance block to the fence or use a stop block attachment, Fig. 6-17. The clearance block or stop block should be attached well in front of the blade, so that the stock being cut

does not get pinched between the block and the blade. See Fig. 6-18. When figuring out the length of the pieces, measure from the edge of the blade to the clearance block or stop block, not the fence itself.

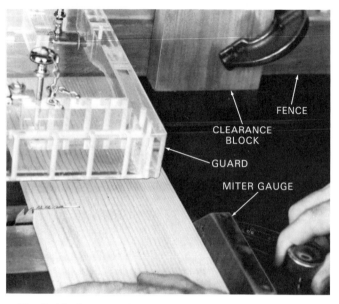

Fig. 6-18. Crosscutting duplicate pieces using a circular saw and clearance block.

Mitering

Angled cuts may be made across pieces of stock by using a procedure similar to crosscutting stock. Miters (45 degree) are commonly used to form 90 degree angles for products like picture frames. The miter gauge should be set to the proper angle of the cut. Check the angle to make sure that it is correct. Some miter gauges

Fig. 6-17. Stop block attachment for a table saw.

may have hold-down fixtures to prevent the stock from moving. Then proceed with the cut as you would when crosscutting stock.

Ripping

Softwood lumber is available in standard widths and lengths. Hardwood lumber is sold in random widths and lengths. In many cases, the width dimensions of your product are not the width dimensions of the stock. In these cases, you must rip the stock to the correct width. Make sure when you are ripping stock that the edge resting against the fence has been planed or smoothed.

Remove the miter gauge from the saw and place it out-of-the-way of the ripping operation. Raise the blade so that it is 1/8 to 1/4 inch above the stock, as in crosscutting. Set the fence using the scale on the front guide bar. Before cutting, use a bench rule or tape measure to verify the ripping width. This is done by measuring from the tooth set to the fence. Adjust the distance as necessary.

Place the guard in position, making sure the splitter and anti-kickback fingers are properly positioned. Lay the stock flat on the table with the true edge next to the fence. Make sure a push stick is at hand (if it is needed) before turning on the saw. A push stick is required for pieces less than six inches wide. Turn on the saw and push the board slowly into the blade. Apply forward pressure only on the piece between the blade and the fence. Continue pushing the board until its entire length has been cut, and then turn off the saw. Wait until the blade stops rotating before removing pieces of wood from around the blade. Be sure to use the splitter for ripping operations. See Fig. 6-19. The SPLITTER acts as a metal wedge in the saw kerf and separates the two pieces being cut to help prevent binding.

Ripping Accessories

Accessories allow you to do your work more safely and accurately. All of the following devices are useless unless installed and adjusted prior to the ripping operation. Always think the process through before starting the saw.

Some fences are equipped with a device that may be used instead of a push stick. This "finger-saving" device holds down the stock while

pushing it past the blade, Fig. 6-20. This device is normally mounted to the fence so that it is available when needed.

Another fixture that may be used when ripping simply holds the stock firmly against the table. This allows the operator to guide the stock using both hands. This fixture may be installed

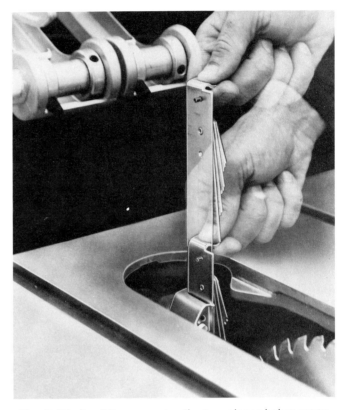

Fig. 6-19. A splitter separates the two pieces being cut to prevent binding.

Fig. 6-20. This finger-saving device holds the wood down while allowing you to cut it.

on the fence when performing ripping operations. In addition, the fixture also prevents kickbacks if the blade binds. Fig. 6-21 shows this fixture in use.

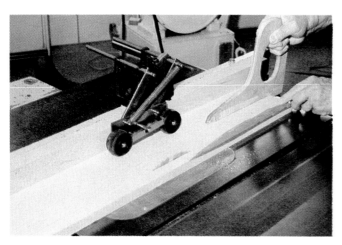

Fig. 6-21. This ripping fixture holds the stock against the table, and also prevents kickbacks if the blade binds.

Another accessory that is helpful when ripping is the OUTFEED STAND, also called a STEADY-REST or DEAD-MAN. See Fig. 6-22. The height is easily adjusted to provide support when ripping long stock.

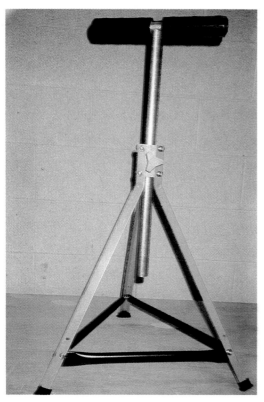

Fig. 6-22. An outfeed stand supports long pieces of stock. Make sure these devices are properly placed and weighted to prevent them from tipping during a ripping operation.

A FEATHERBOARD is a device that is typically made in the woods laboratory. A featherboard is simply a piece of stock with a series of kerfs cut along the grain (not across the grain). When clamped to the table of the saw and properly positioned against the stock being cut, the featherboard guides the stock into the blade by pushing the stock firmly against the fence. See Fig. 6-23.

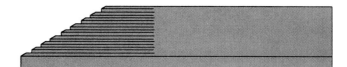

Fig. 6-23. A featherboard is used when ripping stock. It is clamped to the table of the saw.

Beveling

A BEVEL is an angled cut along an edge of a board. The blade must be tilted to cut a bevel on the table saw. Turn the saw tilt handwheel to the correct angle. Always check the saw blade angle with a sliding T-bevel and protractor. The saw-mounted gauge is seldom accurate enough for finish cutting.

Since you will be cutting at an angle, the blade may need to be raised to cut all the way through the stock. Before starting the saw, make sure that the blade does not come into contact with the guard or fence.

Sawing a Rabbet

A RABBET is a type of wood joint commonly used in drawer and cabinet construction. One-half of the thickness of the wood is removed so that another piece can fit into position.

Lay out the size of the rabbet on the end of the stock and set the blade to this height. Place the stock flat on the table with the marked edge next to the fence. Use a push stick to move the board into the saw as if you were ripping stock. Place the surface of the board against the fence and make the second cut as shown in Fig. 6-24.

Cutting a Groove or Dado

Grooves and dados are other types of wood joints used in cabinet construction. GROOVES run parallel to the grain of the wood. DADOS run across the grain of the wood.

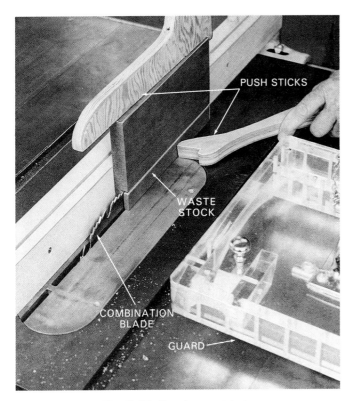

Fig. 6-24. Sawing a rabbet.

Grooves and dados are usually made with a dado head, Fig. 6-25. A DADO HEAD makes a wide cut in a piece of stock. They should not be used to cut through stock. Two types of dado heads are available. One type consists of two saw blades, and a set of chippers with cutting edges varying from 1/16- to 1/4-inch wide. The

Fig. 6-25. Cutting a groove with a dado head. (Guard is removed to view the operation.)

chippers are set up between the saws to the width of the desired cut. Dados or grooves ranging from 1/8- to 13/16-inch wide can be made. The other type of dado head consists of three parts. In this type of dado head, the center piece (containing the cutters) is turned to adjust the blade to the desired width. In either case, a different throat plate must be used to allow clearance for the wider blade.

When cutting a groove or dado, adjust the dado head to the width and depth of the cut desired. Check these settings using a scrap piece of stock. Use a push stick to move the stock slowly into the dado head as in ripping or crosscutting. Make sure that you hold the stock securely, since the dado head is removing more stock than a standard blade.

Cutting a Tenon

A TENON is a wood joint commonly used in furniture construction and cabinetmaking. Material is removed from both sides of the stock. A table saw with a TENONING JIG will cut an accurate tenon safely. A standard rip blade, combination blade, or dado head can be used to cut a tenon. However, a dado head is suggested to reduce the number of steps required.

First, set-up the dado head to the width of the shoulder of the tenon. Install the proper throat plate. Adjust the height of the dado head to the depth of the tenon shoulder. Place the tenoning jig in the miter groove and firmly clamp a piece of scrap lumber, which is the same size as the tenon stock, into the jig. Keep the saw turned off and move the tenoning jig toward the dado head. Stop just as the stock begins to touch the dado head. Adjust the stops on the tenoning jig for the left shoulder and tighten the lock nut, Fig. 6-26A. Repeat this procedure for the right shoulder, Fig 6-26B. Move the jig away from the dado head. Turn on the motor and make a test cut. Adjust the jig as necessary before using the finish stock.

Changing the Blade

Before changing the blade, disconnect the power to the saw and remove the INSERT PLATE (plate around the saw blade, frequently called a THROAT PLATE). Place a wrench on the arbor nut with one hand. Wedge a board under the saw blade with the other hand to

A

B

Fig. 6-26. Cutting a tenon with a tenoning jig. A–Make adjustments for the left shoulder. B–Make adjustments for the right shoulder.

prevent the blade from turning. Many saws provide a second wrench and nut allowing the arbor to be held in place. Turn the nut on the arbor clockwise for removal; most saw arbors have left-hand threads. After loosening the nut, place your index finger on the end of the arbor and unthread the nut onto your finger. This prevents it from dropping into the sawdust below. Remove the nut. Place your index finger on the end of the arbor again and slide the washer onto your finger. Remove the blade being careful that you do not cut yourself on the sharp teeth, or chip the teeth by hitting the table.

Place the new blade on the arbor. Make sure the teeth of the blade point toward the stock and operator when in operation. Put the washer on your finger and slip onto the end of the arbor. Do the same for the nut. Tighten the nut using the wrench.

POWER MITER SAW

The POWER MITER SAW, also called the CHOP SAW, is very useful for accurate crosscutting and mitering. See Fig. 6-27. These saws have an angle gauge that allows you to rotate the movable head to any desired setting from 0 to 45 degrees on either the left or right. Make sure that your fingers are not in the cutting path when using the power miter saw. Also, make sure that the stock is firmly held against the fence and down on the table. After making the cut, do not leave the saw unattended until the blade stops. Some saws have an automatic brake, while oth-

ers have a button on the handle that stops the blade when pushed. The parts of the power miter saw are shown in Fig. 6-28.

Fig. 6-27. Power miter saws are used for accurate crosscutting and mitering. (Delta International Machinery Corp.)

RADIAL ARM SAW

The RADIAL ARM SAW was originally designed for doing very accurate crosscutting at a 90 degree angle, as well as any other desired

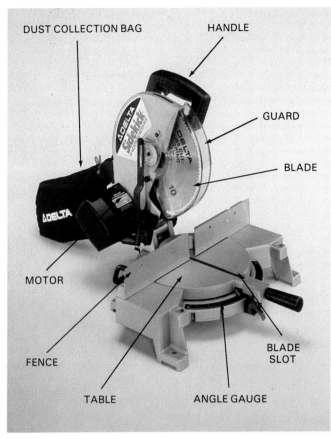

Fig. 6-28. Parts of a power miter saw.
(Delta International Machinery Corp.)

4. Allow the saw blade to reach its full speed before beginning to cut stock.
5. Keep your hand that is not on the motor-blade assembly at least 6 inches from the blade and blade cutting path. Tuck your thumb under your hand. Hold the stock in position with the heel of your hand.
6. Always return the motor-blade assembly to the rear of the saw after making a cut. All saws under Occupational Safety and Health Act (OSHA) regulations must return automatically.
7. Do not leave the saw unattended until the blade has stopped turning. All new saws have an automatic brake to stop the blade.
8. When ripping stock, make sure the splitter and anti-kickback devices are properly adjusted. Make sure to feed the stock into the blade against the blade rotation, and not in the direction of the rotation.

The radial arm saw blade cuts into the wooden table with each cut that is made. Attach a 1/4-inch thick piece of plywood to the original top to reduce damage using small nails or brads. Make

angle. It is now commonly used in the woods laboratory for rough cutting stock to length. The tilting head (motor-blade assembly) makes it possible to cut angles on the ends of stock. In addition, if the overarm is set at an angle other than 90 degrees, nearly perfect compound angles can also be cut. Fig. 6-29 shows a radial arm saw.

A number of accessories that are made for the table saw can also be used with the radial arm saw. These include sanding discs, molding heads, and dado heads. Other accessories are designed just for the radial arm saw such as, jacob chucks, cutoff stops, mitering jigs, belt and drum sanders, and pin router devices.

Radial Arm Saw—Safety and Care
1. Become familiar with the ON-OFF switch, its location, and operation.
2. Make sure the blade guard and sawdust deflector are set properly for the cut that is planned.
3. Check the relationship of the blade to the slot cut into the fence and the groove cut into the table. Adjust the fence as necessary to align all three.

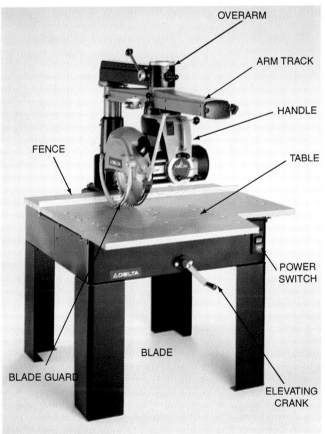

Fig. 6-29. Radial arm saw with parts identified.
(Delta International Machinery Corp.)

sure the nails are not in the blade path. When the plywood top is scored with saw cuts, simply replace it. The crosscutting action of the radial arm saw is somewhat different than the table saw. Stock is pushed through on the table saw; the motor-blade assembly slides on the overarm through the stock on the radial arm saw. When molding or ripping stock, the stock is again pushed through the blade as on the table saw.

Crosscutting

Make sure the blade is properly attached to the motor. As you look at the end of the motor that has a blade attached, the blade should rotate in a clockwise direction. Be sure that the fence and movable portion of the table have been firmly tightened.

When making a 90 degree crosscut, first place a steel square against the fence, aligned with the path of the saw blade. Gently pull the saw along the square with the power turned off. The teeth of the blade should be the same distance away from the square at all points along the blade path. If there is any variance, consult the owner's manual for proper saw adjustment.

After determining the squareness, turn on the power and lower the blade into the table until it makes a cut 1/8 to 1/4 inch in depth. Pull the saw along its entire path. This kerf clearly indicates the blade's path. Then, turn off the saw. Carefully mark and square the desired cutting location on your stock. Align this mark with the cut made in the fence. Make sure the saw kerf will be made in the waste portion of your stock. Firmly hold the stock against the fence, keeping your hands away from the blade path. Turn on the saw and gently pull the saw through the stock. Be prepared to use some backward pressure on the saw carriage as the blade cuts through the stock. Return the saw to its original position and turn off the saw. Check the cut for squareness.

Ripping

When ripping stock, remember that the blade rotates into the stock at the front of the blade, not the back. If the stock is fed from the back of the blade, the power of the motor will force the stock to "shoot" under the blade without being cut, and without your control. This is a very hazardous situation.

Most radial arm saws allow the motor/blade assembly and carriage to be rotated either left or right for in-ripping or out-ripping operations. The width of the stock being ripped and the size of the saw determine whether to set the saw for in-ripping or out-ripping. Disconnect the power to the radial arm saw. Raise the carriage slightly above the table and rotate the head either left or right depending on the width of the cut. Secure the head into position. Loosen the carriage locknut and pull the carriage until the desired width is obtained between the fence and the saw blade. Tighten the carriage locknut. Check this measurement with a rule and adjust as necessary. Reconnect the power and turn on the saw. Lower the blade into the table about 1/8 to 1/4 inch. Rotate the blade guard to approximately 1/4 inch above the stock. Adjust and align the anti-kickback device and splitter. Refer to the owner's manual for specific adjustment procedures. Make sure one edge of the stock has been squared. Place this edge against the fence and feed the stock into the blade. Continue the cut using a push stick, if necessary.

TEST YOUR KNOWLEDGE, Unit 6

Please do not write in this text. Place your answers on a separate sheet of paper.

1. Only the person operating the power saw needs to wear eye protection. True or False?
2. The saber saw will cut _____ lines and _____ lines.
3. The portable circular saw is designed to cut only _____ lines.
4. The _____ is used to hold the kerf open when ripping with a table saw.
5. The teeth of the blades used in a stationary scroll saw always point _____.
6. When making an internal cut with a scroll saw, it is necessary to first drill a small hole in the waste area of the stock. True or False?
7. A bandsaw may be used to make both _____ cuts and _____ cuts.
8. The blade of a bandsaw is continuous. True or False?
9. The two primary cuts made on the table saw are the _____ and the _____.
10. The guard of the table saw protects fingers and hands but also deflects _____ from the eyes.

11. What is a featherboard?
12. On a portable circular saw, a _____ covers the blade at the end of each cut to protect the operator and the saw.
13. When crosscutting with the radial arm saw the blade is pulled through the stock. True or False?
14. A device used to cut a rabbet using a table saw in called a _____.
15. The rip fence and the miter gauge should never be used together unless a clearance block has been properly attached to the fence. True or False?
16. The motor/base assembly on a radial arm saw is called the carriage. True or False?
17. When ripping with a radial arm saw, the stock should be fed into the _____ of the blade.
18. The squareness of a radial arm saw can be checked using a _____.

19. On a radial arm saw, the blade should not cut into the table. True or False?

ACTIVITIES

1. Following safety rules is important. Design a safety poster that can be used with any single piece of portable or stationary equipment discussed in this chapter.
2. Draw sketches that show the shape of crosscut, rip, and combination table saw blades. You may need to reference manufacturer catalogs.
3. Visit a cabinet shop or other woodworking industry. Find out about the types of power saws they use. Report your findings to the class.
4. Visit your local hardware store to see what types of power saws they sell. Make a list of the options offered with a particular saw.

Internal construction of a saber saw. (Skil Corp.)

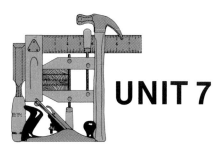

UNIT 7

BORING AND DRILLING

Most woodworking products require one or more holes. They may be for the insertion of a coping saw or jigsaw blade, or perhaps for a dowel or screw. After reading this unit, you will be able to identify the bits most commonly used in the woods laboratory. In addition, you will be able to identify the drills themselves, and demonstrate their proper and safe use.

Holes range in size according to their purpose. A 1/16-inch diameter hole may be used for a small nail, or a 3-inch diameter hole may be used for the installation of a small clock movement. Since one size drill bit cannot generally be used to drill all sizes of holes, there are various kinds and sizes of drill bits that are available.

WOODWORKING BITS

Drill bits can be generally classified into two groups; those that make holes larger than 1/4-inch diameter, and those that make holes smaller than 1/4-inch diameter. Holes larger than 1/4-inch diameter are usually referred to as being BORED. Holes that are smaller than 1/4-inch diameter are usually referred to as being DRILLED. Different bits and tools can be used for each of these processes. Bored holes can be made with a bit brace, hand drill, or power drill using auger bits, Forstner bits, spade bits, and hole saws. Drilled holes can be made with a hand or power drill using a twist drill.

Auger Bits

Until recently, the most common woodworking bit used to bore holes was an AUGER BIT, Fig 7-1. Auger bits have a tapered, square tang that fits into a boring device called a BIT

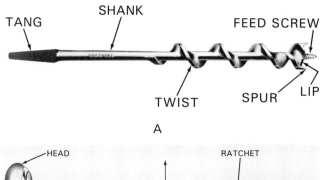

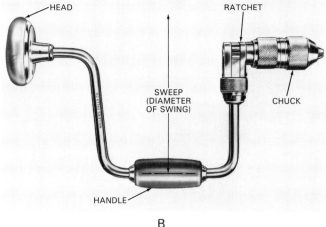

Fig. 7-1. Auger bits and bit braces are used to bore holes. A – Auger bit. B – Brace. (Millers Falls Co.)

BRACE, or BRACE. The number stamped on the tang represents the diameter of the bit in sixteenths of an inch. Auger bits are designed to be used only in wood. They make fairly precise diameter holes. While these bits were generally used in hand boring operations, newer auger bits may allow you to use power drills as well.

Forstner Bits

Another type of bit that is popular in woodworking is the FORSTNER BIT, Fig. 7-2. These bits range in size from 1/4- to 3-inch diameters. Forstner bits make a very clean cut and a flat-bottom hole. Forstner bits are usually used with the drill press.

Fig. 7-2. Forstner bits make flat bottom holes.

Spade Bits

A SPADE BIT is another common type of woodworking bit. See Fig. 7-3A. They range in size from 1/4- to 1 1/2-inch diameters. Spade bits have a very sharp point that is self-starting. They cut stock very quickly. Spade bits are primarily used in power drills and drill presses.

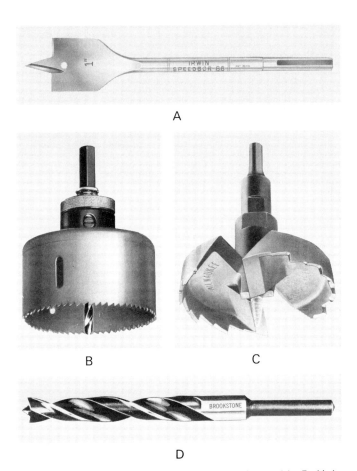

A

B   C

D

Fig. 7-3. Common woodworking bits. A–Spade bit. B–Hole saw. C–Multispur bit. D–Reduced-diameter (cut-down) shank drill bit.

Hole Saws

HOLE SAWS are can-like drilling devices with crosscut teeth on the bottom, and mounted to a shank called an ARBOR. See Fig. 7-3B. They are used for boring holes as large as 5 or 6 inches in diameter. Hole saws are used in power drills and drill presses.

Twist Drill

A common woodworking bit used to drill holes is the TWIST DRILL. This type of bit has straight shank or a reduced-diameter shank. The reduced-diameter shank allows you to use a larger diameter drill bit in a smaller chuck. A 3/8-inch, reduced-diameter shank drill bit, for example, will fit into a 1/4-inch chuck. Twist drills are made either of carbon steel or high-speed steel. Carbon steel bits are commonly used in wood, while high-speed steel bits are commonly used in wood or steel.

Brad Point Twist Drill

Another type of twist drill bit that is being used more and more in woodworking is the BRAD POINT TWIST DRILL, Fig. 7-4. They look like a twist drill, but a point has been filed on the end. This allows the bit to start a hole without straying from the center point.

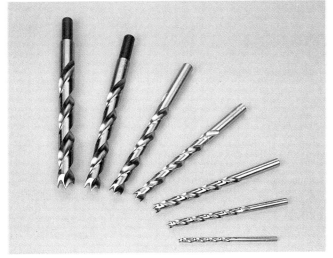

Fig. 7-4. Brad point twist drills are becoming more popular in woodworking.

Countersink Bit

A COUNTERSINK BIT cuts a funnel-shaped recess in the surface of the stock. See Fig. 7-5. This allows the head of a flat head screw to be

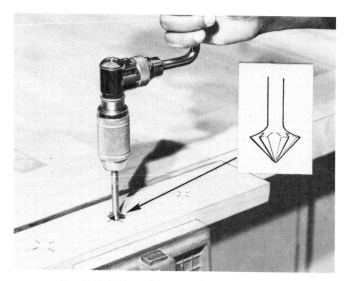

Fig. 7-5. Using a brace and countersink bit.

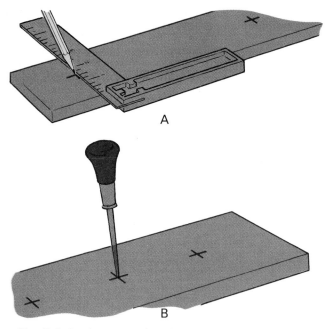

Fig. 7-6. Laying out and marking holes. A–Lay out the correct position with a square and pencil. B–Mark the hole center with an awl.

flush (even) with the surface. When countersinking, make sure that you cut only deep enough so the head of the screw is flush with the surface. Some of these bits not only cut an area for the head of the screw, but also drill the areas for the threads and shank of the screw.

If the screws are to be covered with wood plugs, a counterboring operation must be performed. This is done by counterboring the original holes with a drill bit slightly larger than the screw head. A special counterboring tool may also be used in a portable drill or drill press.

BORING HOLES WITH AN AUGER BIT AND BRACE

Lay out the holes to be bored and mark their locations on the stock with an awl, Fig. 7-6. Clamp the stock in a bench vise, or clamp it to the table top using a wood clamp. In either case, make sure that you also clamp a piece of scrap lumber behind your stock as a back-up board. A back-up board is used to avoid splitting out the back of the stock when the bit cuts through the wood. If a back-up board is not used, bore the hole until the feed screw starts to come through the stock, remove the bit from the hole, and then complete the hole by boring from the other side.

When boring holes, hold the bit perpendicular (90 degrees) to the stock. See Fig. 7-7. Use a try square to check that the bit is boring at 90 degrees to the stock. Use only enough pressure to keep the bit cutting; do not force the auger bit into the stock.

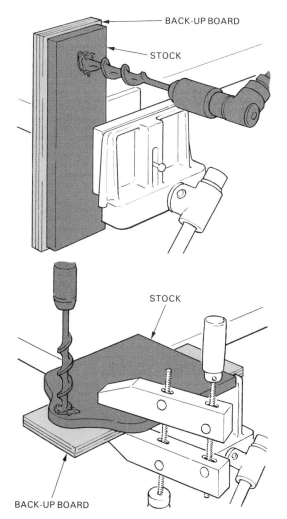

Fig. 7-7. Top. Boring a hole in a horizontal position with a brace and auger bit. Bottom. Boring a hole in a vertical position.

Boring Holes at an Angle

Lay out holes to be bored on the stock and mark the locations with an awl. Make sure that your stock is held firmly in a vise or clamped to the table top. Use a back-up board behind the stock, or complete the hole by boring from the other side, to avoid splitting out the stock. Use a sliding T-bevel set to the desired angle when beginning the boring. You may also want to use it as a guide during boring as shown in Fig. 7-8.

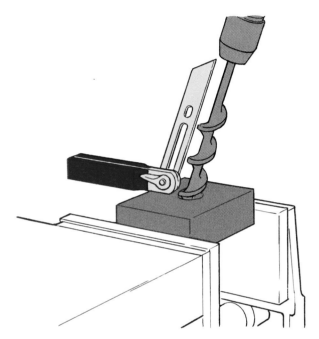

Fig. 7-8. Boring a hole at an angle using a sliding T-bevel as a guide.

HAND DRILL

The HAND DRILL is used to drill small holes and countersink to recess screw heads. See Fig. 7-9. Bits used with a hand drill must have round shanks. The bits are held in a 3-jaw chuck mounted on the front of the drill. The bit is turned with a handle and geared wheels. The size of a hand drill is designated by the capacity of its chuck. This capacity is equal to the largest straight-shank bit that fits into the chuck. A 1/4-inch hand drill is a common size.

Drilling Holes with a Hand Drill

Lay out the locations of the holes to be drilled. Mark the center points with an awl to avoid having the bit slide (walk) across the stock. Hold the bit straight and use only enough pressure to keep the bit cutting, Fig. 7-10. Control the feed rate by applying either more or less pressure on the

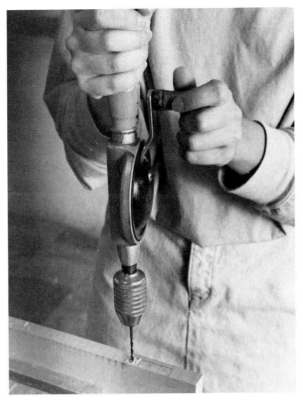

Fig. 7-9. A hand drill is used for small diameter holes.

Fig. 7-10. Drilling with a hand drill.

handle. Use less pressure when drilling hard-wood, or when using small bits. Remove the bit frequently to clear wood chips that may be stuck in the flutes of the bit.

If the hole is to be drilled only part of the way through the stock, apply a piece of masking tape to the drill bit as a depth gauge. If the hole is to be drilled through the stock, use a back-up board to ensure a smooth hole as the bit cuts through the other side of the stock.

PUSH DRILL

A PUSH DRILL is convenient to use when you do not have enough room to turn the crank or handle of a hand drill or brace. See Fig. 7-11. A hole is made by pushing the handle. A strong spring returns the handle to its original position. The special shanks on these bits are called "Yankee shanks." The bits are often stored in the handle. The push drill is a fast and efficient means when making holes less than 3/16 inch in diameter.

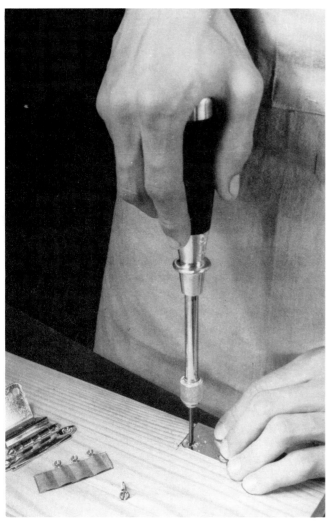

Fig. 7-11. A push drill can be used in areas where there is limited room.

PORTABLE ELECTRIC DRILL

Many people use a portable electric drill for drilling and boring holes because it is efficient and versatile. Fig. 7-12 shows an example of one model of portable electric drill. Portable drill size is determined by the capacity of the chuck.

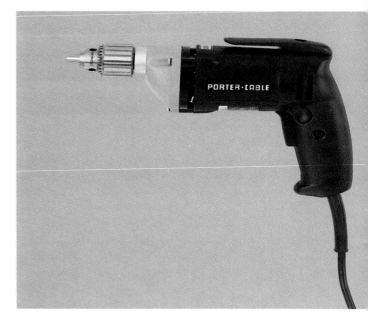

Fig. 7-12. A pistol grip portable electric drill. (Porter-Cable)

Typical sizes are 1/4, 3/8, and 1/2 inch. Some portable drills are variable speed and reversible (VSR), which is ideal for inserting and removing screws. Fig. 7-13 shows a cut-away of a portable electric drill with the parts identified.

Rechargeable, battery-powered drills, Fig. 7-14, and air drills are also available. Battery-powered drills are convenient, since they are not restricted by the length of the cord. However, make sure that the drill is fully charged before using it.

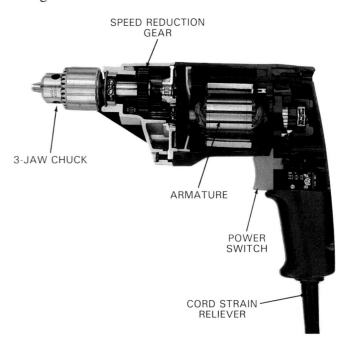

SPEED REDUCTION GEAR

3-JAW CHUCK

ARMATURE

POWER SWITCH

CORD STRAIN RELIEVER

Fig. 7-13. Portable electric drill with parts identified. (Skil Corp.)

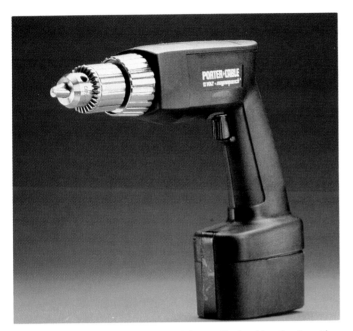

Fig. 7-14. A rechargeable drill is not limited by the length of the cord. (Porter-Cable)

DRILL PRESS

A DRILL PRESS is a power tool used to drill holes in wood and other materials. It can also be used for sanding, routing, shaping, and mortising. Drill press size is twice the distance from the center of the drill bit to the column. A 15-inch drill press, for example, will drill a hole in a piece of stock 7 1/2 inches from the edge, Fig. 7-15 shows an example of a 15-inch drill press.

Various drill speeds can be obtained by either a variable pulley or step pulleys of a drill press. The slowest speed, usually 400-600 revolutions per minute (RPM), should be used to drill 1-inch diameter holes and larger. A speed of 1200 RPM can generally be used to drill holes up to 1/2 inch in diameter.

Drill Press—Safety and Care

1. Unplug the drill press before making adjustments.
2. Clamp all stock to the drill press table before drilling holes. Make sure that you have a piece of scrap lumber under your stock when drilling. Refer to Fig. 3-1.
3. Have your instructor check the setup prior to turning on the drill press.
4. Do not wear loose fitting clothes, neckties, or jewelry when operating the drill press. If you have long hair, tie it back so that it does not get tangled in the rotating chuck.

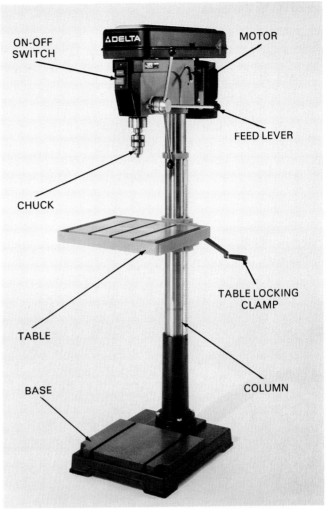

Fig. 7-15. Drill press with parts identified. (Delta International Machinery Corp.)

5. Use approved safety glasses or face shield for all operations. Always have the motor and belt guards securely in place.
6. Always make sure the chuck key has been removed from the chuck prior to turning on the drill.
7. Never use a dull drill bit; a sharp bit will produce better results and is less apt to break.
8. Do not force the bit into the stock.
9. When sanding with a drill press, use a dust mask.

Drilling Flat Stock

Lay out and mark the holes to be drilled as you would when using hand tools. Select the correct size bit, insert it in the chuck, and tighten the chuck with the chuck key. Make sure that you remove the chuck key. Center the table under the drill bit. Adjust the drill press for the proper chuck speed. The speed on some drill presses must be changed while the motor is turned on. Set the depth gauge if you do not wish to drill all the way through the piece. See Fig. 7-16. Place a scrap board under the stock to be drilled and use some type of mechanical holding device (drill press vise or clamp) to hold both pieces in place.

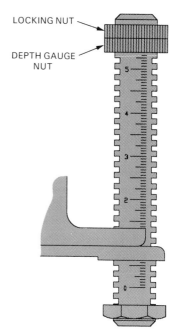

Fig. 7-16. A depth gauge is used if you do not want the holes to go through the stock.

Fig. 7-17. Using a V-block as a fixture while drilling into round stock.

Turn on the drill. Make sure your hands are clear of the path of the drill bit. Bring the bit into cutting position with the feed lever using light pressure. If the hole is deep, remove the bit from the stock several times to pull out the chips and to prevent the bit from overheating. When the hole is completed, return the bit to its original position by rotating the feed lever in the opposite direction. Do not let the feed wheel snap back. Shut off the motor and wait for the chuck to stop.

Drilling Round Stock

Round or irregular-shaped stock should be held in a V-block as in Fig. 7-17, drill press vise, or clamped to the table. If possible, the table can be turned for drilling into large pieces. Follow the same procedures as performed for drilling flat stock.

Drilling Holes at an Angle

When using a twist drill and the drill press to drill a hole at an angle, you must clamp a piece of scrap lumber above the stock being cut. An angle equal to the angle of the drill press table should be cut across one end of the scrap lum-

ber. This angle, which is perpendicular to the drill bit, enables you to cut straight into the stock without straying. Set the drill press table at the correct angle using a sliding T-bevel. Clamp a piece of scrap lumber below the stock and the scrap lumber with the angle above the stock to the table, as shown in Fig. 7-18. Perform the drilling operation as you would when drilling flat stock.

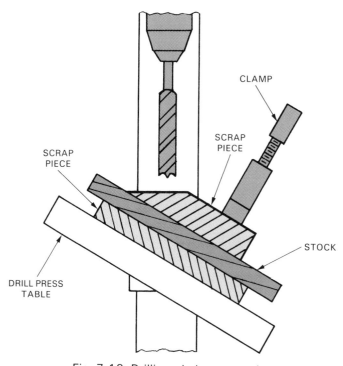

Fig. 7-18. Drilling a hole at an angle.

Fig. 7-19. Left. Drilling a large hole with a circle cutter. Right. Circle cutter.

Drilling Large Holes

A circle cutter or hole saw can be used to drill large holes in stock. Set the cutter or hole saw to the correct size before attaching it to the machine. Make sure the center drill bit is set about 1/4 inch below the cutter so it can guide and anchor the cutter. Adjust the drill press to its slowest speed. Clamp the stock to the drill table and have your instructor check the setup. See Fig. 7-19. Make sure your hands are out of the way before turning on the power. Proceed slowly as you feed the cutter or hole saw into the stock.

TEST YOUR KNOWLEDGE, Unit 7

Please do not write in this text. Place your answers on a separate sheet of paper.

1. A _____ may be used as a guide when boring holes at an angle.
2. A Forstner bit is designed to _____.
3. Describe the operation of the push drill.
4. A _____ cuts a funnel-shaped recess to receive the head of a flat head screw.
5. A drill press can be used for many drilling operations. List five of them.
6. Name six types of drill bits available for the portable electric drill and/or drill press.
7. When drilling round stock, it may be held in a _____, _____, or _____.
8. The portable electric drill is often used because it is _____ and _____.
9. The square shank on an auger bit is called the _____.
10. Forstner bits range in size from _____ to _____ inch diameter.
11. It is necessary to mark the center point with an awl prior to using a spade bit or a brad-point bit. True or False?
12. Hole saws are mounted to a shank called an _____.
13. Screws that will be covered by a plug require a _____ operation.
14. A scrap back-up board is frequently used when boring holes to prevent or reduce splintering as the bit penetrates the stock. True or False?
15. The size of a hand or portable electric drill is designated by its chuck size. True or False?
16. Drill bits are frequently backed out of the stock when drilling deep holes. Why?
17. List four devices designed to hold drill bits while drilling or boring holes.
18. Name two devices for drilling 1 1/2 inch holes or larger.
19. When using a portable electric drill for drilling holes in a piece of stock, the stock should be firmly held by a clamp or positioned in a vise. True or False?
20. A 1/4 inch twist drill helps to guide the circle cutter into the stock. True or False?

UNIT 8

FILING AND CHISELING

A squared edge is easily formed using a saw and a plane. However, different tools must be used for irregular shapes, such as a radius cut on the edge of the product. After studying this unit, you will be able to identify the tools used to form irregular-shaped cuts. In addition, you will be able to safely use these tools in the woods laboratory.

FILES AND RASPS

The most common tool used to form an irregular shape is the FILE. Files come in a variety of styles. Style refers to the file's cut, shape, coarseness, and size. See Fig. 8-1. The CUT of a file refers to the tooth pattern. There are four different cuts—single-cut, double-cut, curved-cut and rasp-cut. The SINGLE-CUT file is primarily

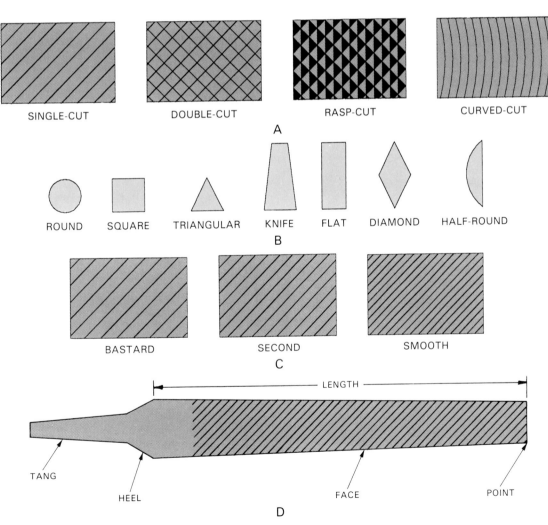

Fig. 8-1. A–File cuts. B–File shapes. C–File coarseness. D–File terminology.

used for sharpening, finish filing, and drawfiling. It consists of parallel, diagonal rows of teeth. The DOUBLE-CUT file is used for rough filing metal. The double-cut file has two sets of diagonal rows of teeth of different coarseness that cross each other. One row is called the OVERCUT, and the other finer row is called the UPCUT. The third file cut is called the CURVED-CUT. Its teeth are curved and it is used mostly in auto body work. The last cut, RASP-CUT, is different from the other files in several ways. The teeth are individually punched separate from one another. They actually cut the material being filed rather than abrading it as the other files do. They should only be used on wood. Most woodworkers do not refer to a rasp as a file, but rather as just a rasp.

Files are further identified according to their type. SHAPE refers to a file's cross-sectional shape. Common types are round, half-round, square, triangular, knife, and flat.

COARSENESS refers to the number of teeth per inch. Three common grades of coarseness are: bastard, second, and smooth.

A typical woods laboratory contains a variety of different files for cutting both wood and metal. Make certain not to use a metal file for cutting wood. A metal file will clog very rapidly when used on wood. The metal files are used for sharpening saws, saw blades, and cabinet scrapers as well as filing off the tips of screws. A wood rasp will dull very quickly and will not provide a smooth surface when used on metal. A very common wood file is called the four-in-hand. This file has a curved side and a flat side. Each side has a double-cut and a rasp-cut.

Shaping Tool–Safety and Care
1. Files, rasps, chisels, and other shaping tools have sharp edges. Prevent the edges from becoming dull. When storing these tools, hang them from the tool board, place them in a drawer with dividers, or roll them in a cloth tool roll.
2. Never use a file with an exposed tang or loose handle. Clean waste material from the teeth for better cutting action.
3. Do not carry chisels, files, or knives in your pockets.
4. Keep both hands away from the cutting path of chisels and knives.
5. Always secure your stock before beginning a filing, chiseling, or cutting operation.

Using a File
Make sure that the file you have selected has a tight-fitting handle. Do not use a file without a handle, because the tang may gouge your hand. Clamp the stock in a vise. Position the edge you are shaping close to the vise to prevent vibration and splitting the wood. Hold the file at an angle to the edge you are shaping. File the edge toward the middle to prevent the opposite edge from tearing out. This is especially important when shaping plywood. Use only enough pressure to remove a small amount on each stroke. Too much pressure will result in the edge of the stock tearing. Try to maintain an average speed of 30 strokes per minute. Control is difficult at higher speeds and you will tire quickly. Use a wire brush or file card to clean the grooves in the file. If the grooves become clogged with sawdust and chips, the file will not cut as well.

When shaping inside curves, use a half-round or round file. A flat file or the flat side of a half-round file can be used to smooth outside curves or straight edges, Fig. 8-2.

SURFORM® TOOLS

Another shaping tool that is similar to a file is the Surform® tool. This tool has a unique

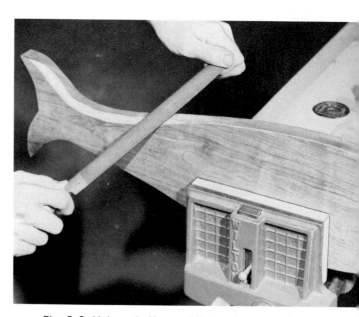

Fig. 8-2. Using a half-round file to shape an edge.

"cheese grater" appearance. It is available in a number of different shapes, including flat, round, curved, long, short and even one for the electric drill. The Surform® allows rapid removal of waste material as well as finish smoothing. The difference among these cuts is in the technique used by the operator. When removing waste rapidly, hold the Surform® at 45 degrees in the direction of the stroke. When removing less material, simply reduce the angle. Reversing the angle slightly makes it possible to get a polished appearance.

Other Wood-Shaping Tools

Four types of cutting tools are commonly used in woodworking. These are the drawknife, spokeshave, gouge, and knife. The tool used for the wood-shaping operation depends on the type of cut being made.

Drawknife

A DRAWKNIFE is commonly used for shaping edges to rough size. The drawknife has a wide blade and handles at both ends. The edge of the blade is sharpened to a keen, beveled edge.

When using a drawknife, make sure that you have the contour that you want cut laid out on the stock. Clamp the stock in a vise, making sure

that you have enough clearance from the vise for your hands when drawing the knife. Grasp each handle with a firm grip, holding the beveled edge of the blade down. Pull the knife towards you with firm, even pressure as shown in Fig. 8-3. When you have completed roughing out the contour, place the drawknife back in its keeper. When using the drawknife, you will be pulling the cutting edge toward your body. Be very careful when using the drawknife.

Spokeshave

A SPOKESHAVE is used for smoothing free-form shapes, such as boomerangs and archery bows. Its original purpose was to smooth spokes for wagon wheels and stocks for guns. The spokeshave has two handles and an adjustable blade that cuts like a plane iron. The blade is also sharpened like a plane iron.

When using a spokeshave, make sure that your curved design or contour is laid out on the stock. Use a saw or drawknife to rough out the shape. Clamp the stock in vise, with the edge to be smoothed close to the jaws. Adjust the blade for a fine cut. Many fine cuts will give you better results than one thick cut. The spokeshave may be pulled toward you or pushed away from you when cutting. Grasp the spokeshave with both hands, either pushing or pulling it along the edge of the stock. See Fig. 8-4.

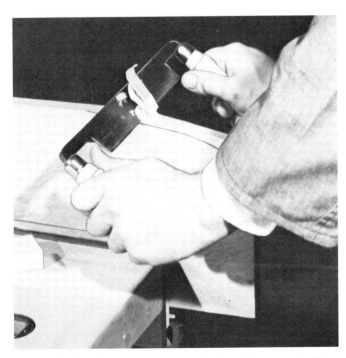

Fig. 8-3. Shaping an edge to rough size with a drawknife.

Fig. 8-4. Shaping a curved edge with a spokeshave.

Gouge

GOUGES are chisels with curved blades. Gouges are generally used to shape the inside of bowls, dishes, or trays.

Lay out the shape to be cut on the stock. Clamp the stock in a vise. Start cutting at the outside edge of the shape and work toward the center. Use firm, even pressure to guide the gouge. Guide the gouge with one hand and push it with the other hand, Fig. 8-5. Make sure that both hands are clear of the cutting edge of the gouge. Roll the gouge as you cut across the grain.

Fig. 8-5. Shaping the inside of a dish with a gouge.

Knife

A sloyd knife or utility knife may also be used to shape wood. A sloyd knife, a straight solid knife, is very popular. A utility knife with interchangeable blades can also be used to your advantage. Make sure that your knife is sharp. A sharp knife cuts wood easier and safer than a dull knife.

CHISELS

Two principle types of chisels are used for woodworking. See Fig. 8-6. The SOCKET chisel is made for heavy work. Its handle is tapered to fit into a cone-shaped recess at the end of the chisel blade. A socket chisel is usually driven with a mallet. A TANG chisel is used for lighter work. The back end of the blade is tapered to a point (tang) that fits into the handle. The width of the cutting edge of a chisel ranges from 1/8 to 2 inches. Chisels are ground and honed to a sharp, 25 to 30 degree beveled edge for general purpose work.

Chisels can be used to trim and shape stock, as well as make wood joints. Make sure that your stock is secured in a vise. Determine the direction of the grain. Most cuts will be with the grain of the stock. When making very fine cuts, hand pressure is usually enough. A mallet should be used for heavier cuts. Do not use a hammer, since the steel face of the hammer can damage the chisel handle. Turn the bevel edge of the chisel up to make convex cuts, paring cuts, and to start dado and rabbet joints, Fig. 8-7. Turn the bevel down for better control of the cut when making concave cuts, or when making finishing cuts in wood joints, Fig. 8-8.

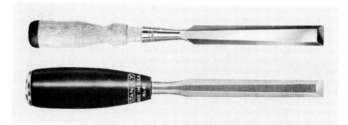

Fig. 8-6. Above. Socket chisel. Below. Tang chisel.

Fig. 8-7. Starting a dado joint with the chisel bevel turned up.

Fig. 8-8. Cutting a dado joint to with the chisel bevel turned down.

TEST YOUR KNOWLEDGE, Unit 8

Please do not write in this text. Place your answers on a separate sheet of paper.

1. _____-cut files have parallel rows of teeth running diagonally across the surface, while _____-cut files have two rows of teeth crossing each other, running diagonally across the surface.
2. When shaping plywood with a file, it is important to file at an angle toward the middle and then complete the job from the other side. Why?
3. A spokeshave was originally used to _____.
4. A spokeshave is sharpened like a _____ iron.
5. Gouges are chisels with _____ blades.
6. When sharpening a wood chisel, the bevel should be about _____ degrees.
7. When using a wood chisel to start a dado joint, the beveled edge should be pointed _____.

ACTIVITIES

1. Make a list of the different kinds of files, rasps, chisels, and knives found in your laboratory.
2. Cut a slight curve on one edge of a softwood scrap, using a coping saw or jigsaw. Clamp this scrap in a vise. Use a rough cut and a smooth cut rasp to round over first the straight edge, then the curved edge. If a Surform® is available, try the same procedure using it.
3. Securely clamp a softwood scrap in a vise. Using a chisel equal or wider than the thickness of the stock, make some cuts with hand pressure and some using a mallet. Notice how the cut changes when the bevel is reversed.

Workshop bench and tool panel with various woodworking tools.

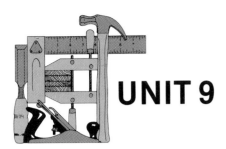

UNIT 9

HAND PLANING

Planes are frequently overlooked in the construction of a product. However, without true surfaces, edges, and ends, it would be very difficult to construct a square product. After reading this chapter and practicing the basic hand planing techniques, you will be able to square a board and to cut a chamfer using a hand plane. In addition, you will be able to adjust the plane iron to make a proper cut. You will also be able to identify the proper plane for various cutting operations.

A plane is used to remove MILL MARKS (marks made by the cutting knives of a planer or jointer) from the surfaces and edges of stock. A plane may also be used to remove warp and other surface imperfections from the stock.

PLANES

PLANES are used to smooth the surfaces and edges of boards, and also to make wood joints. All types of planes operate basically the same way. Cutting is done with a sharp steel blade-like device called a PLANE IRON. On some planes, another piece of steel called the PLANE IRON CAP is fitted to the plane iron. This is used to break the wood shavings into curls, while deflecting them out and away from the plane. Fig. 9-1 shows the parts of a plane. Various sizes and types of planes are available.

Jointer Planes and Fore Planes

Fore planes and jointer planes are used to joint (smooth) the edges of long pieces of stock when preparing for gluing. Jointer planes are 22- to 28- inches long; fore planes are approximately 18 inches long. Fig. 9-2 shows a variety of planes.

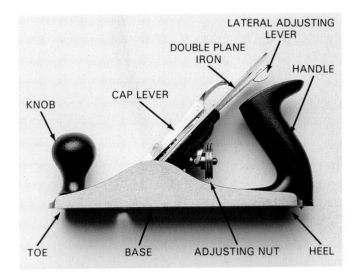

Fig. 9-1. Parts of a hand plane.

Jack Planes and Smooth Planes

Jack planes and smooth planes are very similar. They are both used for smoothing the face surfaces of the stock. The primary difference is their size; jack planes are 11- to 15-inches long and smooth planes are 6- to 10-inches long. The jack plane is used for general-purpose work, Fig. 9-2.

Block Plane

The block plane is used to surface the end grain of wood. It is about 4- to 6-inches long. The block plane is smaller and lighter than other planes. See Fig. 9-2. The block plane is designed to be used with one hand.

Router Planes and Rabbet Planes

The router and rabbet planes are used to make wood joints. The ROUTER PLANE consists of a frame with two knob-type handles and an attached blade. It is used to deepen a dado or groove, and to remove the waste from a dado after the two parallel shoulder cuts have been

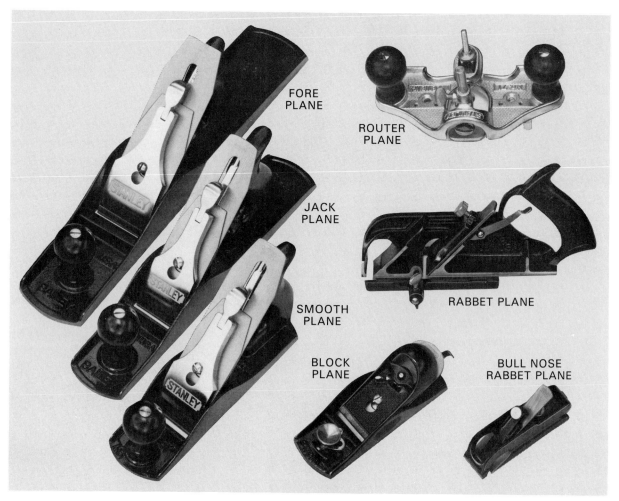

FORE PLANE

ROUTER PLANE

JACK PLANE

RABBET PLANE

SMOOTH PLANE

BLOCK PLANE

BULL NOSE RABBET PLANE

Fig. 9-2. Types of hand planes.

made using a back saw. The RABBET PLANE is used to cut rabbet joints. It consists of a metal frame, a fence, and a two position plane iron. The plane iron is the full width of the frame and can normally be mounted in two positions. The front, or forward position, is used for cutting stop rabbets. The back, or rear position, is used for all other cutting. A fence may be positioned to provide for cutting rabbets to accurate widths. Some rabbet planes also have a depth stop allowing exact depths to be cut. A router plane and a rabbet plane are shown in Fig. 9-2.

CARE AND ADJUSTMENT OF PLANES

Sharp planes give you much better results when planing stock. You must keep your plane sharp and properly adjusted. When the plane is not being used, lay it on its side to protect the plane iron. This also protects the workbench from damage.

Check the plane for sharpness and adjustment before using it. Remove the double plane iron

(blade) by lifting the cap lever. A DOUBLE PLANE IRON consists of the plane iron and plane iron cap that are held together with a screw. See Fig. 9-3.

Replace the blade. Sight along the bottom, or sole, of the plane from the front. Adjust the blade with the lateral adjusting lever so that it is parallel to the sole. This adjustment allows for even thickness shavings. Adjust the depth of cut with the adjustment nut so that the cutting edge of the blade is barely visible. A clockwise direction lowers the blade. Test the plane on a piece of softwood clamped in a vise. A thin shaving indicates a light cut, producing the smoothest surface.

SQUARING A PIECE OF STOCK

The pieces of a product that are to be glued and/or assembled must have true surfaces, ends, and edges. Care must be taken to follow a planing procedure to avoid unnecessary damage

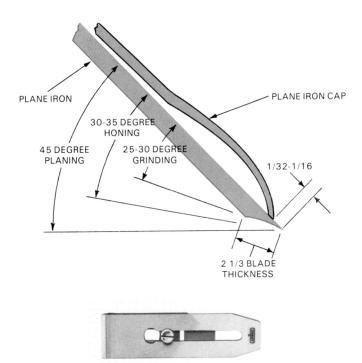

Fig. 9-3. Assembled double plane iron.

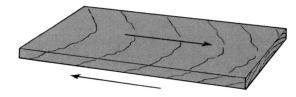

Fig. 9-4. Note direction of wood grain indicated by arrows.

to the stock. The first step in a hand planing operation is to true a surface, called a FACE. Next, square an edge to the first face. When this has been completed, square an end to *both* the first face and first edge. The fourth step is to square the second end with the first face and edge. Then, the second edge is squared with both ends and the finished face. Finally, the last face is planed square to all the edges and ends. If this procedure has been followed correctly, both faces will now be parallel to each other and square to both ends and edges. Remember the following steps for hand planing a piece of stock true and square.

1. Face.
2. Edge.
3. End.
4. End.
5. Edge.
6. Face.

Planing a Surface

Always plane with or across the grain of the wood to obtain the smoothest surface. A ragged or torn surface normally indicates planing against the grain, a twisted wood grain, or a dull plane iron. Examine the edges of the board to determine the direction of the surface grain. The direction of the edge grain may also be deter-

mined by looking at the surface grain. Notice that the grain on the top surface runs opposite to the bottom surface. See Fig. 9-4.

Make sure that your plane is sharp and properly adjusted. It should cut easily and smoothly. Clamp your board in a vise. Plane the best surface first. Check for high spots using a straightedge or blade of a square, as shown in Fig. 9-5.

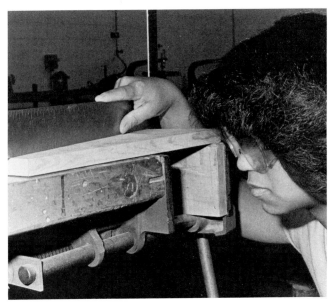

Fig. 9-5. Above. Using a square to check a surface for straightness. Below. Planing a surface with a jack plane.

Remove the high spots by planing diagonally across the surface of the board. Hold the plane level. Apply pressure on the knob of the plane at the beginning of each stroke. Gradually shift the downward pressure to the handle (heel of the plane) as you progress to the other edge. Follow through at the end of each stroke with pressure on the heel. Overlap about one-third of the width of the previous stroke with each succeeding stroke until the entire surface has been covered. Continue with this procedure until the surface is smooth. Frequently check the surface for straightness with a square or rule. The surface of the board must be straight and true before planing an edge. This first smooth surface becomes the WORKING SURFACE, or FACE.

Planing an Edge

Select the best edge of the stock and determine the direction of its grain. Clamp the board in a vise close to the edge. Plane along the edge by holding the plane level and at a slight angle to the edge. This provides a shearing cut. Check along the length of the edge for accuracy with a straightedge. Check the edge with a try square, making sure it is square to the working face. See Fig. 9-6.

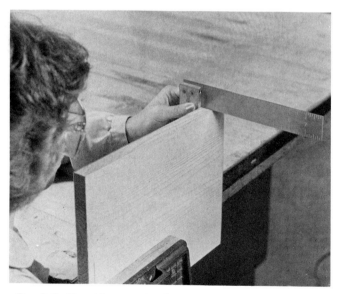

Fig. 9-6. Checking an edge for squareness. Make sure the handle of the square is flush with the working face.

Planing the First End

Planing end grain requires a very thin shaving made with a sharp plane. A block plane is best for planing end grain. The plane iron of a block plane consists of a one-piece blade. The plane

iron has a lower angle than other planes. In addition, the sharpened bevel should be on the top side to deflect the shavings.

Square a line across the end of the stock. Clamp the stock in a vise near the layout mark. Set the block plane to make a fine cut. Use light, uniform pressure while holding the plane level. Push the plane from the edge to the middle of the stock. Then, plane from the other edge to the middle of the stock as shown in Fig. 9-7. Be careful not to plane across the end in one direction only. This will result in splitting the opposite corner.

Fig. 9-7. Planing end grain with a block plane. Plane from the edge to the middle and then from the other edge to the middle.

The ends of narrow stock may be planed by clamping a back-up board against the opposite edge for support. You can then plane in one direction.

Another method of planing end grain is to plane or cut a slight bevel on the edge that has not yet been planed. This procedure allows you to plane in one direction toward the bevel. Make sure that the bevel is not deeper than the amount of material to be removed from the edge. When the end is square, begin working on the unplaned edge.

Planing the Second End

Measure the length of the stock from the square end. Use a square to mark a straight line. Cut the stock to length with a backsaw. Make sure that you cut on the waste side of the line. Square this end, following the same procedure used for planing the other end. Remember to always check the squareness of the stock using the edge and surface that have been squared.

Planing the Second Edge

Square the second edge of the stock after squaring both ends. Lay out the width of the board from the finished edge. Draw a line along the length of the board. You may be able to use the marking gauge for narrower pieces. If necessary, cut the stock to rough width (approximate finished width plus 1/8 to 1/4 inch) using a ripsaw. Plane the second edge to the line and square to the face. Remember to use the working surface to check for the squareness of the edge and ends.

Squaring the Second Surface

If the stock is thicker than 1/8 inch, use a marking gauge to mark the desired thickness of the stock. Place the head of the marking gauge on the working surface when laying out the thickness. Plane the second surface to this line. When finished, both surfaces should be parallel and square with both ends and edges.

PLANING CHAMFERS AND BEVELS

Chamfers and bevels are commonly used along the edges of stock to "dull" the "sharp" edge. A CHAMFER is an angle cut made part of the way across an edge. A BEVEL is an angle cut made across the entire edge.

Use a marking gauge to lay out lines around the edges of the stock. Clamp the board in a vise close to the lines. Hold the plane at the desired angle and plane the chamfer or bevel to the layout lines. See. Fig. 9-8.

Fig. 9-8. Planing a chamfer.

Radius and Chamfer Planes

Two small hand-held planes have been recently added to the woodworking laboratory. These are wooden planes with a brass angled sole and two cutters or blades. The RADIUS PLANE has curved cutters to make a curved or round cut. The CHAMFER PLANE has a flat cutter to cut a flat surface. The cutters are set at a slightly different depths. The first blade makes a rough cut; the second blade makes the finish cut. Either of these tools can quickly relieve the sharp edges of freshly squared stock.

USING A RABBET PLANE

A RABBET PLANE is used to make rabbet (L-shaped) joints along the edges of stock. A rabbet plane has an adjustable fence for the width, and a depth stop for the depth of the cut.

Set the guides on the rabbet plane to the desired dimensions of the rabbet. Clamp the stock in a vise near the edge to be planed. Hold the rabbet plane against the edge of the stock. Use firm, even pressure to push the plane across the stock. Remove only a small amount of stock each pass. Continue cutting until the wood joint reaches the predetermined depth. See Fig. 9-9.

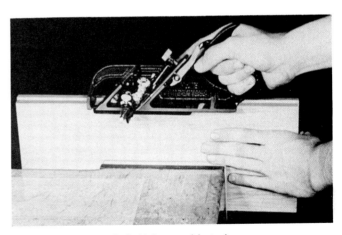

Fig. 9-9. Using a rabbet plane.

USING A ROUTER PLANE

A ROUTER PLANE is used to smooth the bottom of wood joints such as the dado, groove, and lap. Clamp the stock in a vise so the joint to be planed is accessible. Place the plane over the joint and set the depth stop and blade for a thin cut. Push or pull the plane across the joint to smooth the bottom. See Fig. 9-10.

Fig. 9-10. A router plane and its parts. (Woodcraft Supply)

Fig. 9-11. Grinding a plane iron using a special grinding fixture.

SHARPENING PLANE IRONS

Sharpening includes both grinding and honing. GRINDING shapes the cutting edge to a hollow-ground (curved shape made with the grinding wheel) bevel. HONING, or WHETTING, on an oil stone further sharpens the cutting surface to a fine edge.

Grinding is necessary when the cutting edge loses its hollow-ground bevel or becomes nicked. Plane irons are usually ground to a 25 to 30 degree bevel for general-purpose work. This forms a bevel that is about 2 1/3 times the blade thickness.

The plane iron is ground by clamping it in a special fixture that is moved across a grinding wheel. See Fig. 9-11. Each pass of the grinding wheel should remove very small amounts. Continue the grinding process until a small burr appears behind the bevel. Dip the plane iron in water frequently to keep it cool. Excessive heating during grinding draws the temper (hardness) from the blade.

When you have completed the grinding operation, you will need to hone the blade to remove the burr. Apply a few drops of oil to a clean oilstone. Place the plane iron into the special honing jig, making sure the bevel of the plane iron lays flat on the oilstone. Push the plane iron and jig along the length of the oilstone several times. See Fig. 9-12. Then, turn the plane iron

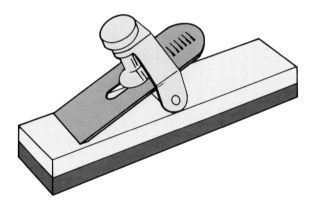

Fig. 9-12. Honing a plane iron.

over (do not remove from the holding device), place it flat on the oilstone and stroke the other side to remove the burr. The plane iron should be honed to 30 to 35 degrees. Repeat this process until the cutting edge can slice the edge of a piece of notebook paper with a clean cut.

When you have completed the honing operation, slightly round the corners of the cutting edge on the side of the oilstone. This prevents the edges from digging into the stock while in use.

SCRAPING A SURFACE

A CABINET SCRAPER is used to smooth flat surfaces after planing. It is also helpful before sanding to smooth rough places around knots and curly grain, and to remove the mill marks left by the planer or jointer. Cabinet scrapers may have handles. The scraper should be held at an angle of about 75 degrees as shown in Fig. 9-13.

Fig. 9-13. Using a cabinet scraper.

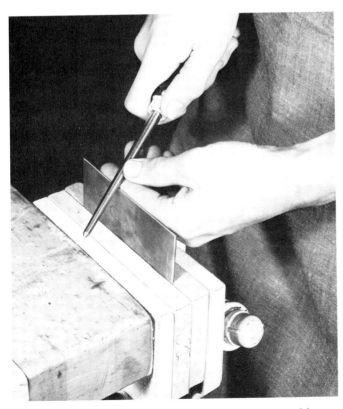

Fig. 9-14. Turning the edge of a hand scraper with a burnisher.

Sharpening the Hand Scraper

A hand scraper can become dull after prolonged use. You should keep it sharp to have the best results. Clamp the scraper in a vise and draw file across the edge. Then, pull a burnisher (hardened steel rod) across the edge several times, holding the burnisher at 90 degrees to the edge. See Fig. 9-14. Gradually raise the burnisher to about 85 degrees. This burnishing process turns over the edge forming a "burr." This burr becomes the new cutting edge.

TEST YOUR KNOWLEDGE, Unit 9

Please do not write in this text. Place your answers on a separate sheet of paper.

1. _____ are used to smooth the surfaces and edges of boards, and also to make wood joints.
2. List six different kinds of planes.
3. The plane should be laid on its side when not in use. True or False?
4. Torn wood indicates planing _____ the grain, a _____ wood grain, or a _____ cutting edge.
5. When planing, check for accuracy with a _____, and test for squareness with a _____.
6. A _____ is often used for planing end grain.
7. Describe the difference between a chamfer and a bevel.
8. L-shaped joints that are made along the edges of stock are made using a _____ plane.
9. A router plane is used to smooth the bottom of joints such as _____, _____, and _____.
10. List three places where you might use a cabinet scraper.
11. Why should you frequently dip the plane iron in water while grinding it?
12. Describe the procedure used to hone a plane iron.
13. List the six steps, in order, for hand planing a piece of stock true and square.
14. Referring to Fig. 9-1, the base of a plane is also called the sole. A rectanglular shaped opening in the sole is called the throat. List five other parts.
15. All planes have their plane irons set in the frame at the same angle. True or False?

16. Some cabinet scrapers are held in a special frame while others are held in your hand. What is the angle the scraper should make with the surface while cutting?

17. A radius plane will quickly remove the sharp edges that remain after squaring stock. True or False?

ACTIVITIES

1. Prepare a paper on the history of planing tools and machines.

2. Select a plane from the tool storage area. What kind of plane did you choose? Remove the plane iron from the plane body. Look at the angle or bevel cut on the plane iron. Does it fit into the plane body bevel up or down? Why? Place the plane iron in the plane body. What is the angle created by the plane iron and the bottom of the plane? Adjust the plane iron. Have your instructor check your adjustments.

3. Cut a small piece of softwood about 4-inches long, 3-inches wide and 3/4-inch thick. Check all edges, ends, and surfaces for squareness. Choose the best face. Clamp the board with this face up in a vise. Plane the surface true. Continue planing and squaring each face, edge, and end until the board is true and square. (If this activity is carefully completed you will have a sanding block to use with a one-quarter sheet of abrasive paper.)

4. Cut a 1/4-inch chamfer around one surface of the block you squared in Activity 3.

5. Select a scrap of softwood with clearly visible mill marks from the jointer or planer. Clamp this board in a vise with the face up. Use a cabinet scraper to remove the mill marks. Turn the board over and try removing the mill marks with just abrasive paper. Which produces the best surface? Which is faster? Which is easier?

Specialty planes such as these can be used in certain situations. (Woodcraft Supply)

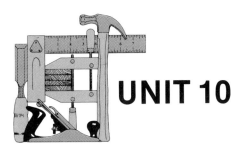

UNIT 10

POWER PLANING

Edges and faces of stock can be smoothed using hand tools or power tools. However, power tools can smooth the stock more efficiently when used properly. After reading this unit, you will be able to identify the power planing tools used in a typical woods laboratory. After the instructor demonstrates the proper set-up and technique, you will be able to properly use the power planers in your laboratory.

THE JOINTER

A JOINTER is used to remove warp and other surface imperfections from the edges and faces of stock. This makes the stock straight and true.

Straight and true stock is necessary to ensure that other operations, such as sawing and drilling, will also produce square cuts and holes. The jointer is also used to cut chamfers, bevels, rabbets, and tapers.

The size of the jointer is specified as the length of its KNIVES. The knives are the parts of the jointer that actually do the cutting. A jointer usually has three knives, which revolve in a CUTTERHEAD at about 4500 RPM. A jointer, as shown in Fig. 10-1, is equipped with an infeed table, outfeed table, fence, and cutter guard. The INFEED TABLE, or front table, is adjusted to the desired depth of cut. It is adjusted with either the handwheel or an adjustment lever

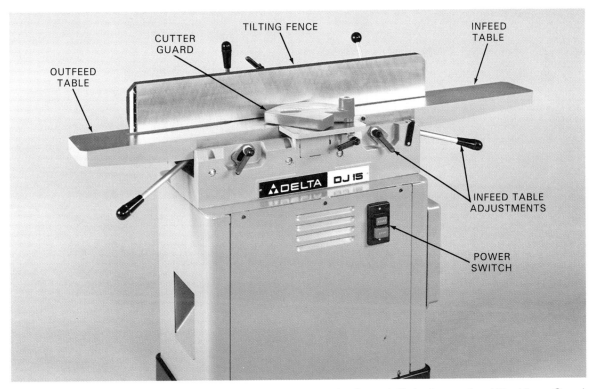

Fig. 10-1. A jointer is used to surface the face, edge, or end grain of wood. (Delta International Machinery Corp.)

located below the infeed table. The OUTFEED TABLE must be set even with the cutting edges of the knives at their highest point in their rotation. The outfeed table should be locked in this position if straight cuts are desired. The FENCE is used to guide stock as it is pushed from the infeed table to the outfeed table. The fence may be moved in or out to accommodate different widths of stock. It may also be tilted to make angular cuts. The CUTTER GUARD is positioned over the cutterhead to protect the operator from injury, and protect the edges of the knives from damage. The cutter guard is spring loaded. When stock is fed across the jointer, the guard only exposes a small amount of the cutterhead and knives. Fig. 10-2 shows a cross-sectional view of the jointer.

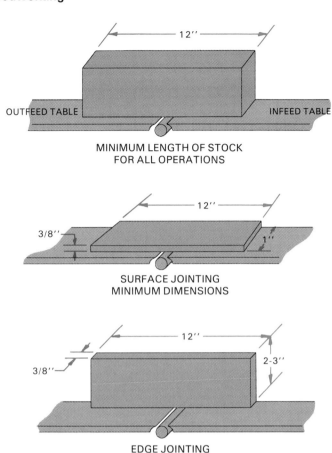

MINIMUM LENGTH OF STOCK
FOR ALL OPERATIONS

SURFACE JOINTING
MINIMUM DIMENSIONS

EDGE JOINTING
MINIMUM DIMENSIONS

Fig. 10-3. Minimum stock dimensions for the jointer.

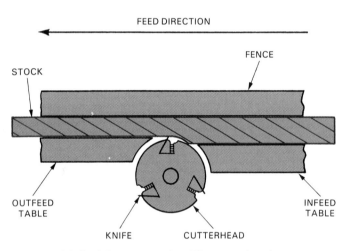

Fig. 10-2. Jointer operation. The cutterhead rotates clockwise, while the stock is fed into it.

Stock Size and Depth of Cut Limitations

Stock to be smoothed on a jointer should be at least 12-inches long. This allows a good portion of the stock to be on the outfeed table as the last portion of the stock is leaving the infeed table. When jointing the surface of stock, the minimum surface width should be 1 inch and the minimum thickness should be 3/8 inch. When jointing the edge of stock, the minimum surface width should be 2 to 3 inches and the minimum thickness should be 3/8 inch, Fig. 10-3. This allows you to keep your fingers well above the cutters. Variations of these minimums are possible with the use of special jigs and fixtures designed for the operator's protection.

Stock that projects beyond the length of the infeed table by more than 18 inches should be

jointed by two people. The operator should be in control of feeding the stock, while the assistant should balance the weight of the stock. It is good practice to carefully plan your work to avoid jointing short pieces. Stock that is 48- to 60-inches long is a manageable length. Stock that is 10- to 12-feet long should be cut into two or three manageable pieces prior to jointing, unless the long lengths are necessary for the product.

The depth of cut depends on the width and hardness of the stock, as well as the feed rate. Generally, lumber that is hard and wide should be fed slowly into the jointer. Maximum recommended depth of cut for hardwoods is 1/32 to 1/16 inch. Softwoods may be jointed using a 1/16 to 1/8 inch depth of cut.

Jointer–Safety and Care
1. Always secure permission from the instructor before using the jointer.
2. Only use stock that is free from knots and splits on the jointer.
3. Keep your hands at least 4 inches away from the knives and cutterhead.

4. Use a push stick for planing flat surfaces and jointing narrow edges.
5. Make sure that the area beyond the infeed table is clear before turning on the motor.
6. Jointer knives must be kept sharp. Dull knives cause vibration and poor cuts.
7. Feed the stock so that the knives cut with the grain.
8. Surface cupped stock with the concave side down. This allows you to have two points of the stock in contact with the table.
9. Do not attempt to operate the jointer without the guard in proper position.

Jointing Edges

Adjust the fence so it is square with the infeed table. Place the handle of a try square on the infeed table and rest the blade along the fence. See Fig. 10-4. When the fence is in the proper

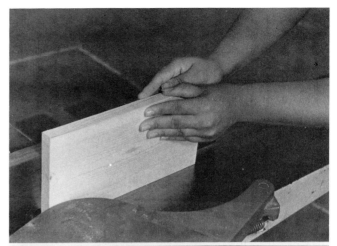

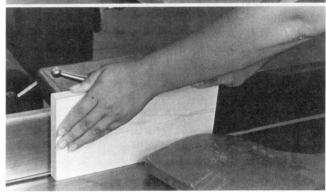

Fig. 10-5. Jointing a board. Above. Applying pressure on the fence and infeed table. Center. Applying pressure on the fence and both tables. Below. Applying pressure on the fence and outfeed table.

Fig. 10-4. Adjusting jointer fence square with table.

position, lock it in place. Set the depth of cut for 1/32 to 1/16 inch using the handwheel or adjustment lever. You might want to check your setup at this time by using a piece of scrap lumber of the same species. When you have determined that you have the correct setup, inspect your finish stock to determine the grain direction. Turn the stock so the knives will cut with the grain.

Make sure the guard is in its proper position over the cutterhead. Place the stock on its edge on the infeed table. Rest the surface of the stock against the fence. Stand to the left of the jointer

and turn on the motor. Refer to Fig. 10-5 as you read the next few sentences. Hold the stock firmly against the fence and infeed table while pushing it over the cutterhead. When about a foot of the stock has passed over the cutterhead, lift your left hand from its original position and apply pressure on the stock against the fence and outfeed table with that hand. Use both hands to apply pressure against the fence and outfeed table at the end of the stroke.

Narrow pieces can be jointed safely by using a push stick, Fig. 10-6. Make sure that you have the push stick in hand before starting the jointing operations. The left hand should be lifted across the cutterhead to apply pressure to the piece against the fence and outfeed table.

Fig. 10-6. Jointing a narrow board with a push stick.

Chamfering and beveling can also be done with the jointer. Set the fence to the desired angle using a sliding T-bevel as a guide. Then, lock the fence in place. When jointing the edge to the desired angle, make sure that surface of the stock is held firmly against the fence.

Planing Surfaces

The surface, or face, of the stock must be jointed to provide a true surface when laying out other measurements. The first surface, or working surface, is smoothed with a jointer. Set the depth of cut for 1/32 inch. (A smaller depth of cut is required since you will be removing stock from a larger surface area than when edge jointing.) Turn the stock so the knives will cut with the grain. Make sure that you have a push stick or push shoe in one of your hands. It will be needed when planing surfaces. See Fig. 10-7. Step to the side of the jointer, make sure the guard is in its correct position, and turn on the motor.

If the stock is warped, place it on the infeed table with the cupped surface down. Use a push

Fig. 10-7. Smoothing the surface of stock using a push shoe.

stick to apply pressure against the fence and infeed table while pushing the stock over the knives toward the outfeed table. Gradually shift the pressure to the outfeed table as the cut is completed. Continue to push the stock across the jointer until the guard snaps back over the cutterhead.

Rabbeting

Rabbets may be formed on the jointer, although there may be more efficient methods of forming the joint. Move the fence toward the rabbeting platform on the left side of the machine. Adjust the fence to the width of rabbet desired. This distance is measured from the end of the knife, not the edge of the table. Lock the fence in place. Set the depth of cut to 1/16 of an inch and push the stock over the cutterhead. See Fig. 10-8. Reset the depth of cut for additional cuts until the desired depth of rabbet is obtained.

PORTABLE POWER PLANES

The PORTABLE POWER PLANE is designed mainly for edge jointing stock, such as doors and plywood panels. It is used in a manner similar to the hand plane. A MOTOR rotates a cutter that precisely removes the desired amount of stock. The planer has an adjustable FENCE

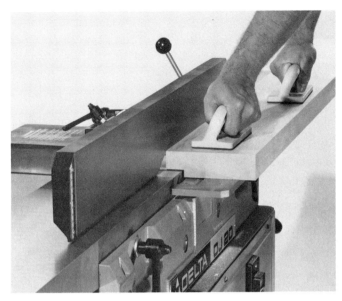

Fig. 10-8. A rabbeting platform is used when making rabbets along the edge of the stock. Note that this operation requires removal of the guard. Always secure your instructor's permission before attempting this operation. Use extreme care when performing the operation and replace and adjust the guard when finished. (Delta International Machinery Corp.)

to set the width of cut, and an adjustable FRONT TABLE to set the depth of cut. See Fig. 10-9. Some portable power planes have a removable fence that allows for surface planing.

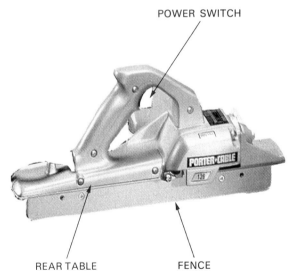

Fig. 10-9. A portable power plane is more efficient than a hand plane. (Porter-Cable)

Planing Edges

Clamp the stock securely in a vise. Make sure that the edge to be planed is accessible. Set the depth of cut on the plane for 1/16 inch. Rest the table of the plane on the edge of the stock. Turn on the motor and allow the plane to obtain full

speed. Push the plane across the edge applying pressure against the fence. Follow through at the end of each stroke. Turn off the motor when completed with the operation. Make additional cuts as necessary.

PLANER OR SURFACER

The PLANER, or SURFACER, is used to machine stock to exact thickness. A planer is equipped with a CUTTERHEAD that usually contains three knives, similar to a jointer. However, unlike the jointer, the planer cuts the stock on the top surface. The size of a planer is specified by the length of the knives and the thickness of the stock it will accept. Common planer sizes for the woods laboratories are 12, 18, and 24 inches. See Fig. 10-10.

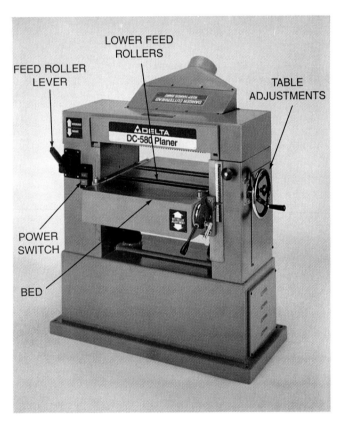

Fig. 10-10. A planer is used to surface stock. Note the positions of the controls. (Delta International Machinery Corp.)

A planer is equipped with four feed rollers— two infeed and two outfeed. The UPPER IN-FEED ROLLER, which is milled or corrugated, and LOWER INFEED ROLLER pull the stock through the cutterhead. The CHIP BREAKER and the PRESSURE BAR hold the stock down as it is fed through the machine, Fig. 10-11.

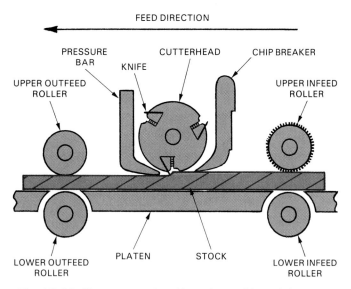

FEED DIRECTION

PRESSURE BAR
CUTTERHEAD
CHIP BREAKER
KNIFE
UPPER OUTFEED ROLLER
UPPER INFEED ROLLER
LOWER OUTFEED ROLLER
PLATEN
STOCK
LOWER INFEED ROLLER

Fig. 10-11. Planer operation. Note the position of the parts.

Depth of cut is set by adjusting the table. The smooth outfeed rollers grasp and pull the stock as it passes below the cutterhead. The combination of the infeed and outfeed rollers ensures a smooth, even feed of the stock across the cutterhead.

Planer—Safety and Care

1. When using the planer, never surface a piece of stock shorter than the recommended minimum length. Consult the instructor or operation manual if this information is not posted on the machine. The minimum length of stock to be used with most planers is 12 to 16 inches.
2. Hold the stock in a horizontal position and with both hands as it is fed into the planer.
3. Feed stock so the planer knives cut with the grain.
4. Wide stock and hardwood stock should be fed at slow speeds. The depth of cut should also be reduced.
5. Inspect the stock for defects. Make certain the stock does not contain any nails or paint, and that it is warp-free.
6. Never look into the mouth of the planer while it is running. If stock gets caught or turns sideways, stop the machine before lowering the table. Then remove the jammed material.

Planing Stock

The stock to be planed must have one true face or surface. This face is first smoothed on the jointer. The cupped shape of defective stock will not be

removed by using only the planer. The feed mechanism of the planer will flatten the stock before the stock enters the cutterhead. As the stock leaves the planer, it will return to its original shape. Measure the stock at its thickest point to determine its dimension. Set the planer for this thickness minus the depth of cut. For example, if the stock is 13/16-inch thick and depth of cut is 1/16 inch, set the planer to 12/16, or 3/4, inch. The recommended depth of cut is 1/32 to 1/16 inch for hardwoods and 1/16 to 1/8 inch for softwoods. Make sure that your stock is long enough to pass through the planer without getting caught. The minimum length of stock to be used with most planers is 12 to 16 inches.

Position the stock so the knives will cut with the grain. Make sure the true surface is down. Grasp the board with both hands, one on each side of the stock. Hold the stock horizontally and allow the infeed rollers to pull the board across the cutterhead. Make sure that you do not have your fingers between the stock and the infeed table. Stand to the side of the stock as you feed it; do not stand directly behind the stock, Fig. 10-12. Walk to the back side of the planer to receive the board. Reset the depth of cut and make additional cuts until the desired thickness is obtained. When planing stock that is 6 feet or more in length, either use an assistant to "tail-off," or use an outfeed stand to support the stock. If the stock is not properly supported, the

Fig. 10-12. Stand to the side of the stock as you feed it into the planer. (Delta International Machinery Corp.)

weight of the stock pushing downward could result in an uneven finish thickness or damage to the planer.

TEST YOUR KNOWLEDGE, Unit 10

Please do not write in this text. Place your answers on a separate sheet of paper.

1. List four uses of a jointer.
2. The _____ table must be set even with the cutting edge of the jointer knives.
3. The _____ is used to guide stock as it is pushed from the _____ table to the _____ table.
4. Cupped stock must first be smoothed on a _____ before using a planer or surfacer to machine it to the exact thickness.
5. It is possible to cut chamfers, bevels, and rabbets on the jointer. True or False?
6. Why should the cupped surface be placed down when jointing it?
7. Unless a piece of stock has been previously surfaced, one face should be smoothed on the jointer prior to using the planer. Why?
8. The fence on the jointer must be at 90 degrees to the table when cutting a chamfer or bevel. True or False?
9. The guard must always be in place and functioning when using the jointer except when cutting rabbets. The fence is then moved to the outer edge of the table to avoid excess exposure of the cutters. True or False?
10. A piece of stock should not be fed into the planer/surfacer sideways even if the width is above the minimum capacity of the machine. True or False?
11. The rate of feed for softwoods is slower than for hardwoods. True or False?
12. The depth of cut should be reduced when cutting hardwoods. True or False?
13. Stock that extends beyond the outfeed table by 6 feet or more should be handled by "tailing off" or using an outfeed stand. Why?
14. Why shouldn't you have your fingers between stock and the infeed table of a planer?

ACTIVITIES

1. Compare the illustration of the jointer in Fig. 10-1 to the jointer in your wood laboratory. How do they differ? How are they alike? Does your jointer have a handwheel or lever for depth adjustment? Is your fence mounted by the cutterhead or attached to the end of the infeed table? Is there a dust collection hook-up to your jointer? Where is the ON-OFF switch? Are the push sticks and push shoes close at hand?
2. Cut a piece of 2 x 4 dimensional lumber about 3 ft. in length. Set the tables of the jointer even. Disconnect the power and practice pushing the board over the cutter. First, do an edge, then a face or surface. Practice this until you are comfortable with the feel of the guard moving and your stance and hand movement.

   Carefully inspect the edge for knots. Set the jointer to make a 1/16- to 1/8-inch cut. Edge joint the board until the rounded edges have been removed. Adjust the infeed table to make a 1/16-inch cut. Re-inspect the board for defects and place the best face down. Use a push shoe to joint the surface to 1 1/4 inches.
3. Look at the planer/surfacer in your wood laboratory. Who is the manufacturer? Where is the power switch? Does the cutterhead have a brake? Is it manual or electric? Is the dust collector attached to the planer? Where is the adjustment for height of the table? Is ear protection available for the operator?
4. Use the board from Activity 2 and prepare to surface the board using the planer/surfacer. First, measure the thickness of the stock and set the table height of the planer to this distance minus 1/16 inch. Set the feed rate at its lowest speed. Carefully feed the stock into the planer. What happens when the board touches the infeed rollers? Move to the back of the planer and wait for the outfeed rollers to release the wood. Measure your stock. Did the planer remove 1/16 inch? What is the appearance of the surface? Are there any mill marks visible? Increase the depth of cut to 1/8 inch and feed the stock through the planer. Does the machine sound any different with the 1/8 cut than it did with the 1/16 inch cut. Inspect the surface again and note any difference. Increase the feed rate and surface the stock one more time. Develop your own conclusions about the feed rate and depth of cut.

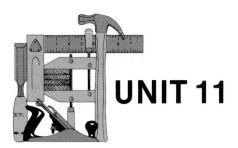

UNIT 11

WOOD JOINTS

When constructing most products, pieces of stock must be joined. A variety of wood joints may be used to join the pieces together. After reading this unit, you will be able to identify the different types of wood joints and their applications. In addition, you will be able to construct these joints using the proper tools and techniques.

Many types of wood joints can be used to fasten pieces of stock together. Glue is used to strengthen the joints. The strongest joints bonded with glue are those that involve the surfaces and edges of the stock. The weakest wood joints usually involve the end grain of the stock. Reinforcement, such as nails, screws, and staples, are commonly used to strengthen some types of wood joints. Wood dowels, plugs, splines, and biscuits may also be used to align and strengthen the joints.

WOOD JOINTS

The type of wood joint selected for a situation depends on many factors. These include:

1. How will the joined pieces be used?
2. What is the required durability of the product on a day-to-day basis?
3. What is the required durability of the product over its expected lifetime?
4. What is the desired or required appearance of the joint?
5. How many joints need to be made for the product?
6. What special tools or equipment are needed to make and clamp the joint?

Many types of wood joints can be constructed. They vary in the amount of complexity involved in making the joint, as well as the amount of strength that can be expected from the joint. The wood joints discussed in the following pages and shown in Fig. 11-1 include the:

- Butt joint.
- Miter joint.
- Lap joint.
- Rabbet joint.
- Dado joint.
- Groove joint.
- Mortise and tenon joint.
- Dovetail joint.
- Plate, or biscuit joint.
- Box joint.

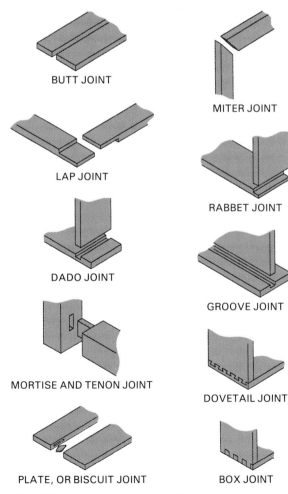

Fig. 11-1. A variety of wood joints can be used to connect pieces of stock.

96

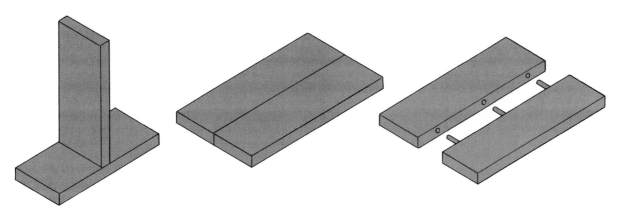

Fig. 11-2. Left. End butt joint. Center. Edge butt joint. Right. Edge butt joint reinforced with dowels.

BUTT JOINTS

Butt joints are used in products where strength is not the primary consideration. Finish or dimensional stock should be used to make accurate butt joints. The term "butt joint" generally refers to stock that is joined with the minimum amount of preparation. Specific terms, such as "end butt joint" or "edge butt joint," refer to the specific part of the stock that is being joined. See Fig. 11-2.

End Butt Joint

An END BUTT JOINT involves attaching the square end of one piece of stock to the surface or edge of another piece of stock. The end grain of stock does not lend itself well to joinery (making wood joints). Unreinforced end butt joints should be used where strength is not a major factor. They are generally used to save time and effort, and where appearance is not important.

The first step in making an end butt joint is to mark a square line across the end of the stock using a square and a pencil. Cut off the scrap stock using a back saw. Use a block plane to true the end, if necessary. Attach this end to the surface of another piece of stock using nails, screws, dowels, or biscuits.

Edge Butt Joints

EDGE BUTT JOINTS are used to fasten two or more pieces of stock edge to edge. These wider pieces can then be used when constructing desk tops, shelves, and other similar products.

Joint or plane the pieces of stock to be joined using a jointer or hand plane. Inspect the stock to determine the direction of grain. You should try to match the grain patterns so the surface grain of all pieces run in the same direction. This allows the wider surface to be planed to a smooth surface. The end grain of adjacent pieces should be opposite each other. This reduces the tendency of the wide piece to warp. Mark reference points on adjacent pieces of stock so they can be easily reassembled before gluing. See Fig. 11-3.

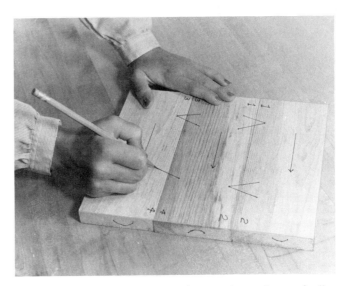

Fig. 11-3. Marking reference points on the surfaces of adjacent boards before joining them to make a wide board.

Edge butt joints for stock that is straight and less than 2-feet long, usually do not require any reinforcement; gluing is sufficient. Unit 14 discusses the gluing and clamping procedures.

Reinforcement is required for edge butt joints that are longer than 2 feet. One of the most common types of reinforcement are dowels. You can easily prepare the edges of the stock for dowels with a doweling jig. Clamp the two adjacent pieces of stock together in a vise with the working surfaces facing outward and edges upward.

The diameter of the dowels should be about one-half the thickness of the stock. Mark the dowel locations across both edges using a square, Fig. 11-4. The dowels should penetrate one-inch deep into each piece. Use a depth gauge on your drill bit, or fasten a piece of masking tape on your bit to control the depth. Adjust the doweling jig and clamp it over one of the layout marks. Drill or bore the first hole. Turn the doweling jig around and clamp it on the opposite side. Use the same layout mark as a guide when

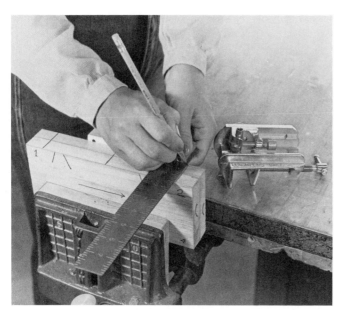

Fig. 11-4. Marking the locations of dowels on the edges of two adjacent boards.

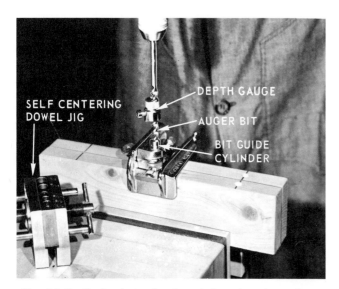

Fig. 11-5. Boring holes for dowels into the edges of two adjacent boards.

drilling the hole in the other piece of stock. Drill all the holes along the edges before removing them from the vise. See Fig. 11-5.

Another method of installing dowels is by using DOWEL POINTS. Dowel points are small, metal, standard-size cylinders with sharp center points. When using the dowel points, you must first drill your dowel holes in one of the pieces being joined. Insert the dowel points in the holes. Press the edge with the dowel points into edge of the second piece. Small indentations will appear along the edge of the second piece indicating where the holes are to be drilled.

Plate joinery, discussed later in this unit, is also an efficient means for strengthening edge butt joints.

MITER JOINTS

MITER JOINTS are used for making corners for frames, installing molding, and similar applications. See Fig. 11-6. Miter joints without reinforcement are very weak joints. They may be strengthened with dowels, feathers, biscuits, or metal fasteners. A doweling jig or dowel points may be useful if using dowels to reinforce the miter joint.

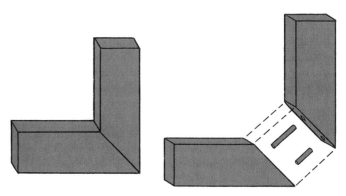

Fig. 11-6. Miter joints form 90 degree angles. Dowels can be used to reinforce the joint.

A miter box is very valuable for making miter joints. Cut the two pieces of stock to the desired width and length. squaring off the ends. Set the miter box to 45 degrees. Cut the end of one of the pieces to that angle. Turn the saw to 45 degrees on the other side of the miter box, and cut off the end of the matching piece of stock. See Fig. 11-7. When the two pieces are fit together, they should form a 90 degree angle.

depth of the joint on each piece using a backsaw or miter box. Cut lightly along the layout lines toward the center using a chisel with the bevel side up. Do this until the waste stock breaks free. Smooth the surface of the joint using a chisel with the bevel side down, Fig. 11-9.

Fig. 11-7. Cutting a miter with a miter box.

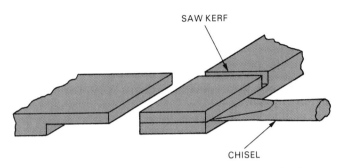

Fig. 11-9. Removing waste stock from a corner lap joint.

LAP JOINTS

LAP JOINTS are commonly used for support purposes, such as supporting a table top. The stock making up the lap joint can be joined at any angle. Lap joints are made by reducing the thickness of each piece to one-half of its original size, and then lapping one piece over the other. Types of lap joints include half lap, cross lap, edge lap, end lap, and corner lap. See Fig. 11-8. Lap joints are very strong when made carefully, since the face of one piece is bonded to the face of another piece.

When making a lap joint, cut two pieces of stock to the desired width and length. Lay out one-half the lap joint on each piece. Cut the

RABBET JOINTS

A RABBET is an L-shaped recess cut at the end or along the edge of the stock as shown in Fig. 11-10. The matching end or the square end of another piece of stock can be fastened into the recess making a strong joint. A rabbet joint is commonly used for making the sides of the boxes and drawers. It is relatively easy to make and assemble.

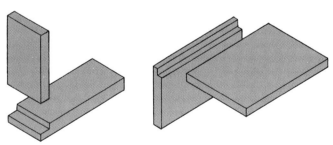

Fig. 11-10. Left. End rabbet joint. Right. Edge rabbet joint.

End rabbets can be made by using a saw with a fixture as a guide. The fixture can be made by attaching a piece of stock that is the same thickness as the desired rabbet to one end of a piece of scrap lumber. Lay out the width of the rabbets on the stock with a try square and the depth with the fixture. Fig. 11-11 shows the depth of an end rabbet being laid out with the fixture.

When the stock has been laid out, clamp the stock and the fixture in a vise. Use the fixture as a guide when sawing the joints to depth with a

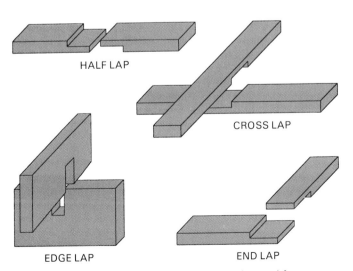

Fig. 11-8. Lap joints are commonly used for support purposes.

Fig. 11-11. Marking the depth of a rabbet joint with a fixture as a guide.

Fig. 11-13. Cutting an edge rabbet with a rabbet plane.

Fig. 11-12. Using a backsaw to cut a rabbet to depth with a fixture as a guide.

backsaw. Then, cut each joint to width with a backsaw or miter box as shown in Fig. 11-12.

A rabbet plane can be used to make edge rabbets. Set the rabbet plane guides to the required width and depth of the joint. Use uniform pressure to push the plane along the edge of your stock with the grain, Fig. 11-13. Do not try to cut the entire depth in one pass; several small passes will give you better results.

Rabbets can also be made using power tools. A dado head can be used with the table saw or radial arm saw. Set the dado heads to the correct width and adjust the fence for the proper width. Attach a strip of wood along your fence. This strip prevents the dado head from cutting into the fence. When cutting the rabbet, use several passes over the dado head, each one increasingly deeper.

A jointer can also be used to cut a rabbet if it is equipped with a rabbeting table. Refer to Unit 10 regarding the procedure for cutting a rabbet on a jointer.

Another method for cutting rabbets with power tools is by using the router. The router can be placed in a router table, a special rabbeting router bit can be used, or a fence could be attached to the router's base to guide a straight bit. In addition, a straightedge could be attached to the stock to provide a guide for the router base. Each of these routing techniques work very well. Normally, it is possible to set the micrometer adjustment to the desired depth of the rabbet, and then make several light passes until the depth is achieved. The width of the rabbet will depend on the width of the bit, the placement of the fence, or the pilot guide on the router base.

DADO JOINTS

A DADO is a square-cornered recess that runs across the grain of the stock. It is similar to a rabbet, except that it is not located along the edge or end of the stock. Dados are commonly used to hold shelves in cabinets. See Fig. 11-14. It is also used for drawer slides.

Lay out and mark your stock using a square and a pencil. Clamp a straightedge next to the

layout line. Secure the stock and straightedge in a vise. Cut one side of the dado to depth using a backsaw. Move the straightedge, clamp it into position, and cut the other side of the dado. See Fig. 11-15.

Remove the waste stock (area between the kerfs) with a chisel. Hold the chisel bevel side up, and start the cuts from each side and working toward the middle. See Fig. 11-16. Use a mallet, striking the chisel with light, even blows. When you have roughly formed the dado, turn the chisel over for better control. Use a mallet to

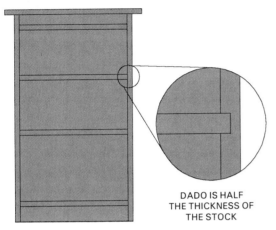

DADO IS HALF
THE THICKNESS OF
THE STOCK

Fig. 11-14. Dado joints are frequently used to support shelves. They offer better support than nails or screws.

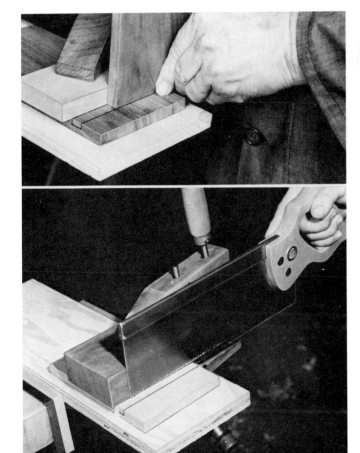

Fig. 11-15. Above. Clamping a straightedge as a guide for sawing a dado. Below. Using a straightedge as a guide for cutting a dado to depth with a backsaw.

Fig. 11-16. Removal of waste stock from a dado. Above. Starting the cut with the chisel bevel held up. Center. Using the chisel with its bevel held down. Below. Completing the cut with a router plane.

tap the chisel down into the dado at close intervals. Continue working from the edges to the middle of the stock to avoid chipping out the ends of the joint.

You can plane the dado to finished depth using a router plane. Adjust the blade and depth stop for the required depth of cut. Pull or push the router plane across the dado using firm, even pressure. Once again, work from the edge of the dado to the middle.

Dados can also be made using power tools. You can use the dado head on a table saw. You can also use a router with a straight bit to form dados. One method is to use a straightedge as a guide to form the sides of the dado. Another method to form a dado is to cut the edges using a backsaw and then cleaning out the dado using the router.

GROOVE JOINTS

A GROOVE is exactly like a dado, except that a groove runs along the grain of the stock. One of the most frequent uses of a groove is to hold drawer bottoms.

When making a groove, lay out the sides of it using a marking gauge as shown in Fig. 11-17A. This will ensure that the sides are parallel. Clamp a straightedge along the layout line, together with a piece of scrap lumber beneath as a support. Clamp the supporting board in a vise. Use the straightedge as a guide when cutting the groove to depth with a backsaw. See Fig. 11-

17B. Move the straightedge to the other layout line, clamp it in position, and make the second cut.

Remove the waste stock using a chisel with the bevel side up. Use light taps on the chisel with a mallet. Start from the ends and work toward the middle of the stock. Turn the chisel over for better control. Tap the chisel into the groove to the approximate depth at several locations. Use firm, even pressure to push the chisel with the grain and along the groove. See Fig. 11-18. Use only enough strokes to cut to the required depth. You can also use a router plane to complete the groove.

Grooves can also be formed using power tools. The dado head can be used on the table saw, or the router can be used in a similar manner as when cutting a dado.

MORTISE AND TENON JOINTS

MORTISE AND TENON JOINTS are commonly used in furniture construction. When accurately made, the joint is very strong. The joints consists of two parts; the MORTISE, or rectangular recess, and the TENON, or rectangular projection. The tenon fits in the mortise. See Fig. 11-19. There are two types of mortise and tenon joints–blind and through. The tenon of a blind mortise and tenon joint is hidden. The tenon of a through joint is partially exposed. This type of joint is difficult to make with hand tools. However, when power tools are used, the mortise and tenon joint is made rather easily.

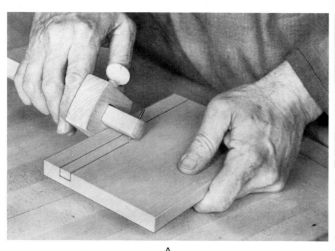

A   B

Fig. 11-17. A–Laying out a groove with a marking gauge. B–Cutting a groove with a backsaw.

Fi. 11-18. Removal of waste stock from a groove. Left. Starting the cut with the chisel bevel held up. Right. Using the chisel with its bevel held down.

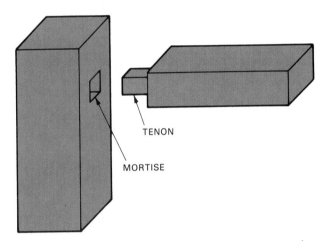

Fig. 11-19. The mortise and tenon joint is commonly used in furniture making.

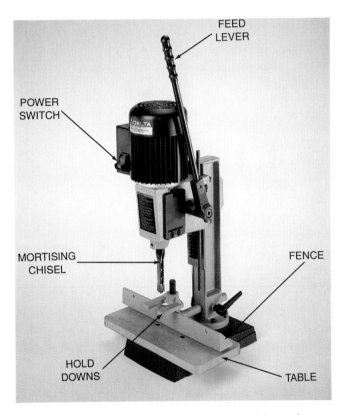

Fig. 11-20. A stand-alone mortising tool. (Delta International Machinery Corp.)

Three different methods can be used when making a mortise and tenon joint. In each case, the mortise should be made first. When using the first method, lay out the size of the mortise on the stock. Uniformly space marks for holes. Use a doweling jig as a guide to drill holes to the required depth, plus 1/16 inch. Smooth the corners and surfaces with a chisel.

The second method utilizes a stand-alone mortising tool. See Fig. 11-20. The mortising tool consists of a set of hold downs and a mortising chisel. The mortising chisel is a hollow, square chisel that is fitted with a special drill bit. The chisels are available in standard sizes ranging from 1/4 inch to 1/2 inch in 1/16-inch increments. When using the mortising tool, the stock must be held firmly in position. The mortising chisel is slowly brought into the stock. The drill bit bores the stock and the chisel squares the sides.

A router with a mortising bit and a simple jig will allow you to rapidly and accurately produce a mortise. The ends of the mortise can be squared using a chisel after completing the routing operation.

The tenon can be easily produced using hand tools or the table saw. The hand tool procedure is similar to the layout and cutting of a half-lap joint. Mark both sides of the stock carefully before removing the stock. The tenon should fit

0

Exploring Woodworking

snug into the mortise that was previously cut. Even though the joint is snug, there should still be room to allow for glue. When using a table saw to cut the tenon, a special tenoning jig should be used. See Unit 6 for more information on this set-up.

DOVETAIL JOINTS

The DOVETAIL JOINT is primarily used for drawer construction. It is widely used for high-quality furniture and cabinets. A dovetail joint consists of wedge-shaped projections that fit into a matching recess. Fig. 11-21 shows a dovetail joint. It can be cut carefully by hand. However, the most efficient means of making a dovetail joint is by using a router and dovetail jig.

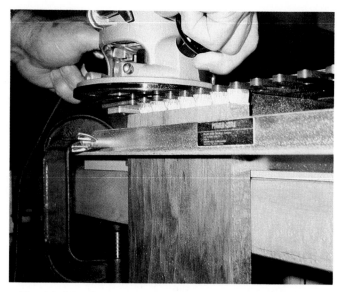

Fig. 11-22. The template guide should follow the finger template from one side of the stock to the other.

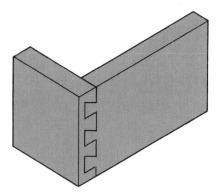

Fig. 11-21. A dovetail joint is used for drawer corners in high-quality furniture. The fingers interlock, giving the stock rigidity and a good appearance.

When making a dovetail joint, select two pieces of stock to be joined. Mark one as the FRONT or BACK, and the other as SIDE. Clamp the FRONT piece against the guide pin on top of the jig. Then, place the piece for the side against the guide pin on the front of the jig. The inside surface for each piece should be facing out. Clamp the finger template on top of the jig. Attach the template guide to the router base and adjust the bit to the depth recommended by the manufacturer.

Begin at one side of the clamped stock. Insert the template guide into the finger template from the front only. Turn on the router and follow the finger template from one side of the stock to the other. See Fig. 11-22. Turn off the router and remove it from the finger template by pulling backward only. See Fig. 11-23.

Fig. 11-23. The template guide is fastened to the bottom of the router base.

Notice that the two pieces of stock are offset when they are cut together. They will match when you put them together to make the completed joint.

PLATE JOINERY

PLATE, or BISCUIT JOINERY is becoming one of the most popular methods of making joints for all types of products. This process was developed in Europe in the 1950s. It allows you to make butt joints that do not shift during clamping, yet give you strength similar to that of a spline or dowel joint. Fig. 11-24 shows several

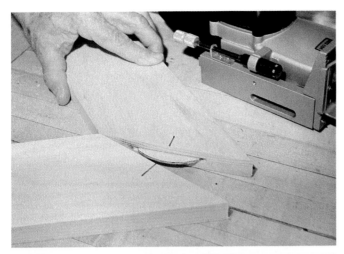

Fig. 11-24. Biscuit joinery has many applications.

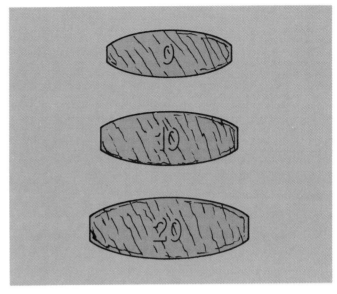

Fig. 11-25. Biscuits are available in three different sizes.

Fig. 11-26. A plate joiner is used to cut the recesses that accept the biscuits. (Porter-Cable)

types of joints that benefit from the use of biscuit joinery.

The BISCUIT, or PLATE, is a flat football-shaped piece of beech. They are available in three sizes–0, 10, and 20–with 20 being the largest, Fig. 11-25. The biscuit fits loosely in a semicircular slot cut by a special tool called a PLATE JOINER. See Fig. 11-26. When a water-based adhesive is added to the groove, the compressed biscuit swells and tightens the joint. Edge-joined material has less problems with expansion and contraction than other reinforcement methods, such as dowels or splines, because the grain of the biscuit runs diagonally. Plate joints can be made quickly and easily with the proper tools.

Plate Joiner–Safety and Care
1. Always keep both hands behind the cutter blade.
2. Start the motor before beginning the plunge cut.
3. Perform a dry run to check the setup, including clamping, fence adjustment, etc. A DRY RUN is a test run of the operation with the plate joiner unplugged.

Making a Plate Joint

When making a plate joint, make sure that the two joining surfaces are flat, smooth, and clean. Place the joining surfaces together and mark the desired biscuit location on both pieces. Make a pencil mark about 3/4-inch long on both pieces. A straightedge or a square may be used as shown in Fig. 11-27. If more than one joint is to be made, number each joint for assembly purposes.

A

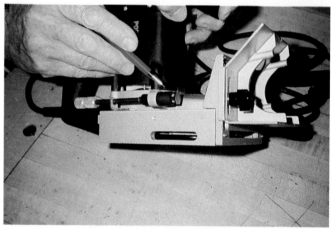

B

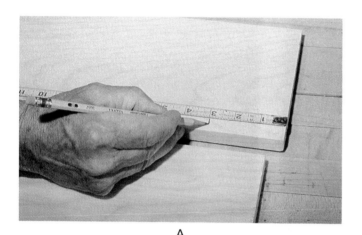

A

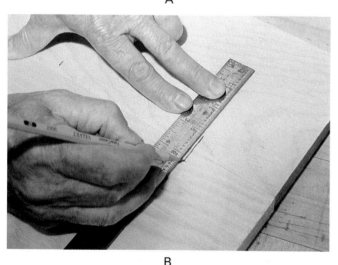

B

Fig. 11-27. Marking the position of the biscuits. A–Lay out the position on one piece of stock. B–Transfer these marks using a straightedge or a square.

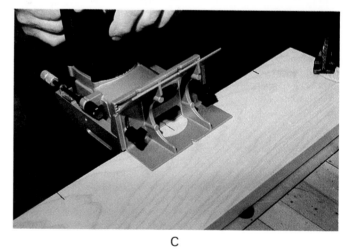

C

Fig. 11-28. Preparing the plate joiner. A–Carefully adjust the fence. Note the carbide-tipped blade beneath the fence. B–Adjust the depth of cut according to the size of biscuit being used. C–Align the mark on the fence with the layout mark on the stock.

Separate the pieces and firmly clamp the first piece to be cut in a vise. Do not try to hold the piece by hand while cutting. Carefully adjust the fence on the plate joiner to cut approximately at the center of the stock. Be aware of the carbide-tipped blade just below the fence. Adjust the depth of cut to the size of the biscuit being used. Cut grooves on all pieces of stock as previously marked. Fig. 11-28 shows the process of adjusting and cutting a recess for a biscuit.

Insert the biscuits into the grooves and dry assemble the stock, Fig. 11-29. If the alignment is correct, apply a water-base glue into the grooves and onto the mating surface of one

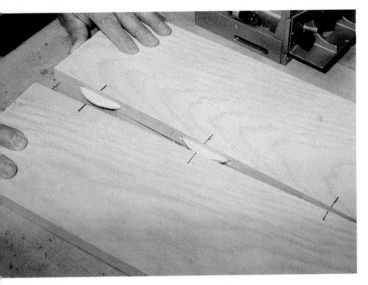

Fig. 11-29. Always dry assemble parts before gluing.

piece. Insert a biscuit into each groove. Apply glue into the mating groove on the other piece of stock. Assemble the pieces, align your original marks, and clamp. Allow the glue to set before removing the clamps.

BOX JOINTS

BOX JOINTS are used to make strong, yet decorative corners. The box joint consists of a series of rectangular-shaped projections on the edge of one piece and mating recesses along the edge of a second piece. See Fig. 11-30. The projections and recesses of the second piece are offset the width of one segment, so the two pieces will match when they are assembled.

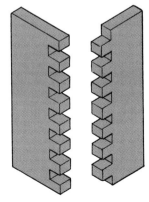

Fig. 11-30. Box joints make strong, yet attractive corners.

Box joints are usually made using a fixture on the table saw. They can also be made using a router and router table.

TEST YOUR KNOWLEDGE, Unit 11

Please do not write in this text. Place your answers on a separate sheet of paper.

1. _____ is used to strengthen most wood joints.
2. The strongest wood joints fastened with glue are those involving the _____ and _____ of wood, and the weakest joints are those involving _____ of wood.
3. A _____ joint involves the square end of one piece of wood being attached to the surface of another piece of wood.
4. When making edge butt joints, the surface grain of all boards should _____.
5. In edge butt joints, end grain of adjacent boards should be opposite to _____.
6. Describe the use of dowels in a wood joint.
7. A special tool is required to make a plate joint. True or False?
8. A plate joint is similar to a joint held together with _____, but is much stronger and faster to make.
9. The small wooden plate used in plate joinery is called a _____.
10. A dovetail joint can be cut using either a router or by hand. True or False?
11. _____ joints are formed with two pieces that have 45 degree cuts at their ends.
12. List three power tools that can be used for making a rabbet joint.
13. A dado head can be used only for making dados. True or False?
14. The finish depth of a hand-cut dado can be made using a _____.
15. A groove is exactly like a dado, except that a groove runs along or with the grain of the stock. True or False?
16. The mortise can be made either by hand or by using a special mortising attachment on the _____.
17. The rectangular recess of a mortise and tenon joint is called the _____.
18. The dovetail joint is used primarily for _____ construction.
19. Box joints are very strong because of the increased gluing surface. True or False?
20. The biscuits used in plate joinery are available in three different sizes. What are these sizes?
21. What type of wood is used to make the biscuit in plate joinery?

22. Along with the router and dovetail bit what two other devices are needed to cut dovetails?
23. What power tool is normally used to make box joints?

ACTIVITIES

1. Make a list of the various joints described in this unit. Describe the appearance of each joint, its strengths and weaknesses, and the tools needed to build it.
2. Look at several pieces of furniture at your home. List the joints that are used to construct the furniture. Make sketches of the joints.
3. Make the following wood joints using a 1 x 2 piece of pine and hand tools: edge butt, end butt, half lap, miter, rabbet, and dado.
4. Prepare two edge butt joints, one using dowels and another using the plate joiner. Answer the following questions. Why are dowels or biscuits used? Which method is faster? Which method is easier?
5. Construct a dovetail joint using two pieces of softwood about 5- or 6- inches wide and about 1-foot long. Use the router and dovetail jig.

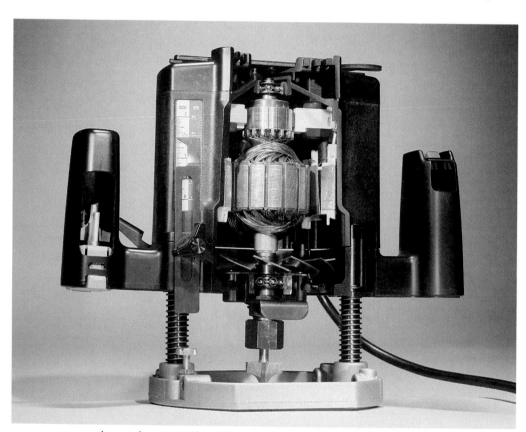

Internal construction of a portable plunge router. (Skil Corp.)

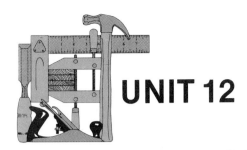

UNIT 12

ROUTING AND SHAPING

In general, the tools and equipment that have been previously discussed are used to size stock. Even though this might be adequate for some products, many products are given a better appearance through the use of the shaper or router. After studying this unit, you will be able to identify shaping and routing bits. You will also be able to safely set-up and operate the hand-held router and the stationary shaper.

PORTABLE ROUTER

The PORTABLE ROUTER, Fig. 12-1, is one of the most versatile pieces of woodworking equipment. It can be used to shape the edges of wood frames and paneling, rout grooves and mortises, and trim veneer and plastic laminates. The portable router can also be used with jigs and fixtures to plane edges, and for cutting specialized shapes using a template.

The size of a portable router is indicated by its horsepower rating and by the capacity of its chuck (bit shank diameter). The spindle of the router revolves at very high speeds, frequently 20,000 to 30,000 RPM (revolutions per minute).

Router Bits

Router bits are made from high-speed steel with carbide cutting edges. Silicon carbide is an extremely hard material. This material allows the bit to stay sharp much longer than standard high-speed steel bits.

SHAPING BITS are used to form decorative edges. Inside curves are formed with cove bits. Outside curves are formed with round over or beading bits. See Fig. 12-2. Rabbets, chamfers, and combination curves can also be formed on edges using different bits. Shaping bits are guided along the edge of the stock by several methods. A fence can be attached to the base of the router, allowing the cutter to penetrate into the material the desired amount. Many bits have a pilot tip that extends below the cutter shape. The pilot tip follows the edge of the stock, producing the desired depth. A third method of

Fig. 12-1. Parts of a router. (Porter-Cable)

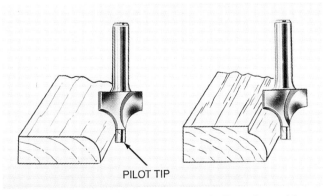

Fig. 12-2. Typical shaping bits. Left. Round over bit. Right. Beading bit.

control involves using a bushing and a template. The bushing is guided around the template while the cutter moves through the stock.

ROUTING BITS are used to cut dados, grooves, veins, coves, and mortises in the surfaces and edges of wood. Fig. 12-3 shows a straight bit that can be used for dados and grooves. These bits can be guided with a fence attached to the base, or with a template and guide. They are often used without the use of any type of guide. This is called FREEHAND ROUTING and requires a great deal of skill.

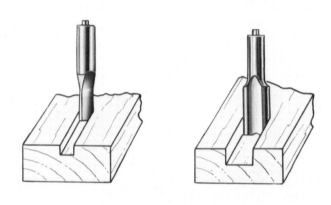

Fig. 12-3. Routing bits. Left. Single-flute, straight bit. Right. Double-flute, straight bit.

Special bits are available for trimming veneer and plastic laminates. Others are used to make dovetail joints, hinge and lock mortises, and special cuts.

Installing Bits and Adjusting the Base

The router bit must be installed in the chuck before adjusting the base and cutting any stock. First, disconnect the power cord. Loosen the locking handle and base so that you have easy access to the chuck. Tighten the locking handle so that the router base does not move when inserting the bit. Then, insert the bit into the collet chuck. Position the bit so that the maximum amount of the bit shank is inside the chuck, but not touching the bottom of the cluck. If the shank touches the bottom of the cluck, it should be raised 1/32 to 1/16 inch to prevent its loosening while cutting. Firmly tighten the chuck. Loosen the router base and set the bit to the required depth with the depth adjustment. The depth adjustment is very useful when using routing bits, such as the straight bit. Tighten the base

locking handle and make any other necessary adjustments before starting the motor.

A fence may be used when using routing bits. Insert the fence adjustment bars into the router base and tighten the lock screws. Then, move the fence to the required width and tighten the lock nuts. When measuring the distance from the fence to the cutter, be sure to measure to the outside of the arc made by the cutter. It is easy to measure closer to the bit shank, resulting in an improper adjustment.

Plug in the router and test your adjustments on a piece of scrap stock. Make sure that the scrap stock is firmly secured in a vise or clamped to the table top.

Router–Safety and Care
1. Turn off the router motor immediately after making each cut.
2. Disconnect the power cord before making any adjustments.
3. Grasp the router firmly, holding the cutter bit away from you, before turning on the motor.
4. Tighten screws and nuts securely when making adjustments. Since the router is a power tool, screws and nuts may have a tendency to vibrate loose during operation.
5. Handle the router carefully. Lay it on its side on a bench away from the work area to prevent accidentally knocking it on the floor. An alternative to laying it on its side is to place a block of wood under the base so that the bit does not contact the table top.
6. Use only sharp router bits. Protect the cutter bits from damage by returning them to their holder immediately after use.
7. Wear a face shield or goggles when using the router. Many types of safety glasses do not prevent wood chips from falling behind the lenses and into your eyes.
8. Wear ear protection when using a router due to the high noise level.

Shaping an Edge
One of the shaping bits will be used to shape an edge of the stock. Choose a bit, install it in the router, and adjust the depth of cut. Clamp a practice piece of stock in a vise and firmly grasp both router handles as shown in Fig. 12-4. Turn on the motor and lightly push the router toward

Fig. 12-4. Shaping an edge with a round over bit.

the edge of the stock, allowing the bit to make a short cut. Turn off the router and make any adjustments, if necessary.

Hold the router handles with both hands, turn on the router, and push or pull it around the edge of the stock. The feed direction of the router depends on whether an inside or outside cut is being made. Remember that the router bit is rotating clockwise as viewed from above. The feed direction should be against the rotation of the bit as it contacts the surface of the stock. Therefore, the router should be fed in a counterclockwise direction for an outside cut and clockwise for an inside cut. See Fig. 12-5. Move the router with moderate speed, applying very light pressure against the stock with the tip of the bit.

Heavy pressure will result in excess friction, causing the bit to overheat. When this occurs the edge of the stock may be burned. Complete the edge and turn off the motor.

When routing the outside of a piece of stock, be sure to rout the end grain first and then the edges. Most of the splintering that may have occurred when routing the end grain will be removed as the edges are routed. An alternative to this method is to attach a scrap piece of stock to the edge and allow the router to complete its cut in the scrap. The set-up for this procedure is similar to an edge butt joint, except the scrap stock is clamped, not glued. This procedure should also be followed if all sides of a surface are not being routed, for example, the top of a night stand. The rear edge is usually not routed.

Cutting a Groove

A straight bit is used to cut grooves. Select the correct size bit, install it in the router, and adjust the depth of cut. Attach the fence to the router base and adjust it to the desired width. Make sure that the router is unplugged when inserting the bit and adjusting the fence. Clamp a piece of scrap stock in a vise and turn on the router motor to make a trial cut. Grasp both router handles and make a short cut. Make adjustments to the depth of cut and fence setting, if necessary. Push or pull the router along the edge of the stock using pressure against the fence, Fig. 12-6. Complete the groove and then turn off the motor.

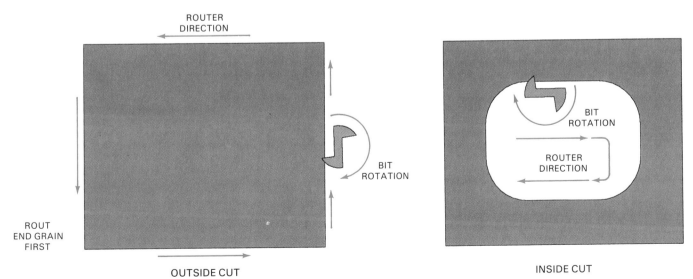

Fig. 12-5. When making an outside cut, rout the end grain first. Progress in a counterclockwise direction. Use a clockwise direction when routing an inside cut.

Fig. 12-6. Using a fence as a guide for cutting a groove with a straight bit.

Fig. 12-7. A laminate trimmer is used to trim plastic laminates. (Porter-Cable)

Using Templates

Irregular shapes can be cut with a router by using a TEMPLATE and template guide, called a BUSHING. The template is either attached to the stock to be cut, or the stock is secured in the template. Two templates that are commonly used are the dovetail template and the door hinge template. The bushing is attached to the bottom of the router base. A router bit with a pilot tip or a small bearing located above or below the cutter may also be used when using a template.

A template may be made by cutting the desired shape out of a piece of 1/8- or 1/4-inch hardboard or plywood. Clamp the stock to a bench and fasten the template to it. Attach the template guide to the router base. Insert the desired bit in the router chuck and tighten it securely. Adjust the bit to the required depth, plug in the power cord, and turn on the motor. Hold the bushing next to the template and push or pull the router around the template. Work from the outside of the template inward. Complete the cut, turn off the motor, and unplug the router.

Trimming Plastic Laminates and Wood Veneer

A router or laminate trimmer can be used to trim plastic laminates and wood veneer. A LAMINATE TRIMMER is a special type of router used specifically for this purpose. See Fig. 12-7. It is similar to a router in both operation and appearance. When using a router or laminate trimmer to trim plastic laminate or veneer, either a special bit or guide must be used. Both of these devices control the side-to-side movement of the bit.

When laminating plywood or other base material, the laminate should be cut about 1/2 inch larger than the base material. Adhere the plastic laminate or wood veneer to the plywood surface with the appropriate adhesive.

Insert a trimming bit in the chuck and tighten it securely. Adjust the bit. Clamp the stock to the bench or secure it in a vise. Firmly grasp the router, connect the power cord, and turn on the motor for a trial cut. Lightly push or pull the router toward the stock until the pilot tip or ball bearing guide touches the edge. Check the cut and make any necessary adjustments. Continue moving the router around the stock to complete the cut, turn off the motor, and disconnect the power cord.

Overarm (Pin) Router

The OVERARM ROUTER, also called the PIN ROUTER, is a fast and efficient means of producing repetitive work, such as cut-outs, grooving, lettering, and edging. Other overarm routers are a stationary power tool that may use a portable router motor as its source of power. Some models of overarm routers have a built-in power source as shown in Fig. 12-8.

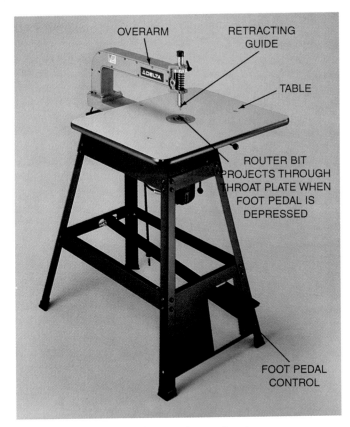

Fig. 12-8. Overarm inverted router.
(Delta International Machinery Corp.)

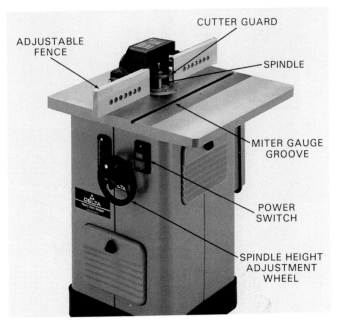

Fig. 12-9. Parts of a wood shaper.
(Delta International Machinery Corp.)

A guide pin that matches the diameter of the router bit follows a groove previously cut into a template. This template is placed below the material to be routed. As the template moves along the pin, the overarm-mounted router bit shapes the stock. Fences and other accessories may be added to expand the capabilities of this machine.

SHAPER

A SHAPER is used to shape the edges of both straight and irregular cuts. It is commonly used to form edges, make moldings, and cut grooves. Templates can be used when making duplicate parts. Fig. 12-9 shows a shaper with its parts identified.

The size of a shaper is specified by the diameter of the spindle that holds the cutters. Common spindle sizes are 1/2, 3/4, and 1 inch. Many machines allow the use of different sizes of spindles. The outside diameter of the shaper cutter knives vary a great deal, depending upon their use. Many cutters have larger spindle holes (center holes) as the outside diameter or overall thickness of the cutter increases. The height of

the spindle is adjustable to allow for varying depths of cut. Once the desired height is determined, the spindle is locked into place.

The cutter and spindle are rotated by a motor-driven belt. Cutter speeds range from 5000 to 10,000 RPM. Some machines have variable speeds. They provide the best cutter speed for the type of material being cut, the thickness of the cut, and the size of the cutter. The cutter normally turns in a counterclockwise direction, but many machines are equipped with reversing switches.

Straight stock is usually held against the fence. The shaper fence is divided into two parts: the FRONT FENCE and the REAR FENCE. Both parts of the fence are separately adjustable. Curved stock is fed against a depth guide collar attached to the spindle, and one or two fulcrum pins.

Shaper Cutters

Three-lip solid cutters are available in a variety of shapes, including straight, round over, cove, bead, combination, tongue and groove, flute, and door lip. See Fig. 12-10. Some cutters may be purchased for either left-hand or right-hand operation. Cutters are made of high-speed steel with carbide-tipped cutting edges to increase their durability.

113

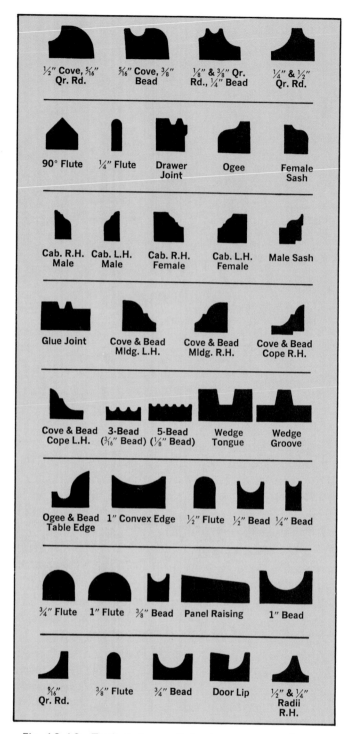

½" Cove, ⁵⁄₁₆"
Qr. Rd.　　⁵⁄₁₆" Cove, ³⁄₈"
Bead　　⅛" & ³⁄₈" Qr.
Rd., ¼" Bead　　¼" & ½"
Qr. Rd.

90° Flute　　¼" Flute　　Drawer
Joint　　Ogee　　Female
Sash

Cab. R.H.
Male　　Cab. L.H.
Male　　Cab. R.H.
Female　　Cab. L.H.
Female　　Male Sash

Glue Joint　　Cove & Bead
Mldg. L.H.　　Cove & Bead
Mldg. R.H.　　Cove & Bead
Cope R.H.

Cove & Bead
Cope L.H.　　3-Bead
(³⁄₁₆" Bead)　　5-Bead
(⅛" Bead)　　Wedge
Tongue　　Wedge
Groove

Ogee & Bead
Table Edge　　1" Convex Edge　　½" Flute　　½" Bead　　¼" Bead

¾" Flute　　1" Flute　　⅜" Bead　　Panel Raising　　1" Bead

⁵⁄₁₆"
Qr. Rd.　　⅜" Flute　　¾" Bead　　Door Lip　　½" & ¼"
Radii
R.H.

Fig. 12-10. Typical shapes, 3-lip shaper cutters. Cutters are shown half size. (Delta International Machinery Corp.)

Installing Cutters

When possible, cutters should be installed so that they cut from the bottom of the stock. This allows the stock to act as a partial shield. Spacing collars may be used above or beneath the cutter to hold the assembly in the proper position. If irregular shapes are to be cut, a depth guide collar must be placed above or beneath the cutter. This regulates the depth of cut and guides

the stock as it is fed across the shaper, Fig. 12-11. When cutting irregular shapes, one or two fulcrum pins must be installed to aid in starting the cut.

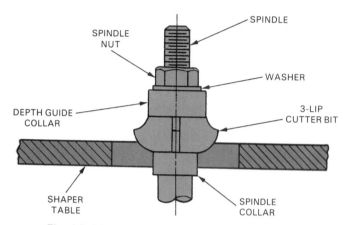

Fig. 12-11. Installing a bit on a shaper spindle.

When installing a cutter in a shaper, disconnect the power cord or turn off the disconnect switch. Remove the top spindle nut. Select the desired cutter and install it on the spindle. Spacers are generally necessary either above or below the cutter. These should be placed on the spindle prior to replacing the spindle nut.

Shaper—Safety and Care

1. Know where to place your fingers and hands before turning on the motor. Always keep them well away from the cutters.
2. Use only stock that is free of warp, loose knots, and other defects. Make sure the stock is at least 16-inches long. Use a featherboard or other device to help hold stock less than 4-inches wide or 1-inch thick.
3. Be sure the cutter revolves toward the stock and in the direction of the grain.
4. Always use a fulcrum pin (guide pin) to help start stock against the depth collar. This will help prevent kickback of the stock.
5. Check adjustments carefully before you turn on the motor.
6. Feed stock at moderate speed. Use only sharp cutters.
7. Have your instructor check your set-up prior to operating the shaper.

Forming Straight Edges

Best results when using a shaper are obtained after practicing on a piece of scrap stock. Select a defect-free piece of stock that is at least 16-inches long. Install a suitable cutter on the spindle. Set the fence in a position so the cutter is correctly aligned with the edge of the stock. Move the fence parallel to the miter gauge slot on the table and tighten it securely. Inspect the grain of the stock to determine its direction. Turn the stock so the *cutter knives cut toward the stock* and in the direction of the grain. See Fig. 12-12.

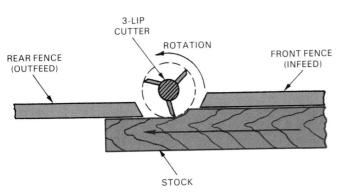

Fig. 12-12. Offset of the shaper fence as an entire edge is shaped (top view).

The process of forming a straight edge with a shaper is similar to that of jointing an edge with a jointer. Place the stock on the shaper table and turn on the motor. Hold the stock against the table and the fence and push it over the cutter. When about 2 inches of the stock passes the cutter, turn off the motor and adjust the second part of the fence to the formed edge. Turn on the motor and continue the cutting stroke. When about 8 inches of the stock passes the cutter, move one of your hands to the other side, then

the other hand, and complete the cutting stroke with both hands pressing against the second part of the fence. This procedure ensures that your hands will not pass directly over or in front of the cutter. See Fig. 12-13.

Forming Irregular Edges

Select a piece of scrap stock and saw a curve on one edge. Install a suitable cutter and a depth guide collar on the spindle. Fasten a fulcrum pin in the table. The FULCRUM PIN acts as a guide and support when starting the cut. Turn the stock so the cutter knives cut toward the stock and in the direction of the grain.

Position Ring Guard

Place the stock on the shaper table and turn on the motor. Hold the stock firmly against the fulcrum pin and push it toward the depth guide collar into the cutter knives. Fig. 12-14. *Be sure the knives revolve toward the stock*. Continue to push the stock forward with light pressure against the depth guide collar. Complete the stroke by keeping light pressure against the depth guide collar while pushing the stock past the cutter. Turn off the motor after the cutting stroke has been completed.

Fig. 12-14. Shaping a curved edge of wood against a depth guide collar on the spindle of a wood shaper. Note the fulcrum pin and the guard.

TEST YOUR KNOWLEDGE, Unit 12

1. The size of a portable router is indicated by its _____ rating and by the _____.

2. Some router bits are _____-tipped, giving them greater durability than standard high-speed steel bits.

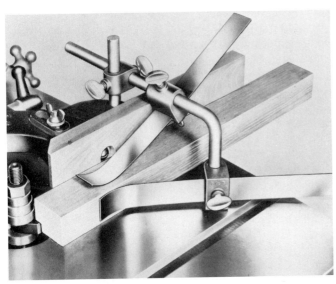

Fig. 12-13. Shaping a straight edge of wood against the fence of a wood shaper.

3. Irregular shapes can be cut using the portable router by using a _____ and a _____ _____.

4. The size of a wood shaper is indicated by the diameter of the _____ which holds the cutter.

5. The wood shaper spindle is adjusted _____ for the depth of cut.

6. Speed of a shaper spindle is usually 5000 to 10,000 RPM. True or False?

7. When shaping straight stock, the stock is usually held _____ _____ _____.

8. When possible, shaper cutters should be installed from the _____ so the stock can act as a partial shield.

9. The _____ _____ acts as a guide and support when starting irregular cuts on the shaper.

ACTIVITIES

1. Inspect a router from your tool cabinet. What is the brand name? How many horsepower and amps? What is the size of the chuck? Does it have a standard base or a plunge base?

2. Remove the router bits from tool storage. Look at the various shapes. How many straight cutters are there? Sketch some of the shapes. Sketch profiles that can be obtained by combining different bits. Do some of the bits have pilot tips or ball bearing guides? Are any of the cutting edges carbide tipped?

3. Remove a router and a simple shaping bit from tool storage. Mount the bit in the chuck and tighten. Adjust the bit. Shape the outer edge using a scrap piece of softwood at least 3/4-inch thick x 6-inches wide.

Make several light passes rather than one wide pass. Did the wood splinter on the ends? Did the router pull through the work? Are there any burn marks on the edges?

4. Identify the following parts on the shaper:
   A. The ON/OFF switch. Is there a reversing switch?
   B. The spindle adjustment wheel. How is the spindle locked into position?
   C. Locate the spindle. What size is it?
   D. Look at the fence. Are both sections in a straight line? If not, why not?
   E. Where is the guard? How does it protect the operator?

5. Identify the following parts that are used with the shaper.
   A. A typical cutter. Sketch its profile. What direction does it rotate?
   B. A spacing collar. How does this fit on the shaper? Does it fit above or below the cutter?
   C. What other accessories are available in your laboratory for the shaper?

6. Select a small diameter cutter and appropriate spacing collar. Mount them on the spindle. Adjust the fence to a straight line with the cutter in its proper position. Position the guard, hold downs, or featherboards. Select a clear scrap piece of stock measuring 2 x 4 x 36 inches. Determine the direction of the grain. Readjust the hold downs and guard to allow shaping the edge of the board. Adjust the spindle height to take a cut from the bottom of the board. Lock the spindle height. Have your instructor check your set-up. Make the cut. Answer the following questions:
   A. Are there any burn marks? If so why?
   B. Did the grain splinter?
   C. Is the profile what you expected?

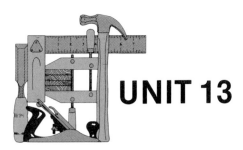

UNIT 13

WOOD TURNING

Many common items are produced by turning. Some of these include balusters for stairs, rails for chairs, bowls, and lamp bases. After reading and studying this unit, you will be able to identify the different parts of a wood lathe and the common turning tools used with it. In addition, you will be able to design and turn items mounted either between centers or on the faceplate.

Items such as those previously mentioned are shaped on a wood lathe. The shaping process is called WOOD TURNING. Stock is shaped with special tools called TURNING TOOLS. The tools are supported by a TOOL REST as the stock revolves.

WOOD LATHE

The size of a wood lathe is determined by the swing and the bed length. SWING is the largest diameter piece of stock that can be turned on the lathe. The BED LENGTH is the maximum distance between the centers of the headstock and tailstock. A common-size lathe is one with a 12-inch swing and a bed length of 48 inches. See Fig. 13-1.

Lathe Speeds

All stock turned on the lathe should be started with a slow speed, 400 to 1000 RPM. A slow speed is required because stock is often mounted off-center and is not balanced. If it is turned fast, excessive vibration could throw the stock off the lathe. A faster speed can be used when the stock has been turned to a cylindrical shape.

In general, a slower speed should be used for large pieces than is used for small pieces. A max-

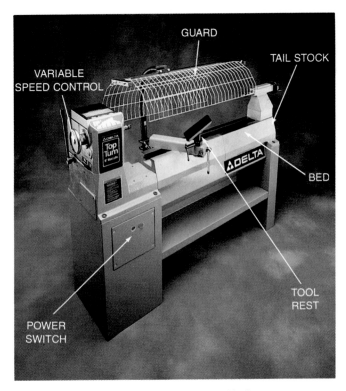

Fig. 13-1. Parts of a wood lathe.
(Delta International Machinery Corp.)

imum speed of 600 RPM should be used for stock that is 8 inches or more in diameter. Small stock measuring 4 inches or less in diameter can be turned at higher speeds. Small stock can be turned at 1000 to 1500 RPM after rough turning to balance the piece.

TURNING TOOLS

Six shapes of turning tools are commonly used by wood turners, Fig. 13-2. The tools are available in various widths, thicknesses, and lengths. The type of tool used is determined by the task that is to be performed. A skew, for example, is commonly used to make finishing cuts on stock.

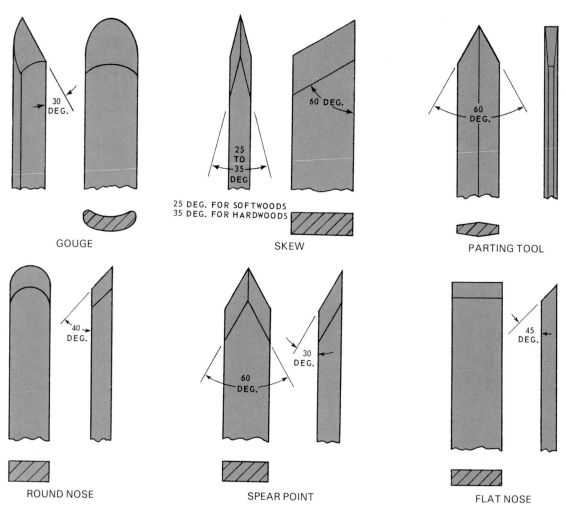

30 DEG.

25 TO 35 DEG

25 DEG. FOR SOFTWOODS
35 DEG. FOR HARDWOODS

GOUGE

60 DEG.

SKEW

60 DEG.

PARTING TOOL

40 DEG.

ROUND NOSE

60 DEG.

30 DEG.

SPEAR POINT

45 DEG.

FLAT NOSE

Fig. 13-2. Turning tools.

Turning tools cut best when the bevels are hollow-ground and honed to a sharp edge with a slipstone. Additional grinding may be necessary when a tool is nicked or loses its hollow-ground bevel. Honing should be done at frequent intervals while turning.

Gouge

A GOUGE is generally used to cut rough stock to a cylindrical shape. A gouge cuts rapidly, but does not produce a smooth cut or surface. When using a gouge, the convex side should be held down. The tool should be rolled 30 to 45 degrees in the direction it is being moved along the tool rest. The cutting edge should be slightly ahead of the handle when making cuts. The bevel at the gouge should contact the stock before the cutting edge. This is easily accomplished by lowering the tool handle 10 to 15 degrees. As the bevel rubs the stock, raise the handle until the cutting edge begins to remove the material. See Fig. 13-3.

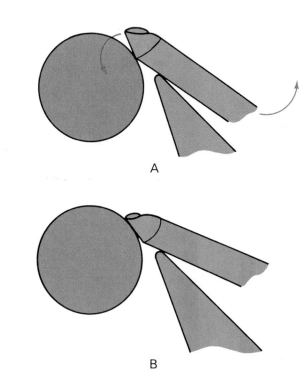

A

B

Fig. 13-3. A—Move the gouge into the wood until the bevel touches it. B—Raise the handle and move the edge into the wood.

Skew

The SKEW is used to make finishing or smoothing cuts, cut beads and V-shaped grooves, and to square shoulders. The skew is placed flat on the tool rest with the bevel down. The tool should be held almost level with the center of the stock. The handle can be lowered slightly. Gently push the cutting edge into the stock. Only the edge contacts the material. The skew scrapes the material rather than cutting it.

Parting Tool

The PARTING TOOL is a special tool that is thinner at the edges than in the center. This shape allows you to push the tool straight into the stock without binding. As the name indicates, the tool is used to part or separate the finished part from the rough stock. It is also valuable in establishing initial diameters prior to cutting special shapes. This procedure provides relief for the other cutting tools while establishing the finished depth.

Round Nose, Spear Point, and Flat Nose

These chisels are used when the tool shape fits the contour of the work. As with the skew, these tools usually make a scraping cut. They are held flat on the tool rest, approximately level with the center of the stock. The tool is pushed gently into the stock with only the edge contacting the material.

Each of these tools is ground to a special contour. Whenever the shape you are turning matches one of these contours, these tools can be used to increase speed and uniformity. Many turners will custom grind a special shape they will be repeating into the profile of a flat tool, such as a bull nose. You should use extreme care when sharpening a tool with a special contour in order not to destroy the original profile.

WOODS FOR TURNING

Several different woods can be used for turning in the woods laboratory. Commonly used woods include birch, mahogany, hard maple, oak, and walnut. You must first decide the purpose for the turning. Is it to be a table leg, or perhaps a candy bowl? The purpose determines many variables. If the turning will support a product structurally, the stock must be kiln dried and straight grained with minimal defects. If, however, the product is only decorative (such as the bowl), defects and "wild" grain patterns can enhance the finished appearance. Many professional bowl turners use freshly cut wood that has been discarded because of defects. This "wet" wood turns very easily and the defects add character to their work.

Gluing Stock for Turning

Several pieces of stock may need to be glued together for some products. This is done to achieve the desired rough stock size, to make allowance for the product design, for decorative purposes, to stabilize a defect, or even to allow separation of pieces after turning. Whenever stock is glued for turning, only flat and true pieces of stock should be glued together. If the mating surfaces are not flat, the stock could separate while turning. This separation could destroy the product or cause personal injury. Use a good white or yellow glue to glue stock for turning. Do not attempt to turn glued stock until the glue has set for at least 24 hours.

Many times different types of woods are glued together prior to turning to give a decorative appearance. In some cases, turnings are thin at one end and larger at the other. This procedure allows you to use small pieces of stock that may have otherwise been discarded.

If you are face plate turning, you can glue a piece of scrap to the good stock. This allows screws to be placed into the scrap without damaging the final product. Many turners glue a piece of notebook paper between the scrap and the good stock for easier separation later. Some spindle-turned material will be separated after turning and attached to a flat surface for decorative purposes. When this technique is utilized, two pieces of stock can be glued together, separated with a piece of notebook paper. The two pieces are easily separated after turning. Use care to place the center points of both centers on this glue line to assure equal separation.

Professional wood turners commonly use defects for design. However, a loose knot could separate while turning, causing a hazard. The defect is glued in place using a special adhesive specifically designed for lathe turning. This adhesive, called *cyanoacrylate,* can be extremely hazardous when it comes into contact with the skin. Cyanoacrylate sets almost immediately, allowing for repairs to be made to the stock while only briefly shutting the lathe off.

Wood Lathe–Safety and Care

1. Roll up your sleeves and tie up long hair so they do not become entangled in the rotating stock.
2. Clamp your work securely and check the setup by hand before turning on the motor.
3. Always begin cutting the stock with a slow speed.
4. Always wear safety goggles and/or a full face shield.
5. Stop the lathe often to lubricate and check the tailstock.
6. Keep the tool rest close to the work. The tool rest should never be more than 3/8 inch away from the stock.
7. When cutting the stock, keep tool handles angled downward.
8. Keep tools sharp.

SPINDLE TURNING

Spindle turning is used to make products such as balusters, rails, and lamp bases. When spindle turning, the stock is mounted between the lathe centers. Select a piece of stock and cut it about an inch longer than the completed product. Fasten the piece in a vise and draw diagonal lines across the corners of both ends. Then, mark the centers with a punch. Cut saw kerfs about 1/8 inch deep along the diagonal lines at one end. If the thickness and width of the stock is greater than two inches square, plane or saw off the corners prior to turning. This decreases the amount of time required for rough turning

Fig. 13-4. Using a mallet to seat a spur center in the end of a piece for spindle turning.

and reduces hazards. Drive the SPUR (headstock) CENTER into the kerfs with a mallet as shown in Fig. 13-4.

Insert a CUP (tailstock) center into the tailstock spindle. Some cup centers, called DEAD CENTERS, are stationary. These types of centers require the use of grease or wax as a lubricant. Some tailstock centers have bearings that rotate with the stock. These bearing centers require little or no lubrication.

Mount the spur center and the stock in the headstock spindle. Insert the cup center in the other end of the stock. Turn the stock by hand to seat the cup center in the end of the stock, and then lock the tailstock into position.

Adjust the tool rest so that it is parallel to the the center of the stock and about 1/8 inch away from it. Make sure that the tool rest is not below the center of the stock. Turn the stock by hand to see that it clears the tool rest. Set the lathe at the slowest speed and turn on the motor. The speed of some lathes may need to be adjusted after turning on the lathe.

Place the gouge on the tool rest, positioning one of your hands on the blade and the other hand on the handle. The hand on the blade should have your thumb over the blade and forefinger under the blade. Turn the blade slightly to make a SHEARING cut. Move the gouge carefully along the tool rest using your forefinger as a guide. See Fig. 13-5. Make additional cuts with the gouge using the same method until the piece becomes cylindrical. When the space between the stock and the tool rest reaches 3/8 inch, stop the lathe and readjust the tool rest.

Use a skew with a SCRAPING cut to smooth the cylinder. A scraping cut is made by turning the skew's cutting edge at a right angle to the piece. Move the skew along the tool rest using a similar motion as when using the gouge to achieve a smooth, uniform cylinder. Scraping cuts are easier to make with the skew than shearing cuts. Scraping cuts are recommended until you have had enough experience using the lathe. Shearing cuts are made with a skew by raising the tool rest above center and turning the cutting edge of the skew at an angle to the stock. The cutting edge then cuts as a knife.

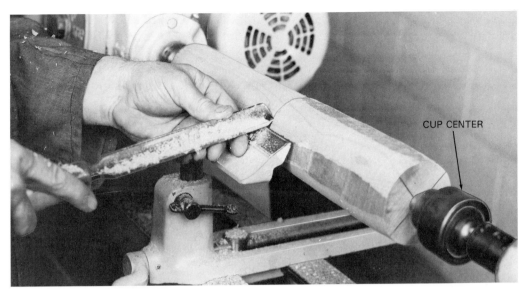

Fig. 13-5. Rough turning spindle stock with a gouge. Note the position of the hands and angle of the lathe tool.

Use a parting tool and outside caliper to lay out the necessary diameters along the cylinder. See Fig. 13-6. Then, use other tools to form the desired shape to complete the piece.

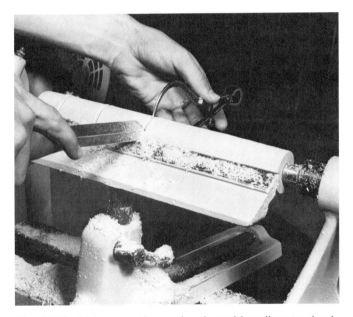

Fig. 13-6. Using a parting tool and outside caliper to check diameters. The lathe must be stopped when checking the diameter.

Fig. 13-6 illustrates using the caliper and the parting tool while the stock is rotating. This is a common procedure used by many *experienced* turners. This procedure should not be attempted by beginning students. The lathe should be turned off to make measurements when learning to turn wood.

When the desired shape has been completed, certain finishing operations should be completed prior to removing the stock from the lathe. The first of these operations is sanding. Two cautions must be considered at this time. First, your hand will be contacting the turning material. Make certain not to allow any clothing or rags to pull your fingers into the stock. Also, sanding and polishing generates some frictional heat that can burn your fingers if you apply too much pressure. Secondly, as with any sanding operation, care should be taken not to inhale the dust or to allow excessive dust to build up on the surface of your skin. Use a NIOSH-approved breathing mask and position a fan to blow the dust away from you.

Many lathes are equipped with reversing switches. This capability allows for faster sanding. Do not reverse the direction of rotation while the lathe is turning. This could cause damage to the lathe or cause personal injury.

The grit size used for sanding depends on two factors—the type of wood and the quality of the finish achieved using the lathe tools. Generally, start with 80 to 100 grit paper and end using 180 to 220 grit paper. Do not use steel wool as it can easily wrap around the stock. Old sanding belts can be cut into strips and used for sanding. Sanding belts have a cloth backing and, when cut into strips, allow you to hold the ends while sanding. This can reduce or eliminate friction burns.

When the spindle has been carefully sanded, some finishes can be applied while the stock is still mounted between the centers. French polishing, explained in the headstock turning section of this unit, is an excellent finish. Many turners use a wax finish. The wax finish is simple, fast, and very effective for many turnings. While the spindle is rotating, apply the wax directly to the turning. Allow a slight build-up of wax. Press a clean cloth on the wax while the spindle is turning. The friction melts the wax, pushing it into the pores of the wood surface. Applying more or less pressure with the rag can vary the shade of the finish. Be careful not to allow the cloth to pull your hand into the stock.

HEADSTOCK TURNING

Headstock turning is used to make products such as bowls. When making a small bowl, select a piece of turning stock that measures about 1-inch thick by 5-inches square. In addition, select a smaller piece of scrap stock to use as a separation piece. The scrap stock is used to provide a waste area for screwing the stock to the faceplate. Cut both pieces to a circular shape. Then, attach the scrap to the stock with a piece of

Fig. 13-7. Attaching stock to a faceplate with wood screws.

paper between the two pieces. Glue and clamp the pieces of stock and paper securely, allowing them to dry overnight. The two pieces can later be easily separated using a chisel. Attach the faceplate to the scrap stock using No. 12 wood screws as shown in Fig. 13-7.

Remove the spur center from the headstock and screw the faceplate on the headstock spindle. Set the lathe to its slowest speed. Some lathes must be rotating in order to change the speed. If this is the case with your lathe, adjust the speed before mounting the stock to the spindle. Adjust the tool rest so that it is parallel to the center of your stock and about 1/8 inch away from it. Turn the stock by hand to make sure that it clears the tool rest. Rough turn the outside of the bowl with a gouge, and then smooth it with a round nose tool. See Fig. 13-8A.

Reset the tool rest so it is parallel to the face of the bowl. Position a round nose tool on the tool rest and begin cutting at the outside edge of the bowl. Move the tool carefully along the tool rest toward the center. See Fig. 13-8B. Remember to scrape from the larger diameter to the smaller diameter when making internal cuts, and from the smaller diameter to the larger diameter when making external cuts. Continue with additional cuts using the same method to obtain a wall thickness of about 1/4 inch and a bottom thickness of about 3/8 inch.

Remove the tool rest. Fold a piece of medium or fine abrasive paper (sandpaper) into a small pad. Use the pad to smooth the bowl using a lathe speed of 1500-1800 RPM.

Apply a French polish finish to the bowl using a combination of linseed oil and shellac. Place a piece of paper under the bowl to protect the lathe from the finishing materials. Set the lathe to a speed of 600 RPM and turn on the motor. Fold a clean cloth into a small pad, apply a small amount of linseed oil to the pad, and rub the oil into the surfaces and edges of the bowl as shown in Fig. 13-8C. Apply shellac to the bowl with the pad held lightly against the surfaces. When the bowl is coated, increase the speed of the lathe to about 1200 RPM while increasing the pressure on the pad. Use a few drops of linseed oil on the pad as a lubricant. When the finish becomes shiny, turn off the lathe and remove the bowl.

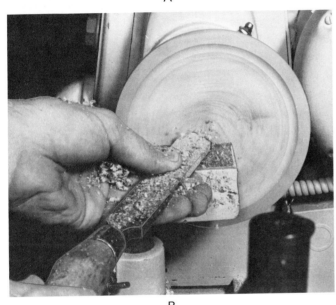

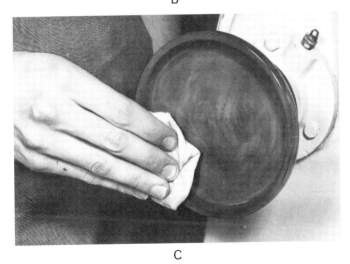

Fig. 13-8. Headstock turning. A–Shaping the outside of a bowl with a round nose tool. B–Shaping the inside of a bowl with a round nose tool. C–Applying a French polish to a bowl.

Allow the finish to harden overnight. It will probably be necessary to apply a second coat of French polish after the first coat has thoroughly dried. Apply a coat of wax after both coats of finish have dried.

Chuck for Turning Small Pieces

An improvised chuck can be used to turn small pieces of stock. The chuck is made by cutting a piece of scrap stock so that it is 1-inch thick by 6 inches in diameter and drilling a 3/4- to 1-inch hole in the center of the flat surface. The chuck is then fastened to a faceplate with wood screws.

Select a piece of turning stock that has slightly larger diameter than the hole in the chuck. Drive the piece into the hole with a mallet. Mount the faceplate to the headstock, and then turn it to the desired shape. See Fig. 13-9.

Fig. 13-9. Turning a small piece of wood held in a chuck.

LATHE DUPLICATOR ATTACHMENT

When several parts with the same design are needed, a LATHE DUPLICATOR ATTACHMENT can be used. This device can be attached to most lathes. Most lathe duplicators have a guide that follows either the original part or a template that is a silhouette (outline) of the original part. See Fig. 13-10. The template is usually

Fig. 13-10. Duplicate parts can be easily made using the lathe duplicator attachment.
(Delta International Machinery Corp.)

made from plastic or hardboard. The rough stock is simply placed between the centers, the lathe is turned on, and the guide is moved along the template. An exact copy is then turned between the centers.

TEST YOUR KNOWLEDGE, Unit 13

Please do not write in this text. Place your answers on a separate sheet of paper.

1. Cylinders, spindles, bowls, and other cylindrical items are shaped using a process called _____ _____.
2. The size of a wood lathe is determined by the _____ , which is the largest diameter piece that can be turned, and by the _____ _____, which is the longest length of stock that can be turned.
3. List three woods commonly used for turning.
4. All work turned in the lathe should be started with a _____ speed.
5. The gouge cuts rapidly and does not produce a smooth cut or surface. True or False?
6. The skew is used to make _____ cuts.
7. A parting tool is used primarily to cut _____ into the stock.

8. Turning tools cut best when the bevels are _____ and _____.
9. Always turn the stock by hand to see that it clears the _____ _____ before turning on the lathe.
10. When turning a product such as a bowl, the stock and separation piece are attached to a _____.

ACTIVITIES

1. Select three different lathe cutting tools. Make a sketch of each. Briefly describe how and why each is used.
2. Select a piece of stock approximately 2 inches square and 12 inches long. Prepare the ends for spindle turning. After your instructor has approved your end preparation, place the stock between the spindles and turn the stock to a cylindrical shape. What tools did you use? What was the appearance of the stock that was removed? Was it shavings or dust? Did using a different tool cause a different surface appearance?
3. Use the cylindrical stock turned in the previous activity. Lay out several spaces approximately 1 1/2 inches apart. Use the parting tool to make a 1/2-inch deep cut at each of these marks. Use a gouge to carefully form a bead from one cut to the next. Repeat the procedure using a skew. Examine the finish. Which has the smoothest appearance? Which was easier to make? Continue making beads between each of the marks.
4. Use the cylinder with the beads from Activity 3. Cut coves to the same depth as was used for the beads. The outside diameters of the coves should be the same as the beads. Practice using different tools. Observe the stock that is removed.
5. Continue making beads and coves of different diameters and lengths until you are proficient in cutting both coves and beads using different tools. You may want to start with a new cylinder when the diameter becomes less than 3/4 inch.

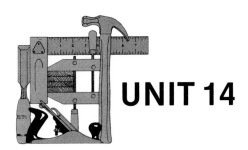

UNIT 14

FASTENERS, ADHESIVES, AND CLAMPING

Pieces of stock must be fastened together for most products. This is done using fasteners and adhesives. Clamps must also be used to hold the stock in position while the adhesive sets. After reviewing this unit, you will be able to identify nails and screws commonly used in woodworking. In addition, you will be able to select the proper fastener for a particular product and identify its size and length. You will also be able to describe the different types of adhesives used in woodworking, and be able to select and use the appropriate adhesive for your application.

NAILS

Most of the nails we use today are made from mild steel using automatic machines. Other nails can be made from copper, brass, and aluminum. Some types of nails have a coating, giving them better weather resistance and holding power.

Nail size is indicated by the letter "d" which is the English symbol for penny. Nails sizes range from 2d, which are 1-inch long, to 60d, which are 6-inches long. Lengths of smaller nails increase 1/4 inch for each additional d. A 4d nail, for example, is 1 1/2-inches long, a 6d nail is 2-inches long, and an 8d nail is 2 1/2-inches long. A wire gauge system is used to determine the diameter of the nails.

Nails are generally sold by the pound. The COMMON nail, which has a flat head, is used in framing and rough construction. The BOX nail also has a flat head, but its shank is smaller in diameter. It is less likely to split the wood when driving it. FINISH nails have small round heads that are usually set below the surface of the stock. The CASING nail, which is heavier than

the finish nail, has a small, tapered head that is also set below the surface of the stock. Fig. 14-1 shows a variety of nails commonly used in woodworking.

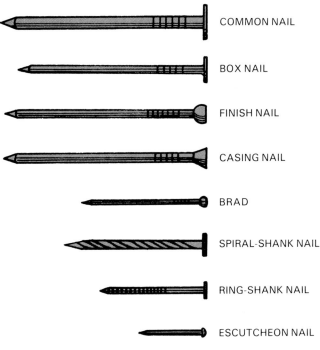

Fig. 14-1. Kinds of nails.

Finish nails that are smaller than 2d are called BRADS. Common or box nails that are smaller than 2d are commonly referred to as WIRE NAILS. Brads and wire nails are available in many gauge sizes. A No. 16 brad is about 1/16 inch in diameter and is almost twice the weight of a No. 20 brad. The ESCUTCHEON nail is used for purposes such as fastening decorative plates around hinges and locks. It has a half-round head that is left exposed when driven into the stock. Escutcheon nails are usually made from copper or brass. SPIRAL-SHANK or

RING-SHANK nails have spiral or straight "threads." These types of nails provide very good holding power.

NAIL HAMMERS

The CLAW HAMMER is used to drive nails in cabinetmaking and carpentry. Its size is indicated by the weight of the head. Sizes of hammer range from 5 to 20 ounces. A 10-ounce hammer works well for driving small nails. However, a 13- to 16-ounce hammer is needed when driving larger nails.

Nail Sets

Nails sets are used to set the heads of finish and casing nails below the surface of the stock. Nails sets are available in tip sizes ranging from 1/32- to 1/8-inch diameter.

Hammer – Safety and Care

1. Always wear approved safety glasses or goggles when you are driving nails.
2. Use a claw hammer for driving or removing nails. Do not use it for breaking concrete or similar activities.

Driving Nails

Nails used for cabinet construction are usually driven straight into the stock. Nails used in rough framing are often driven at an angle to increase the strength of the joint. Driving nails at an angle is generally referred to as TOENAILING. Toenailing is usually practiced when fastening the end of one piece of stock to the surface of a second piece.

Nails should be offset (staggered) to help prevent splitting the stock. Clinching (bending over) nails can be done to increase the strength of the joint. When driving nails into hardwood, drill a small hole into the stock before driving the nail. If the correct size drill bit is not available, cut off the head of a nail and use the nail as a drill bit.

Use a 10- to 13-ounce hammer when driving finish nails. Select two pieces of stock and clamp one of the pieces in the vise. Use light taps of the hammer to start driving two nails into the surface at one end of the second piece. Place the piece with the nails over the piece in the vise, holding the ends flush with each other. Drive each nail, keeping your eyes on the nail, not the

hammer head. Strike the nail squarely with the face of the hammer to avoid bending the nail. Drive each nail until the head is slightly exposed. Then, use the nail set to drive the head below the surface of the stock. Fig. 14-2 shows the procedure used to drive finish nails.

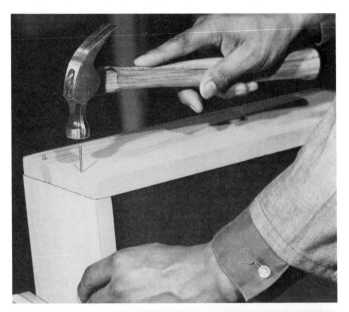

Fig. 14-2. Above. Driving a finish nail with a claw hammer. Below. Driving a finish nail head below the wood surface with a nail set and claw hammer.

Pulling Nails

Small nails, 8d or less, can be removed with a claw hammer. Place a piece of scrap stock next to the nail and hook the nail with the claw of the hammer head. The scrap stock is used to protect

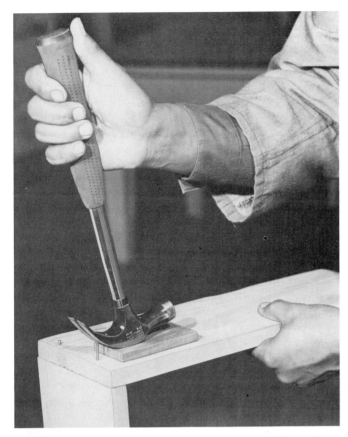

Fig. 14-3. Pulling a nail with a claw hammer. Note the piece of scrap stock between the stock and the hammer.

the surface of your product, Fig. 14-3. Large nails, often called SPIKES, can be removed using a special steel bar, called a WRECKING BAR.

SCREWS

Screws are used to fasten hardware to pieces of stock when the product needs to be disassembled or when extra holding power is required. As screws are turned (driven) with a screwdriver into holes drilled in the stock, they make a threaded recess in the wood. This gives the screws a great deal more holding power than nails.

Many kinds of screws are made from wire in automatic screw machines. The screws are made from a variety of materials, including steel, brass, and aluminum. They can be finished with zinc chromate, copper, nickel, or chromium to give them better weather resistance capabilities and holding power or decorative appearance. Sizes of screws are indicated by wire gauge and length. Screws range in length from 1/4 to 6 inches, and in gauge size from 0 (smallest) to 24.

FLAT HEAD screws are designed so the heads fit flush with the surface of the stock or slightly below it. The entire screw is measured to determine its length. Heads of ROUND HEAD screws fit on top of the stock. The length is determined by measuring from the bottom of the head to the tip of the screw point. Heads of OVAL HEAD screws are partially recessed into the surface of the stock. The length of oval head screws is determined by measuring from the point of the recess to the tip of the screw point. Fig. 14-4 shows how to determine the length of flat head, round head, and oval head screws.

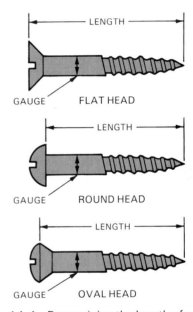

Fig. 14-4. Determining the length of screws.

A variety of screw head recesses are available. The most common types of recesses are slotted, Phillips, or square (Robertson). Other types of screw head recesses include Torx, hex socket, security, and a combination.

Screwdrivers

Screws with slotted heads are driven with a standard screwdriver. A variety of sizes should be available to fit different sizes of screws. The tip of the screwdriver should fit the width and length of the screw slot. A screwdriver that is too large can damage the screw slot and tear the wood. A screwdriver that is too small does not give you enough leverage and can break. Screwdriver tips are available for use in the brace, electric, pneumatic, or rechargeable drills. Phillips head or square head screws work the best when using these types of drills, since they are less likely to slip when being driven.

Installing Screws

Holes should be drilled in the stock prior to driving screws. This is especially true when using hardwoods. Two different size holes must be drilled. The CLEARANCE HOLE should be the same size as the shank of the screw. The PILOT HOLE should be a bit smaller than the root diameter (smallest diameter) of the screw threads. The pilot hole should be drilled first, followed by the clearance hole. This procedure locates the center of the second hole better. Fig. 14-5 provides a chart that can be used to determine the correct hole sizes for screws. When using flat head screws, the upper edge of the clearance hole should be countersunk so that the screw head fits flush with the surface of the stock.

Some drill bits are available that drill both holes and the countersink at one time. The size of these types of bits correspond to the size of screw being used, Fig. 14-6.

Many times you may want the head of the screw below the surface of the stock. A plug is then placed over the screw head to conceal it. This is called COUNTERBORING. Special bits can be used to drill just the counterbore, or you can use a bit that drills the clearance hole, pilot hole, and counterbore hole. After the screw has been driven into the stock, a plug is glued in place over the screw, and sanded smooth with the surface. Plugs can be made

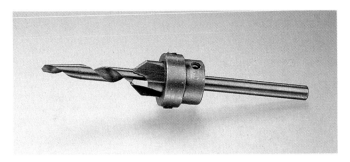

Fig. 14-6. This special drill bit drills a pilot hole, clearance hole, countersink, and counterbore in one operation.

using a plug cutter. Use the same type of stock for the plug as you are using for the product. Be sure to position the plug so that the grain is running the same direction as the stock.

OTHER TYPES OF FASTENERS

A variety of fasteners can be used for joining pieces of stock. Some types, such as the swivel (lazy susan bearing), allow pieces of stock to rotate while being attached. Other types are stationary fasteners, not allowing the pieces of stock to move. Fig. 14-7 shows an assortment of fasteners. A description of some of them follows.

A. **Hanger bolt**–Used to fasten legs to a table with an attachment plate.
B. **Lag screw**–Used to hold braces and other supports.
C. **Stove bolt**–Used to fasten parts that may need to be disassembled.
D. **Corrugated fasteners**–Used to reinforce miter and end butt joints of softwood.
E. **Upholstery tacks**–Used in unexposed areas to hold webbing and fabrics in place.

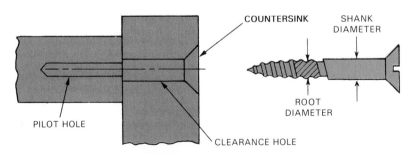

NO. OF SCREW	1	2	3	4	5	6	7	8	9	10	12	14	16	18
CLEARANCE	5/64	3/32	3/32	7/64	1/8	9/64	5/32	11/64	11/64	3/16	7/32	15/64	17/64	19/64
PILOT	–	1/16	1/16	5/64	5/64	3/32	7/64	7/64	1/8	9/64	5/32	5/32	3/16	13/64

Fig. 14-5. Drill sizes for common screws.

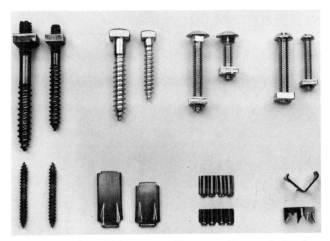

Fig. 14-7. Special fasteners. Top row. Hanger bolts, lag screws, carriage bolts, and stove bolts. Bottom row. Dowel screws, splines, corrugated fasteners, and chevrons.

F. **Cup hooks**–Used for hanging items, such as cups or keys. They are screwed into the stock.
G. **Screw eyes**–Used when the product is to be hung on a wall.
H. **Rubber headed nails**–Used to cushion a lid, or as the feet for a small product.
I. **Upholstery nails**–Used in exposed areas to hold upholstery covering in place.
J. **Swivel (lazy susan bearing)**–Allows two pieces to rotate, yet be fastened together.
K. **Staples**–Used as a permanent means of fastening thin items to stock.
L. **Chair brace**–Used to strengthen chair joints.
M. **Tilt-base leg glide**–Used at the base of a chair leg.
N. **Carriage bolt**–Used to hold heavy pieces of stock together. A nut is used to hold the bolt in place.
O. **Attachment plate**–Used to fasten a leg to a table with a hanger bolt.

STAPLES

A staple is made by bending wire into a "U" shape or modified "U" shape. A variety of types, sizes, and finishes of staples are available. Most types of staples can be bought in strips for easy loading into the stapler.

Staples generally provide more holding power than tacks or small nails because they have two legs that "bite" into the stock. The staple legs follow the cut of the point on each leg. Different types of points are used so that the staple legs

will flare in or out. This flaring action gives them better holding power. Fig. 14-8 shows how a special type of long staple with flaring legs clings to the stock. Some staples are clinched on the back of the stock.

Staples are used for many purposes including fastening roofing, insulation, ceiling tile, and upholstery materials. Staples are commonly used in industry since they are an economical and efficient means of fastening materials to one another.

STAPLE CROWN (SIDE VIEW)

Fig. 14-8. Cutaway of a driven staple with points flaring out.

Staplers

Staplers have been developed for many different uses. Some staplers are spring driven, and work well for light to medium applications. Other staplers are air driven, and work better for heavy applications.

Stapling

A strip of staples is loaded in a stapling gun or stapling hammer with the points facing downward. The stapler should be held firmly against the stock to resist the kickback action of the stapler. A trigger mechanism generally activates the stapler, driving the staple into the stock. Fig. 14-9 shows two examples of when staples can be utilized.

Fig. 14-9. Stapling with a pneumatic stapler. Left. Light wood assembly. Right. Attaching a trim strip. (Porter-Cable)

NAILERS AND NAILING

Nailers are similar to staplers. They are used to drive a variety of nails quickly and efficiently. Nailers are most commonly used for heavy construction work. The nails are fastened together in strips. The strip is then loaded into the nailer with the points facing downward. The nailer is held firmly against the stock and activated with a trigger. Fig. 14-10 shows a pneumatic nailer being used for heavy construction.

Fig. 14-10. Using a pneumatic nailer. (Porter-Cable)

GLUE BLOCKS

Glue blocks are small pieces of stock that are used to strengthen wood joints. They are generally attached with an adhesive or metal fasteners. Glue blocks help to square a product, and add a great deal to its strength. Glue blocks are often used to attach the top of a dresser or cabinet to the base. This method allows for the different expansion and contraction that occurs in wood since the grain is usually running in different directions.

WOOD DOWELS

Dowels are cylindrical pieces of stock, usually made of birch. They are available in diameters ranging from 1/8 inch to 1 inch, and in 3- or 4-foot lengths. Dowels are commonly used to reinforce stock that would otherwise be fastened together with just adhesive. Short dowels specifically made for joinery have spiral grooves along their length. The grooves allow air to escape and forces adhesive to the bottom of the holes during the clamping process.

If short dowels are not available, and you plan to cut your gluing dowels from a standard piece of stock, you must allow for the air to escape from the joint when gluing up. Cut a saw kerf in the side of each gluing dowel using a back saw before inserting it into the stock. This allows the air to escape. If this is not done, the air will force glue out of the joint, or may even separate the pieces being joined.

FEATHERS

A FEATHER is a thin strip of wood used to reinforce and aid in the assembly of a corner joint. A saw kerf must first be cut across a corner joint. The feather is then fastened into the groove with adhesive, locking the two pieces together.

SPLINES

A SPLINE is a thin, rectangular strip of stock that is inserted into grooves or saw kerfs made in the adjacent parts of a joint. Splines strengthen and aid in the assembly of the joint. Splines are similar to a feather, except that a spline can be used to reinforce any type of joint, not just corner joints. Fig. 14-11 shows examples of feathers and splines.

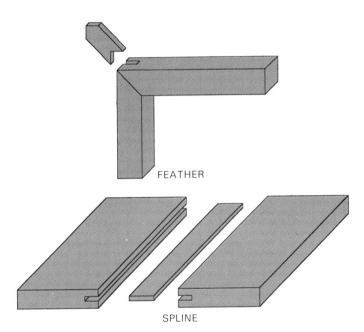

FEATHER

SPLINE

Fig. 14-11. Comparison of a feather and a spline.

BISCUITS

BISCUITS, or PLATES, are used in plate joinery. Chapter 11 provides additional information about plate joinery. A biscuit is a product made of compressed beech wood, and looks like a small, flat football. When inserted into a specially cut slot that is filled with a water-based adhesive, the plate expands making a very strong joint. A joint that is joined using this process is affected very little by the natural expansion and contraction of the stock.

ADHESIVES

Adhesives, or glues as they are commonly referred to, are used to bond materials together. A variety of adhesives are available. Some adhesives are actually stronger than the stock itself. Always read the manufacturer's directions before using any glues, cements, or adhesives.

Adhesive Safety
Adequate ventilation is recommended when applying most types of adhesives. Never directly breath the fumes from any adhesive. In addition, some adhesives, such as contact cements, are extremely flammable. Do not use them near an open flame. Have a properly rated fire extinguisher readily available. Carefully read the manufacturer's precautions on the label.

Rubber Cement
Rubber cement is used to bond paper, cardboard, felt, and other light, porous materials. It is especially useful in woodworking for bonding patterns to stock. Rubber cement is available in liquid form.

When using rubber cement, you have two options for application. If you want a temporary bond, apply the rubber cement to just one surface, and immediately bond it to the other part. The parts may be separated easily later. If you want a permanent bond, apply the rubber cement to both pieces and allow them to dry. When the pieces are no longer tacky, bond the two pieces together.

Contact Cement
Contact cement is commonly used to fasten plastic laminate or veneer to solid stock or plywood surfaces. It is available in liquid form that can be applied with brush, roller, or spray gun. It is also available in an aerosol spray can. One or more thin coats should be applied to the surfaces of both pieces. Two coats are usually needed for dry or porous surfaces. The contact cement should be allowed to dry until it has a dull appearance. The cement bonds as the two pieces come into contact with each other. For this reason, you must make sure that your pieces of

stock are in the proper position while placing them in contact with each other.

You can keep the pieces of stock separated by placing dowel rods or kraft paper between them. When the cement has dried to a dull appearance, carefully position the two pieces. Begin at one end and press the two pieces together. Move toward the other end, pressing from the center outward. Slowly remove the dowels or kraft paper as you progress. Roll the surface with a large dowel or rubber roller to remove any air pockets.

Plastics Cement

Plastics cement can be used for a variety of repair jobs. These types of cements are usually available in tubes. AIRPLANE CEMENT is a common type of plastics cement. It sets quickly and hardens overnight to form a waterproof material. It can be used to bond porous or impervious materials.

White Liquid Resin Glue

White liquid resin glue (polyvinyl acetate), or white glue as it is commonly called, is available in convenient squeeze bottles and large containers. This type of glue is the most common type of glue used for furniture and cabinet construction. It can be applied easily at temperatures above 60 degrees Fahrenheit. White glue is strong and has good gap-filling qualities. It sets and dries in about 30 minutes. When clamping the pieces to be joined, apply only enough pressure to bring the joint together. Excess pressure will force the glue from the joint, leaving you with a weak joint.

White glue dries by moisture absorption and evaporation. It dries to a flexible, colorless material. The biggest disadvantage of white glue is its lack of moisture and heat resistance. All excess glue should be removed with a wet cloth before it has dried. If excess glue still remains after it has dried, remove it before sanding to prevent clogging the abrasive paper.

Animal Glue

Animal glue, or hide glue, is made from animal hooves and hides. It is one of the oldest types of glues. Animal glues are available in liquid and dry forms. The liquid form is usually packaged in plastic squeeze bottles for easy ap-

plication and storage. The dry form is seldom used because it is difficult to prepare. It must be dissolved in water, heated to about 140 degrees Fahrenheit, and applied hot.

Hide glue is excellent for furniture and cabinet construction. It is not waterproof, and therefore, should only be used for interior work. Liquid hide glue requires approximately 3 to 4 hours of clamping time at temperatures above 70 degrees Fahrenheit.

Plastic Resin Glue

Plastic resin glue (urea-formaldehyde) has a great deal of moisture resistance and is very strong if correctly used. It is a good glue to use for products that are exposed to a considerable amount of moisture for a short period of time.

This type of glue is available in powder form. It is mixed with water to a creamy consistency. Plastic resin glue is easy to use and dries to a hard, brittle substance with a light brown color. It dries slowly, by chemical change, which allows plenty of time to clamp the pieces of stock together. Use only stock with well-fitted joints since this type of glue does not fill gaps very well. Use this type of glue only on non-oily woods. Work should be clamped for at least 6 hours at a minimum temperature of 70 degrees Fahrenheit. Additional heat can be used to shorten the amount of time required for setting. Certain compounds of plastic resin glue are used with electronic gluing equipment.

Aliphatic Resin Glue

Aliphatic resin glue (yellow glue) is a cream-colored, nonstaining liquid resin glue. It is very popular with cabinet shops and furniture makers for applying veneers. See Fig. 14-12. This type of glue is available in ready-to-use form. It can be purchased with a brown color added if desired. It is a very strong glue that resists heat and chemicals and sands easily. Aliphatic resin glue does not immediately bond, making adjustment of veneer possible. This glue sets in about 45 minutes at temperatures above 70 degrees Fahrenheit, but can also be used at temperatures as low as 40 degrees Fahrenheit. One of the biggest disadvantages of aliphatic resin glue is its inability to

132

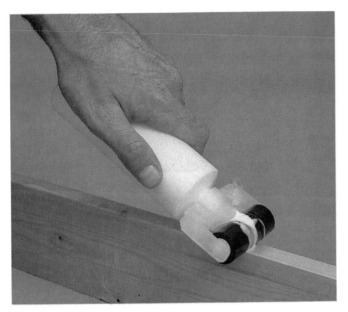

Fig. 14-12. A convenient method of applying adhesive to the edge of stock.

resist moisture. However, it is a good glue for interior work.

Resorcinal Resin Glue

This is powdered glue that is mixed to a creamy consistency with a liquid catalyst and water immediately before use. It is a very strong, waterproof glue. Therefore, it is commonly used with materials that are subjected to large amounts of moisture. Resorcinal resin glue creates an unwanted dark glue line. It requires 12 to 16 hours of clamping time at a minimum temperature of 70 degree Fahrenheit.

Casein Glue

Casein glue is made from milk curd. It is available in powder form, cold water is added, allowed to stand a few minutes, and then mixed to creamy consistency for use. It is a strong glue, requiring moderate clamping time. Casein glue can be used at low temperatures, but it works better at warmer temperatures. It is water resistant and especially useful with oily wood, such as cypress. Casein glue has a tendency to stain woods like maple and oak.

Epoxy Cement

Epoxy cement is a two-part adhesive–a resin and a hardener–that can include a filler. This adhesive is extremely strong, waterproof, and can be sanded. Epoxy cement has several advantages over other types of adhesives. First, it is very strong. Epoxy cement is commonly used where joints work against one another or where joints are expected to carry large amounts of weight, such as chair legs. Secondly, it can be sanded, especially if a filler has been added. The filler can be tinted to match the wood's color if desired. A third advantage is that the setting speed of an epoxy cement can be controlled. Various hardeners can be added to the resin to increase or decrease the setting speed.

Epoxy cements cure as a result of a chemical reaction. Some epoxy cements set almost immediately, other may require hours to set. Carefully read the manufacturer's instructions before using epoxy cement. Heat is produced during the curing process. This heat can warp certain materials, and can also cause burns to your skin. Use epoxy cements in a well-ventilated area. Goggles should be worn to protect your eyes, and rubber gloves should be worn to protect your skin.

Hot Glue

A hot glue is excellent for temporarily holding parts or gluing pieces together that do not require a strong bond. This type of adhesive is heated in a special glue gun. When it has reached melting temperature it is forced out of the gun by pushing an unmelted cylinder of glue into the gun. As it cools, it forms the bond.

ADHESIVE APPLICATION

Many types of adhesives set very quickly. In addition, some adhesives are very messy to clean up once they are applied. Therefore, you should carefully check the fit of all parts with the necessary clamping devices without using any adhesive during a TRIAL ASSEMBLY or DRY ASSEMBLY.

If dry glue is being used, mix only the amount of glue that you need at the time. Use the correct amount of glue when gluing products. Too much glue will result in excess squeeze out that is messy and wasteful. Not enough glue will result in a "starved" joint, resulting in a weak bond.

Consider the setting time of the adhesive before deciding which type to use. Some adhesives should be closed with clamps 2 to 5 minutes after application. Complicated assemblies should be done in several steps with the aid of a helper.

Apply adhesive on each piece to be joined. Apply it evenly, spreading it from the center toward the edges with a brush, flat stick, or roller. End grain should be given an additional coat after about 1 minute. Fig. 14-13 shows the proper procedure for gluing and clamping pieces of stock.

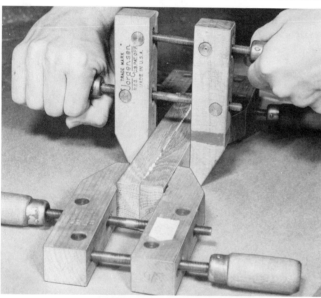

Fig. 14-13. Top. Applying white liquid resin glue on a wood surface with a plastic squeeze bottle. Center. Using hand screws to clamp stock. Note the position of the jaws. Bottom. Using a C-clamp to glue stock.

CLAMPING DEVICES

Clamping devices are available in many different types and sizes. Whatever type of clamp is being used, you should always remove any excess glue squeeze out. Clean off the squeeze out with a damp cloth or sponge immediately after the clamping process. Stain or other finish will generally not soak into the pores of the stock if the glue has not been removed. This leaves an unsightly white area on the stock.

Hand Screws

Hand screws, or parallel jaw clamps, have two adjustable wood jaws that should be carefully set before use. Hand screws are used to hold fixtures and to clamp small pieces of wood. The jaws should be adjusted so that the jaws are parallel with the stock being joined. This distributes the pressure of the clamp evenly.

Spring Clamps

The spring clamp presses against the stock with its fingers that are activated by a strong spring. Some spring clamps are equipped with adjustable fingers for holding irregular shaped work. These clamps are especially helpful for holding small pieces of stock in place. See Fig. 14-14A.

Miter Clamps

Miter clamps are useful for assembling corner joints. Different types of miter clamps are available. Some are used for single corners, while others are used for joining entire frames at once. See Figs. 14-14B and C.

Steel Bar Clamps

Steel bar clamps (cabinet clamps) are used to join several narrow pieces of stock edge-to-edge to form a wider board or panel. They are also used for complete assemblies of cabinets and furniture. Bar clamps can apply a great deal of pressure. You can easily apply 500 to 600 pounds of pressure using a bar clamp. Pieces of scrap stock should be used between the clamp jaws and the stock, or a jaw pad should be used, to avoid damage to the stock.

Space bar clamps 12 to 15 inches apart. When more than two clamps are used, alternate the direction of the clamps to prevent twisting of the panel. Small clamps with scrap stock should be

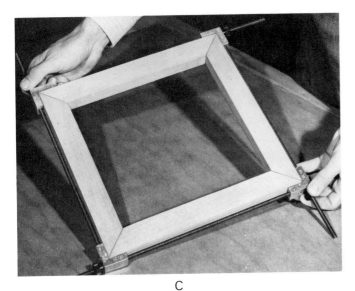

Fig. 14-14. Clamping devices. A–Holding small pieces with spring clamps. B–Forming a corner joint with a miter clamp. C–Gluing an entire frame with a miter clamp fixture.

Fig. 14-15. Gluing narrow stock edge-to-edge to make a wide panel. Note the position of the bar clamps.

Fig. 14-16. Using band clamps to assemble a chair.

placed across the grain to hold the panels straight. See Fig. 14-15.

Band Clamps

Band clamps are used to hold round or irregular-shaped pieces in place. See Fig. 14-16. Any time that you are clamping a product that does not have parallel sides, or the sides are irregular, the band clamp will exert uniform clamping pressure. Chair legs are a good example of an application where band clamps might be preferred.

C-Clamps

The C-clamp has an adjustable screw that holds the stock firmly against the anvil. This is especially useful when holding fixtures and small pieces of stock. Make sure that you place a piece of scrap stock between the adjustable screw and the stock, and the anvil and the stock when using a C-clamp. The stock may be damaged if you apply pressure directly with the C-clamp.

TEST YOUR KNOWLEDGE, Unit 14

Please do not write in this text. Place your answers on a separate sheet of paper.

1. Most of the nails are made from _____.

2. When indicating nail size, the term "penny" is abbreviated with the letter _____.

3. Common nails have _____ heads.

4. Finish nails have small round heads that are usually set below the surface of the wood. True or False?

5. The size of a claw hammer is indicated by the weight of the hammer _____.

6. Nails that are 8d or less can be removed using a _____ _____.

7. _____ are often used on products that need to be disassembled.

8. Screws have better holding power than nails. True or False?

9. The tops of the heads of round head screws should fit flush with the surface of stock. True or False?

10. The pilot hole for a wood screw should be a little _____ than the root diameter of the screw thread.

11. A _____ is made by bending wire to a "U" or modified "U" shape.

12. Dowels are commonly made of _____.

13. A flat, football-shaped piece of beech wood is used in _____ joinery.

14. Epoxy cement usually comes in two parts, a _____ and a _____.

15. Casein glue comes in _____ form and is mixed with _____.

16. Miter clamps are useful in assembling _____ joints.

ACTIVITIES

1. Select a number of different types of nails, including different lengths. Separate them into groups according to type and size. Measure the length and compare with a size chart. Note the difference in the diameters of the shank between common and box nails. Can you tell the difference between the heads of a finish nail and a casing nail?

2. Use two pieces of softwood about 3/4-inch thick and three 6d box nails. Nail the two pieces together at the ends forming an end butt joint. Did you bend a nail? Did either of the two boards split? Did any nail come through the face of the bottom board?

3. Separate the pieces in previous activity and remove the nails. Now, use 4d finish nails, nailing the boards together face to face. Did the nail penetrate the back of the bottom board? Separate and remove the nails.

4. Select several different screws according to length, size, and head style. Do you clearly understand how the length of a screw is determined? Can you tell the difference between a No. 6 and a No. 10 screw?

5. Use a piece of 3/4-inch softwood and drill a series of pilot holes for a No. 8 screw that is 1 inch long. Select a 1-inch oval, flat, and round head No. 8 screw. What happened to the back of the board as the screw penetrated? Did you properly set each screw head?

6. Select several screws, each having different recesses including flat, Phillips, square, etc. Try driving each different type using the proper screwdriver. Which type drives the easiest without slipping out of the recess?

7. Use rubber cement and several small pieces of paper to make a permanent bond and a temporary bond. Try to separate each. Describe what happened when you tried to separate each.

8. Make a list of each of the different type of clamping devices found in your woods laboratory. Briefly describe a use for each.

9. Make a list of the different kinds of glues and adhesives typically found in a woods laboratory. Describe the application for each. What is the set-up time? What are the clamping requirements? Does temperature affect set-up time? What is the moisture resistance of each type of adhesive? Are the fumes or skin contact a problem?

10. Cut several small pieces of 1 x 2 about 10 inches long. Using either white or yellow glue, glue two pieces together with moderate clamping pressure, two with light pressure and two with moderate clamping pressure, two with light pressure and two with the maximum pressure you can achieve using a bar clamp. Allow the glue to set over night and try to break each joint. Describe what happened to each joint. Did the wood tear? Which was the easiest to break?

UNIT 15

SANDING

Wood is sanded to remove tool marks, or MILL MARKS, smooth and shape the edges and surfaces, prepare for the application of finishing materials, and smooth the finishing materials. After reading this unit, you will be able to identify different kinds and grades of abrasive paper. In addition, you will be able to recognize and describe the most common types of sanding equipment used in the woods laboratory.

COATED ABRASIVES

Coated abrasive sheets, commonly known as "sandpaper", are available in a variety of grit sizes and backing materials. Abrasive materials are sifted through screens to obtain uniform size GRITS (particles). These particles are then cemented to paper, cloth, or combination backing. The backing sheets are made in varying weights and degrees of flexibility. The backing sheet is noted with a letter grade:

A–Thin and flexible–150 to 600 grit
C–Heavier than A–100 to 150 grit
D–Heavy–Usually less than 100 grit
E–Heaviest–Used for sanding disks

The abrasive can cover the entire surface or only a portion of it. CLOSED COAT abrasives are those with a grit covering the entire surface. OPEN COAT abrasives are those with a grit covering 60 to 70 percent of the backing surface. This "openness" clogs less and is more flexible.

Coated abrasives are available in a number of different forms including sheets, belts, disks, and drums. Typical sheet size is 9 x 11 inches.

ABRASIVE MATERIALS

The abrasive material, or grit, can be either natural or synthetic (manufactured). The most common abrasive materials are flint, aluminum oxide, garnet, silicon carbide, and emery.

FLINT is made from a natural material called quartz. Quartz is usually mined from large deposits in the earth. Flint abrasive is inexpensive, but lacks the toughness and durability of most other abrasive materials. Sheets of flint abrasive material are a light-tan color and paper backed. They are commonly sold in 9 x 10 inch sheets.

ALUMINUM OXIDE is a synthetic material made in an electric furnace from aluminum ore (bauxite). It is hard, tough, durable, and usually brown in color. The cutting edges of the grit are very sharp. Aluminum oxide abrasive products are best for machine sanding.

GARNET is a natural red silicate mineral. Its color is normally bright orange. It is widely used in the woodworking industry, particularly for finish sanding. Garnet sheets are paper backed, and are tough and durable.

SILICON CARBIDE is a synthetic material that is made in an electric furnace from silica, petroleum coke, salt, and wood sawdust. It is sharp, brittle, and hard; in fact, it is almost as hard as a diamond. Silicon carbide is normally backed with waterproof paper. It is used extensively in production work. Silicon carbide is usually a black or white color. A common trade name for silicon carbide is "wet-or-dry," because it can be used either dry or with a lubricant such as water or mineral spirits. Variations of this product with grits of 1200 or higher are available for polishing applications.

EMERY is also a natural material. Emery is usually cloth-backed, and is black in color. Emery is not recommended for woodworking. However, it is excellent for "sanding" metal, such as removing rust from tool surfaces.

Abrasive Grit Sizes

Standard abrasive grit sizes for most materials are indicated by a number, or by a symbol that represents a grit size. Grit that passes through a screen with 80 openings per linear inch, for example, is 80 grit. It is designated 80(0). The "0" is the grit symbol. Some of the standard abrasive mesh grit sizes are shown in Fig. 15-1. Flint grit sizes are indicated as course, medium, fine, and very fine rather than by number.

CLASS	MESH SIZE	SYMBOL
Very Fine	400	10/0
	360	—
	320	9/0
	280	8/0
	240	7/0
	220	6/0
	180	5/0
Fine	150	4/0
	120	3/0
	100	2/0
Medium	80	1/0
	60	1/2
	50	1
Coarse	40	1 1/2
	36	2
Very Coarse	30	2 1/2
	24	3
	20	3 1/2

Fig. 15-1. Abrasive mesh grit sizes.

STEEL WOOL

Steel wool is made of thin shavings of steel. Steel wool is available in pads and rolls. It is used to smooth intricate and curved surfaces, and to smooth finished surfaces. Grades of steel wool vary from very fine (4/0) to coarse (3).

POLISHING COMPOUNDS

Prepared polishing compounds and powdered abrasives are used to polish finishes. Pow-

dered abrasives are applied with a cloth pad and water or mineral oil. PUMICE, a lava derivative, is one type of polishing compound. It is a white color. Grades FF and FFF are commonly used. ROTTENSTONE is an iron oxide produced from shale. It is reddish-brown or grayish brown in color. Rottenstone is finer that pumice and is generally used after polishing a surface with pumice.

HAND SANDING

The proper technique and sequence are very important when sanding stock. If a product is assembled before the sanding is completed, it may not be possible to produce a good-quality finish at a later time. If you are not careful to sand with the grain of the wood, small scratches can appear after the finish has been applied.

Generally, all exposed surfaces of the stock are sanded after they have been milled to size. Care must be taken when sanding not to sand a joint surface prior to assembly. This could cause a loose fitting joint. Any dents or major scratches can more easily be repaired prior to assembly. After the product has been assembled, additional light sanding may be necessary before a finish is applied in order to remove glue residue.

Final sanding is usually done by hand. It follows the use of cutting tools or machine sanders. Hand sanding removes mill marks, smooths the wood, and prepares it for finishing materials.

Grades 60, 100, and 150 abrasive material can be used for most sanding jobs. Always start with the coarsest grade (lower number), following with finer grades. Carefully tear the abrasive sheet into four equal pieces for most hand sanding operations. Many electric finish sanders are designed to use pieces of abrasive material that have been torn into halves, thirds, or quarters. Fig. 15-2 shows a fixture that can be easily made to gauge and tear abrasive sheets.

When smoothing a flat surface, clamp the piece in a vise. Wrap a piece of an abrasive sheet around a block of wood or fasten it in a sanding block. A sanding block helps to keep the surface of the stock flat while sanding. If you try to hand sand without a block, the abrasive material and

Fig. 15-2. Fixture for tearing abrasive sheets. Used hacksaw blade helps to tear the sheet.

your hand will follow any imperfections on the surface, rather than remove them. Always sand with the grain of the stock, not across it. Sanding across the grain usually cuts deep scratches into the wood that are hard to remove. Fig. 15-3 shows the proper techniques used to sand stock by hand.

When sanding around a curved or irregular-shaped edge, fold a piece of abrasive paper into a small pad so that your thumb or index finger fits the edge. Edges with inside curves may be best sanded by wrapping the abrasive material around a dowel.

Small pieces of stock can be sanded by attaching the abrasive sheet to a piece of scrap wood and clamping the wood in a vise. Hold the small piece in your fingers and move it along the surface of the abrasive material.

POWER SANDING EQUIPMENT

A variety of power sanding machines are available. Some of these are hand held, while others are stationary. These machines allow for very rapid removal of scratches and mill marks. However, it is very easy to remove more surface material than is necessary. This could result in an uneven surface or poorly fitting joints.

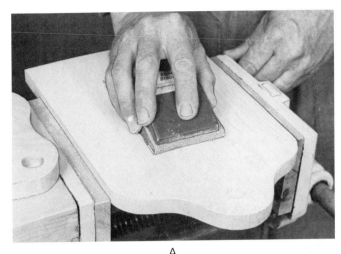

A

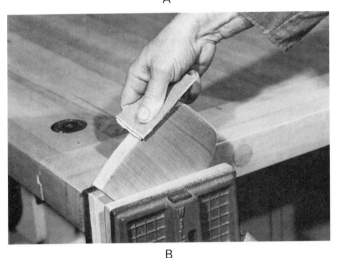

B

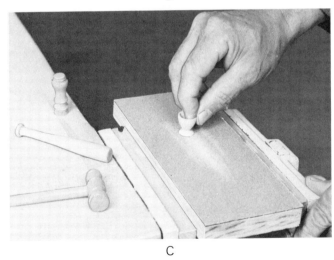

C

Fig. 15-3. Hand sanding. A–Sanding a surface. B–Sanding an edge. C–Sanding small pieces of stock.

Power sanding devices can present the possibility of a health hazard. The dust produced can be extremely hazardous if inhaled. Proper dust collection devices should be in place and operating. Wear a NIOSH-approved respirator when operating a power sander.

Sander—Safety and Care

1. Always check the motor switch to make sure that it is in the OFF position before plugging in the power cord.
2. Unplug the sander when it is not in use. Lay the sander on its side and place it toward the middle of the table top.
3. Use only enough pressure to keep the abrasive material cutting the stock. Excessive pressure can lead to overheating the sander and damaging the motor.
4. When using a belt sander, keep the belt adjusted to the correct alignment and tension.
5. Replace worn sanding sheets, belts, and sleeves when necessary.
6. Keep the sander clean and properly lubricated.

DISK SANDER

The disk sander is useful when shaping edges and ends of the stock. Disk sander size is indicated by the size of the disk. A 12-inch disk sander is a common size. The disk sander is usually equipped with an adjustable table. It can be used with a miter gauge to guide the stock when smoothing bevels and angles.

When using a disk sander to smooth stock, always make sure that the stock comes into contact with the sander while it is moving downward. See Fig. 15-4. If you place the stock along the other side of the disk, the force of the disk may pick up the piece of stock from the table. Allow the table of the sander to support the stock; do not support the stock with your hands. Turn on the motor and move the piece carefully into the disk. Use only enough pressure against the disk to keep it cutting. Move the piece a small amount sideways to reduce the heat caused by friction. When the end of the piece is smooth, remove it from the table and turn off the motor.

BELT SANDERS

Belt sanders utilize a continuous belt covered with abrasive grits to smooth stock. Some belt sanders are stationary, while others are portable. A stationary wide belt sander is generally used in a production setting. The stationary belt sander is commonly used in a cabinetmaking shop. A portable belt sander is usually used at a job site, or where a stationary sander is impractical.

Production Wide Belt Sander

Wide belt sanders are used to smooth mill marks and other imperfections from the faces of planed boards and panels. The size of a wide belt sander is indicated by the width of the abrasive belt. Common widths are 25, 37, and 50 inches.

Fig. 15-5 shows a wide belt sander that is designed to smooth stock efficiently and quickly. This machine is equipped with an adjustable sanding table which moves the stock on a belt under the rotating sanding belt.

Fig. 15-4. Smoothing the end of a piece of stock with a disk sander. Note that the stock is held on the side of the disk that is moving downward.

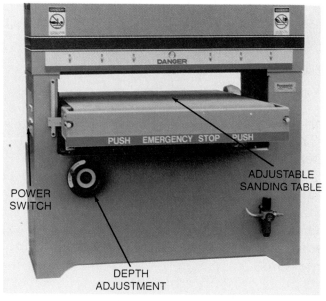

POWER SWITCH

DANGER

PUSH EMERGENCY STOP PUSH

ADJUSTABLE SANDING TABLE

DEPTH ADJUSTMENT

Fig. 15-5. A wide belt sander is used to sand wide pieces of stock efficiently. (Powermatic-Houdaille, Inc.)

Stationary Belt Sander

The belt sander is useful for smoothing the faces and edges of stock. Its size is indicated by the width of the sander belt. A 6-inch belt sander is a common size. The length of the belt varies with the type of sander, so make sure that you purchase a belt that has the correct width and length.

The belt revolves on two cylinders, one adjustable and one stationary. The adjustable cylinder is used to adjust the belt tracking (side-to-side motion) and tension. Belt sanders can be used in both the vertical and horizontal positions. A table is used to hold the stock in the vertical position, and an end stop is used in the horizontal position.

When using the belt sander, carefully lower the piece of stock onto the sanding belt, making sure the end of the piece is held tightly against the stop, Fig. 15-6. Move the stock from side-to-side until it is smooth. Remove the stock from the belt and turn off the motor.

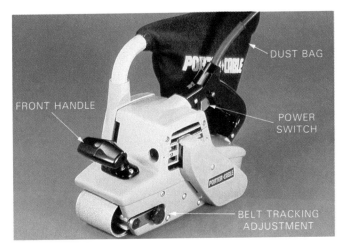

Fig. 15-7. Typical belt sander with parts identified. (Porter-Cable)

over the stock at one side of the stock surface. Turn on the motor and slowly make contact with the surface. Move the sander in the direction of the grain as you sand. Raise the sander at the end of each stroke. Begin the next stroke by lapping halfway across the width of the previous stroke. Continue with successive strokes across the width of the stock.

FINISH SANDERS

Finish sanders are used for one of the last steps in the sanding process. Orbital sanders have an elliptical stroke. Other sanders have straight strokes. Most sanders are designed to use one-quarter, one-third, or one-half sheets of abrasive material. See Fig. 15-8.

Fig. 15-6. Smoothing the surface of a board with a belt sander in its horizontal position.

Portable Belt Sander

The portable belt sander is very useful when smoothing wood faces. The size of a belt sander is indicated by the width and length of its belt. A 3″ x 21″ or a 3″ x 24″ portable belt sander is a common size. The belt rotates on two cylinders. One cylinder is used to adjust the belt tracking and tension. Fig. 15-7 shows a typical portable belt sander.

Make sure that you clamp the stock firmly in a vise when using a belt sander. Hold the sander

Fig. 15-8. Finish sanders. The model on the left uses one-quarter sheets, while the one on the right uses one-half sheets. (Porter-Cable)

Make sure your stock is clamped in a vise before you begin to sand. Begin at one side of the stock surface, moving the sander carefully. Use only enough pressure to keep the sander cutting. Move the sander with the grain of the stock, overlapping each successive stroke. See Fig. 15-9.

A

B

Fig. 15-9. Finish sanders. A—Smoothing the surface of stock with an orbital electric sander. B—Smoothing an irregular surface with a detail sander. (Porter-Cable)

OTHER SANDERS

Drum sanders are special abrasive sleeves that fit onto a rubber cylinder that is attached to a spindle. The spindle is tightened into the chuck of a portable drill, drill press, or a special oscillating sander. Drum sanders are used for sanding the curved edges of stock. See Fig. 15-10.

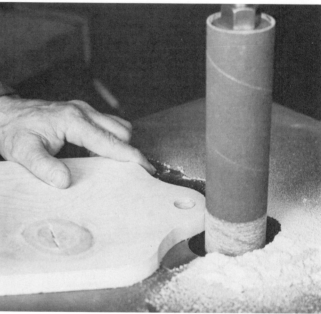

Fig. 15-10. Smoothing curved and irregular-shaped edges. Top. Using a drum sander in a drill press. Bottom. Using a spindle sander.

TEST YOUR KNOWLEDGE, Unit 15

Please do not write in this text. Place your answers on a separate sheet of paper.

1. Coated abrasives are available with both _____ and _____ particles.
2. Open coat abrasives allow chips of wood to fall out and in turn reduce _____.
3. _____ is a natural black material that is excellent for removing rust from metal surfaces. However, is not recommended for wood surfaces.

142

4. Standard abrasive grit sizes are indicated by a number which is the mesh size per linear _____.

5. Always sand with the grain, not across it. True or False?

6. Place materials to be smoothed on the disk sander table so the sander disk cuts in the _____ direction.

7. Belt sander size is indicated by the _____ of the sander belt.

8. _____ sanders are used to smooth mill marks and other imperfections from the surfaces of planed boards and panels.

9. Garnet is a synthetic material made in an electric furnace. True or False?

10. Flint is the only abrasive paper that does not come in standard sized sheets. What size are they?

11. What products are combined in an electric furnace to manufacture silicon carbide sandpaper?

12. What type of abrasive paper is often referred to as "wet-or-dry"?

13. The source of the abrasive material (grit) used to make abrasive paper may be either _____ or _____.

14. The common polishing compounds used in the woodworking industry are _____ and _____.

15. The small (sometimes invisible) dust particles created while sanding can be extremely hazardous if inhaled. True or False?

ACTIVITIES

1. Carefully cut several one-inch squares of several different kinds and grits of sandpaper. Use rubber cement to attach each square to a piece of paper and label the sample according to type of paper and grit size.

2. Walk through your woods laboratory and list each of the different kinds of power sanding devices that are available. Be sure to note the size and type of sanding belt or disk required.

3. Select 1/4 sheets of three different abrasive paper grits–60, 120, and 180. Use a piece of scrap softwood. Sand it with each of the different pieces. Which grit removes material the quickest? Which grit leave the deepest scratches? Which grit produces the smoothest surface?

4. Use the scrap wood and abrasive that appear in the previous activity. Sand it across the grain using 180 grit. Look closely at the surface. Describe its appearance. Now sand with the grain to remove the scratches made when you sanded across the grain. Are the scratches difficult to remove?

5. After your instructor has demonstrated using a power finish sander, practice sanding your scrap of softwood. Notice the size of dust. Is this dust a health hazard? Are surface scratches easy to remove using this sander?

Finish sanders can be used to sand in hard-to-reach places. (Skil Corp.)

UNIT 16

WOOD FINISHING

Finish is applied to stock to protect the surface and enhance the natural beauty of the grain. The type of wood finish used depends on a number of factors, such as the kind of wood, desired appearance, available time to finish the product, and available wood finishing supplies and equipment. After reading this unit, you will be able identify the most common finishes used in a woods laboratory. In addition, you will be able to prepare a piece of stock for finishing and then finish it to a desired appearance.

When using any type of wood finish, it is important that you first apply the finish to a piece of scrap stock of the same kind of wood. Apply the finish according to the manufacturer's instructions.

WOOD FINISHING PROCEDURE

Two series of steps must be followed in order for your product to have the best possible appearance. The first series involves the preparation of the wood surface for the final stain and finish. The second series is the application of stain and protective finish. Care must be taken with each of these steps.

STEPS IN PREPARING A SURFACE FOR FINISHING

1. Remove all mill marks using a cabinet scraper or by sanding the stock.
2. Remove dents by using moisture and heat or by filling.
3. Repair and fill defects.
4. Remove any excess glue from exposed surfaces.

5. If the wood color is not even, or if it is streaked, the surface should be bleached to achieve a uniform shade.
6. Finish sanding the entire surface using 180 to 220 grit sandpaper.

The surface should now be ready to begin applying filler, sealer, stain, and finish protective coatings.

REPAIRING DEFECTS

Nail holes, small cracks, and other small defects must be repaired prior to applying any type of finish. FILLERS are commonly used to repair such defects. Types of fillers include Plastic Wood™, wood putty, water putty, and stick shellac. See Fig. 16-1. These fillers should be used before applying the finish.

Fig. 16-1. Products commonly used in repairing wood defects. Plastic Wood, wood putty, and water putty.

Plastic Wood

Plastic Wood is available in several shades and colors including natural, oak, mahogany, and walnut. It comes in a ready-to-use form.

Use Plastic Wood before any finish is applied. The surface should be clean and dry. Press Plastic Wood into place using a putty knife or small spatula. Fill large holes by placing thin layers into them. Allow each layer to dry before applying the next one. Overfill the hole to allow for shrinkage and sanding. Keep the can covered tightly when you are not using the Plastic Wood.

Caution: Plastic Wood is extremely flammable. Avoid excessive inhalation of fumes. Use only with adequate ventilation.

Wood Putty and Water Putty

Wood and water putties are available in a powder form. They are prepared by mixing the powder with water to form a smooth, thick paste. Mix only a small amount at a time; the putty dries very quickly. Add a small amount of vinegar to slow the setting. Dry colors or water stains can be added if color is required.

Prepare the hole or crack by removing all dirt and grease. Wet the edges to provide a good bond. Use a putty knife to press the mixture into the cavity. Smooth carefully with a wet putty knife or finger. Wait until the putty is dry before attempting to sand it. It may help to moisten the putty with water when sanding.

Stick Shellac and Lacquer

Stick shellac and lacquer are available in a variety of colors. Select a stick that is slightly darker than you expect the wood to be when applying the finish. Dampen a small spot of the stock to help you visualize the color. Use a heated knife, or electrical heating unit to melt the shellac or lacquer and work it into the defect, as shown in Fig. 16-2. Excess stick shellac can be scraped away, and then sanded with the grain.

FILLING DENTS

Most small dents in the stock can be lifted prior to applying the finish. This can be done using water and heat. Lightly moisten the dented area of the stock, place a wet cloth over the dent,

Fig. 16-2. Repairing wood defects with stick shellac.

and apply heat with a soldering iron or household iron.

Water and steam cause the wood fibers to swell and spring back to their approximate original shape. It is not possible to completely repair dents that have torn fibers. When the wood dries, sand it smooth with fine abrasive paper.

PUTTY STICKS

Putty sticks and blending pencils are generally used after applying the finish. They are also used on prefinished surfaces. A variety of colors and types are available, Fig. 16-3. Select a stick that best matches the finished stock. Rub the stick over the hole until it is filled. Wipe off the excess with a cloth pad.

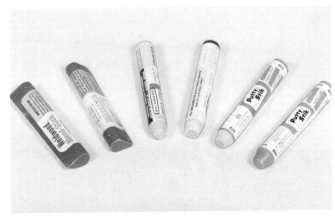

Fig. 16-3. Putty sticks are generally used after applying finish and to fill nail holes in prefinished panels.

BLEACHING WOOD

Wood bleach is commonly used to lighten wood, remove dark streaks, and prepare the surface for special finishes. OXALIC ACID can be used as a mild bleaching solution. Mix the powdered oxalic acid with water to a ratio of 1 part oxalic acid to 20 parts water. The oxalic acid is usually harmless to your skin, but should be kept away from your eyes and clothing. It is generally applied with a cloth pad.

Commercial wood bleach is commonly sold in liquid form in two separate containers. One container holds sodium hydroxide and the other holds hydrogen peroxide. The two solutions are mixed together in small amounts, as needed, by following the manufacturer's instructions. See Fig. 16-4.

Fig. 16-4. Using commercial wood bleach. Bleach has been used on the light-colored area at the left.

When working with commercial bleaches, always wear rubber gloves to protect your hands and arms, and goggles for eye protection. Use the bleach only in well-ventilated areas. If the bleach comes into contact with your skin, wash the affected area immediately using soap and water.

An alternative to oxalic acid or commercial wood bleaches is common household bleach. Household bleach may be used directly from its container. Allow the bleach to soak into the wood until the desired color is obtained.

Most bleaching operations raise the surface grain of the wood. It will be necessary for you to lightly sand after the surface has dried.

SANDING

The stock should be perfectly smooth before applying any type of finish. It is time-consuming to correct surface defects in the stock after applying some finishes. The finished surface will not be any smoother than the surface to which it is applied.

Use a flat sanding block to hold fine abrasive sheets. Always sand with the grain of the stock. Use a TACK RAG to remove all dust and grit from the product. A tack rag is a chemically treated piece of cheesecloth that allows it to remain soft and tacky.

BRUSHES

Brushes are available in a variety of sizes, shapes, and grades. Some brushes have animal hair bristles, while some have nylon bristles. The bristles are usually set in rubber and held in place with a metal ferrule, Fig. 16-5.

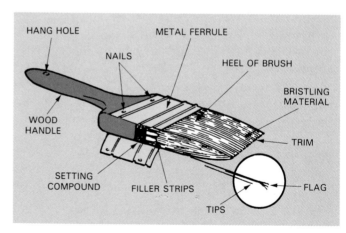

Fig. 16-5. Brush cut-away view showing constructional details.

It is important to purchase good brushes, and to see that the brushes are properly used and stored. A brush that is used regularly for the same type of finish can be stored by drilling a hole through the handle, inserting a wire through the hole, and suspending the brush in a can or jar containing solvent. The brush should be positioned so that the bristles do not touch the bottom of the container. See Fig. 16-6.

Fig. 16-6. Storing brushes in glass jars with rubber lids.

A good way to preserve the quality of a brush is to clean it after every use, dry it off, and store it properly. Remove the excess finish by pulling the brush lightly across the top of a container. Wash the brush in the appropriate solvent and then dry it using paper towel or a cloth. Scrub the brush with soap and water and wrap it with paper or aluminum foil to protect the bristles.

Wood Finishes – Safety and Care
1. Keep sparks and flames away from the finishing area.
2. Place all waste materials and rags in a fireproof, metal container. Finishes should be stored in a fireproof cabinet.
3. Always use an exhaust fan (or work in an area that is adequately ventilated) to remove dangerous fumes while applying or removing a finish.
4. Wear goggles and rubber gloves when handling hazardous liquid such as bleach and finish removers.
5. Clean your brushes and store them properly after each use.
6. Tightly seal finish cans and store them in a metal cabinet.
7. Protect your clothing when finishing.

STEPS IN APPLYING A FINISH

After all surface defects have been repaired and the surface has been smoothly sanded, you are ready to apply the finish. The steps involved in applying a finish are as follows:

1. Select the final finish. This choice should be made after considering the planned service for the product, the various types of finishes, the available equipment, and the amount of space in your woods laboratory.
2. Choose the color stain, if desired.
3. Is a filler necessary? Carefully inspect the surface of the stock. Is it an open-grained or close-grained wood?
4. Dust the surface of the stock using a soft-bristle brush or vacuum cleaner. Be careful not to inhale the dust.
5. Wipe the surface clean with a tack rag.
6. Carefully follow the prescribed procedure for staining, filling, sealing, and applying final finishes you have selected.

WOOD STAINS

Stains are used to emphasize wood grain and impart color into the surface of the stock. Wood stains can be classified according to the solvent or vehicle used in their manufacture. Types of solvents used in the manufacturing process include linseed oil, turpentine, mineral spirits, alcohol, and water.

Oil Stain
Pigmented oil stains contain finely ground color particles, or PIGMENTS, and a liquid, also known as a VEHICLE. The pigments do not dissolve. They are mixed in a vehicle such as linseed oil or mineral spirits. It is a common belief that stain, such as walnut stain, will color the wood to closely resemble walnut stock. However, the color name simply indicates the color, such as brown or reddish-brown. The pigment remains on the surface of the stock, providing uniform color and appearance. Oil stain should be allowed to dry thoroughly and then coated with a sealer (shellac or lacquer) to prevent bleeding of the stain into the finish coats.

Stir the stain thoroughly. Apply it quickly and uniformly, using a soft brush. Flow the stain across the grain, and then make light finishing strokes with the grain. Carefully check the stock for skips or spots that were missed. Allow the stain to set up until the surface appears to be flat or dull (approximately 5 to 10 minutes). Then, wipe the surface with a clean, lint-free cloth with the grain of the wood to bring out the highlights of the grain, Fig. 16-7. Depth of color can be controlled by the amount of stain left on the surface. Use turpentine or mineral spirits for clean up. Allow about 24 hours for oil stain to dry before applying paste wood filler or a finish coat.

Fig. 16-7. Applying oil stain. Wiping with lint-free cloth to bring out highlights.

Penetrating wood stains are made by mixing oil and oil-soluble dyes. One problem that commonly occurs with penetrating stains is that excessive quantities of the stain are absorbed by the end grain. A coat of linseed oil applied to the end grain a few minutes before using the penetrating stain will help to equalize the color.

Non-Grain Raising Stains

Non-grain raising (NGR) stains are made by dissolving colored dyes in glycol and alcohol. Non-grain raising stains will not bleed through a finish, nor will they raise the grain. They dry very quickly, making them popular for spray applications. Their resistance to fading is excellent. However, NGR stains must be stored in nonmetallic containers.

Water Stains

Water stains are made by dissolving water-soluble dyes in water. Four ounces of stain added to one gallon of water makes one gallon of ready-to-use stain. Water stains do not bleach or fade when exposed to sunlight.

Water stains penetrate deeply into the wood, and tend to raise the grain. When using a water stain, raise the grain of the stock by sponging the surface lightly before applying the stain. Allow the wood to dry and then sand lightly with fine abrasive paper with the grain of the stock. Apply additional coats of the water stain to darken the surface. Coat the surface of the stock that has been water stained with shellac or lacquer sealer before applying other finishes.

PASTE WOOD FILLERS

Wood consists of an endless number of interwoven fibers that contain holes or pores. Close-grained woods, such as maple, pine, and basswood, have small pores. These small pores only need to be sealed with finishing materials, such as shellac, lacquer, linseed oil, or synthetic materials before applying finishing coats. Open-grained woods, such as walnut, oak, ash, and mahogany, have large visible pores. These large pores should be filled with paste wood filler to obtain a smooth surface before applying most other finishes. See Fig. 16-8.

Paste wood filler is made from ground silica, linseed oil, turpentine or paint thinner, and drier. It is sold as a heavy paste that needs to be

Fig. 16-8. Paste wood filler being used to fill pores of open-grained wood.

thinned for use. The filler should have a heavy creamy consistency when in use, being thinned by paint thinner or turpentine. Paste wood filler is available in a natural (light buff) color, and in colors such as oak, walnut, and mahogany. The natural filler can be tinted with oil stains. Color of the paste filler should closely match the color of the finished wood.

Mix the paste wood filler to the correct color and consistency when filling an open-grained wood. Try the filler on a scrap piece of stock before using it on your product. You can apply it directly onto the unfinished stock, or apply it to the stock after using a thin coat of sealer. When using the sealer, make sure that it dries before using the filler. Apply the filler along the grain, brushing it into the pores with a stiff brush. If the product is large, coat only a small section at a time. Wait a few minutes until the filler begins to take on a dull appearance, and then wipe off the excess. Rub across the grain using a lint-free cloth, such as cheesecloth, as shown in Fig. 16-9. Use a soft cloth to remove any remaining residue. You can clean out the corners with a piece of cloth wrapped around a pointed stick. Allow the stock to dry about 4 to 6 hours, and then rub lightly with 220 grit abrasive paper.

Fig. 16-9. Excess wood filler being removed, working ACROSS the grain.

SEALERS

Sealers are finishes used as the base coat when filling the pores of close-grained woods such as maple, birch, pine, and cherry. Shellac, lacquer sealer, and sealer stains are commonly used for this purpose.

Sealers are available ready mixed, but are often reduced (thinned) before application. Shellac is reduced with alcohol, and is usually sold as 4-pound cut (4 pounds of shellac solids mixed with a gallon of alcohol). The 4-pound cut is then commonly mixed with an equal part of alcohol to form a 2-pound cut for brush application. Lacquer sealer is usually applied by spraying, Fig. 16-10, but it can also be applied to small products by brushing. Lacquer sealer is reduced with lacquer thinner. Sealer stains are usually reduced with turpentine or paint thinner.

Fig. 16-10. Applying wood stain and sealer by spraying.

WASH COATING is the application of a thin coat of sealer, usually shellac or lacquer sealer. A wash coating is made by mixing 6 to 8 parts of thinner to 1 part of sealer. The wash coating is applied over paste wood filler and some stains to prevent them from bleeding into the finish. A wash coat can also be used on wood prior to applying paste wood filler.

When linseed oil and turpentine, or Danish oil finishes are used, be sure to allow the product to set for about 30 minutes after application. Then, wipe off the excess material and allow the remaining finish to dry 10 to 12 hours. Additional coats are applied in the same way. The linseed oil and turpentine finish penetrates the wood better if it is heated to approximately 140 degrees Fahrenheit before it is applied. When the final coat is thoroughly dry, a coat of wax should be applied. The surface can then be buffed to enhance its beauty and increase its durability.

You can apply sealers with a brush or by spraying. Be sure to follow the manufacturer's instructions for proper application.

TOP COAT FINISHES

A variety of finishes are used for top coats, or oversealers. Varnish, lacquer, and shellac are often used to achieve a natural (clear) or transparent finish. Enamel and paint are used to obtain an opaque finish. Fig. 16-11 shows a variety of finishes commonly used in the woodworking industry.

Fig. 16-11. Commonly used top coat finishes and stains.

You can apply a top coat finish with a brush, roller, or by spraying. Most types of top coat finishes remain on the surface of the wood to form a hard, durable, and protective covering.

When you apply more than one coat of finish, it should be sanded between coats with 6/0 to

8/0 abrasive sheets, or with 3/0 to 4/0 steel wool. Make sure that you tack rag the stock to remove all small particles before applying the next coat.

The final top coat should be smoothed after it has been applied. Sprinkle pumice or rottenstone and rubbing oil on the finished surface. Use a cloth to rub the material over the surface. Wipe off the excess polishing material with a soft cloth. See Fig. 16-12. Apply a coat of wax and buff with a soft cloth to shine.

Fig. 16-12. Using rottenstone and rubbing oil to smooth final coat.

VARNISH and ENAMEL are made from the same basic materials. However, pigment is added to the enamel to give it color and make it opaque. Varnish and enamel are made with natural and synthetic materials, creating a durable and waterproof finish. Drying time varies, but 8 to 10 hours is usually required between coats. Varnish and enamel are reduced with turpentine or mineral spirits.

LACQUER dries fast by evaporation. It is usually applied with spraying equipment, making it adaptable to mass production techniques. Lacquer can be brushed on small products if a retarding (slow drying) thinner is used to reduce it. Lacquer produces a clear, hard, durable, and heat-resistant film. Some lacquers are water resistant. Pigments can be added to make it transparent or opaque.

Lacquer is reduced with lacquer thinner. It should be applied in thin coats. Thick coats dry quickly on the outside, but remain soft on the inside. Lacquer should be allowed to dry about 30 minutes between coats. One caution should be considered when using lacquer: it tends to soften and lift varnish, enamel, and some synthetic finishes. Lacquer should not be used over these materials.

POLYURETHANE is a clear, plastic coating. It dries fast and is highly resistant to abrasion and wear. It can be used on all types of wood used indoors or outdoors. Sealer is not needed when applying polyurethane. It should be applied with a good-quality, clean brush. Two or three coats may be required for new products. Lightly sand between coats to remove the gloss and ensure good adhesion between coats. Tack rag the stock after each sanding and before applying the next coat.

SHELLAC will produce a fine finish if it is applied in thin coats. Shellac should be made as a 2-pound cut, the same thickness as used for a sealer coat. Shellac is one of the oldest finishes. It is a good finish if it is properly cared for, but it is not alcohol or water resistant. Paste wax should be used after the final coat to enhance the shellac's beauty and protect it from moisture.

PAINT is available in a variety of colors with either an oil base or latex (rubber) base. They can be used for both interior and exterior surfaces. Paints are often used to beautify and protect surfaces where an opaque finish is appropriate. Oil-base paint is reduced with turpentine or mineral spirits, and usually requires at least 24 hours of drying time for each coat.

Latex-base paints are thinned with water. The next coat can be applied in a short time. Brushes used for latex-base paint should be cleaned in water immediately after use.

THINNING MEDIUMS

The correct thinner must be used when reducing finishes. Refer to the manufacturer's instructions regarding the proper use of the thinner. Fig. 16-13 shows a variety of thinners used in the woods laboratory.

TURPENTINE is used to reduce oil stains, oil-base paints, varnishes, and enamels. The authentic turpentine is made from yellow pine trees. Substitutes for turpentine, commonly referred to as paint thinners, are made from petroleum.

SHELLAC SOLVENT is a combination of wood and grain alcohol. It is sometimes referred to as denatured alcohol. Shellac solvent should only be used for reducing shellac.

LACQUER THINNER is a clear liquid. It is used as a solvent for lacquer, lacquer sealer, and contact cement. Lacquer thinners have commonly been used as multipurpose cleaners. However, this practice should be avoided whenever possible because of the health hazard posed and the possible damage to the environment.

Extreme care must be taken when disposing of most finish materials, especially when they are in their liquid state.

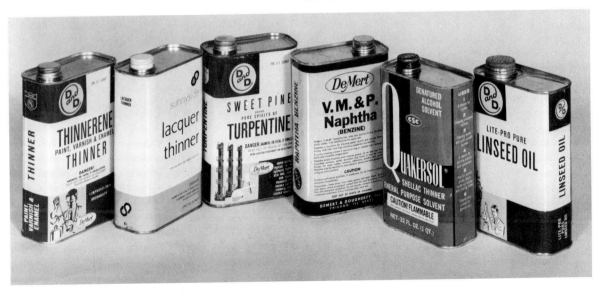

Fig. 16-13. Thinning mediums.

RETARDING LACQUER THINNER is a special thinner used to slow the drying time of lacquer. It is also used to help eliminate "blushing." Blushing is a white or cloudy appearance on a surface caused by trapping small particles of moisture beneath the finish.

LINSEED OIL is obtained from flax seed. It is used to thin some types of paint, as well as being used as a drying agent in paints, fillers, and stains. It can also be used with turpentine as a finish.

FLOCK is pulverized rayon or cellulose acetate that can be sprinkled or blown on a sticky base substance such as enamel or glue. The results of this combination is a velvet-like coating. Flocking can be used on the bottom of small projects to protect furniture, as a decoration, and for a lining in boxes and drawers.

CRYSTALLINE FINISH can be brushed or sprayed on the surface of stock. It is similar to paint or enamel. When the crystalline finish dries, it forms a mass of wrinkles and crystals, making it an interesting and decorative finish.

ANTIQUING, or COLOR GLAZING, is used to make a new product look "old." It consists of a color base undercoat and a color glaze. A variety of color combinations are available. The base undercoat is applied over the surface being finished. It provides a base color for the color glaze. When the undercoat has dried thoroughly, apply the color glaze. Wood tones and other special effects can be obtained using a soft, lint-free cloth to wipe or texture the color glaze while it is still wet. If the effect is not satisfactory, you can wipe off the glaze and start over again. Fig. 16-14 shows the materials that are required when applying an antiquing finish.

SPRAY FINISHES

The spray gun is commonly used in the woodworking industry to produce a protective and beautiful coating with maximum speed. The spray gun atomizes (forms into a fine mist) the finishing material so it can be applied in thin, uniform coats. Correct techniques must be used to be successful when spraying finishing materials.

When spraying, hold the spray gun perpendicular to, and about 6 to 8 inches away from, the surface to be coated. Do not tilt the spray gun up or down, Fig. 16-15. This results in an uneven spray pattern. Use a scrap piece of stock for practice. Begin at one side of the piece and move the gun toward the other side. See Fig. 16-16. Trigger the spray gun ON as you approach the first side of the stock, and OFF as you reach the other side. Make the necessary adjustment with the gun, mixture, or air pressure so the material is "wet" as it is sprayed on the surface. If the material is "dry," adjust the gun or verify the materials have been properly proportioned or blended.

Fig. 16-14. Antiquing kit.

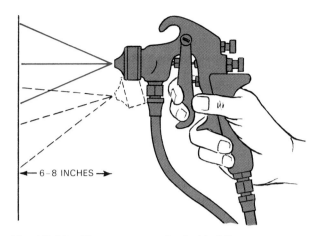

Fig. 16-15. The correct method of holding a spray gun.

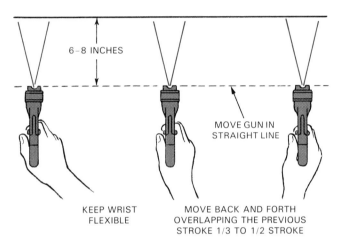

Fig. 16-16. The correct movement of a spray gun.

Continue with the succeeding strokes in the same way. Overlap the previous stroke about 50 percent, Fig. 16-17. When spraying a large panel, spray vertical bands along the ends of the piece first, and then continue with the horizontal strokes.

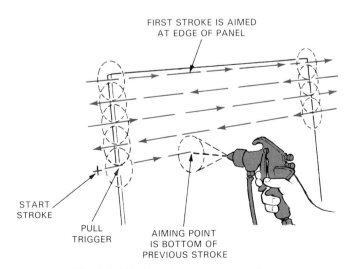

Fig. 16-17. Panel spraying technique.

REMOVING FINISH

Ready-to-use materials are available that can effectively remove finishes from wood or metal surfaces. Refer to the manufacturer's instructions regarding the proper use of the remover before beginning. Cover your workbench with sheet metal, hardboard, or old newspapers before removing a finish. Protect your hands with rubber gloves designed for stripping operations. Always wear eye protection. Make sure the work area is well-ventilated, and use a respirator with organic cartridges.

Use a small brush to apply the remover to one side of the product. Continue applying the remover until the finish begins to loosen. Then, use a piece of burlap, coarse cloth, or coarse steel wool to wipe away the loosened finish. Use a nylon putty knife or spatula if the finish is thick. An old toothbrush or a small brass-bristle brush is helpful to clean around intricate or irregular shapes. Continue with the remainder of your product, removing the finish from one panel at a time. Allow the product to dry 8 to 10 hours, and then smooth it with fine abrasive material.

Many strippers require that the stripped surface be neutralized prior to applying a finish. The neutralization process removes any stripper that could still be in the wood pores, and reduces the possibility of the stripper lifting the new finish when applied. A word of caution when removing finish from stock. Many pieces of furniture have been previously painted with a lead-base paint. If this is the case with the piece of furniture you are working on, stop immediately and allow a professional to continue with the process. The removed residue must be disposed of properly, and proper clothing and breathing devices must be worn during the stripping process.

TEST YOUR KNOWLEDGE, Unit 16

Please do not write in this text. Place your answers on a separate sheet of paper.

1. Why is it important to try a finish on a piece of scrap stock before applying it to your product?

2. Be sure the finishing product is applied according to the _____ instructions.
3. Nail holes, small cracks, and other defects should be repaired _____ applying a finishing material.
4. Plastic Wood handles like _____ and dries like _____.
5. Wetting the edges of a cavity provides good _____ between wood putty and the wood.
6. Use a color of stick shellac that is slightly _____ than you expect the wood to be when you apply the finish.
7. Putty sticks are generally used _____ applying the finish.
8. Oxalic acid can be used as a mild _____ solution.
9. When storing a brush for a short period of time in a can or jar of solvent, the brush should be held so the bristles _____.
10. Wood stains can be classified according to the _____ used in their manufacture.
11. A coat of _____ should be applied to the end grain to prevent excessive quantities of stain from being absorbed into it.
12. Paste wood fillers are used on _____ woods.
13. Wipe _____ the grain when removing excess paste wood filler.
14. _____ are used as the base coat to fill the _____ of close-grained wood.
15. Most _____ remain on the surface of the wood, and form a hard, durable, and protective covering.
16. Paint is available as _____-base or _____-base.
17. List three finish thinning mediums.
18. Hold the spray gun _____ to the surface to prevent an uneven spray pattern.

ACTIVITIES

1. Make a list of the various finish materials available in your woods laboratory. Prepare four columns beside your list. In the first column, list the thinner for each item. In the second column, write the methods of application. In the next column, detail clean-up procedures. In the final column, list any precautions that should be observed.
2. Use a piece of scrap wood from the product you are building. Experiment using different kinds and shades of strains. Make sure to carefully label each sample detailing the procedure you followed.
3. Apply a finish coat to each of the stained pieces after staining. Again, use a variety of finishes and document your procedure.
4. Use a piece of scrap red oak about 4-inches wide and 10- to 12-inches long. Apply a paste wood filler to one half. Allow the filler to dry, then lightly sand. Apply three coats of a clear finish material over the entire piece. Observe the texture of the surface. Is there a difference in appearance? What is the difference? Did the paste wood filler require additional work?
4. Use a piece of scrap pine about 4-inches wide by 10-inches long. Mark the surface using a hammer, a knife, drop it, or anything else to simulate a damaged surface. First, moisten the dents and try to raise them with a hot iron. Which dents could be raised? Which could not? Try using a putty and Plastic Wood for the dents that could not be raised. Prepare the surface for a finish. Apply a couple coats of clear finish. Evaluate each method you used to repair the surface.

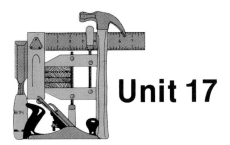

Unit 17

HARDWARE

HARDWARE refers to connectors, fasteners, and pieces of trim that are used in the construction of a product. Hardware is used extensively in furniture and cabinet construction. It is available in many styles and qualities. After reading this unit, you will be able to identify, select, and install various kinds of hardware commonly used with woodworking products. Additional information about some types of hardware is included in Unit 14.

A wide variety of hardware for installation into cabinets and furniture is available. A trip to the local hardware store will provide numerous ideas to be incorporated into your next project. If you plan to use a new item in your next product, purchase a sample before beginning construction. Many items look alike, but you must take little differences into account before construction begins.

HINGES

A HINGE is a device that is generally made by two pieces of metal formed around a pin. The flat portion, or the LEAF, has holes drilled through it. Screws are then inserted through the holes and turned into the stock. The pin, called a HINGE PIN, may be either loose or tight. A loose pin can be removed in order to separate the two leaves, while a tight pin cannot be removed.

There are three major categories of hinges that are commonly used in the woodworking industry today. They are the:

- Butt hinge.
- Surface hinge.
- Concealed hinge.

The number of hinges required on a given product depends on the weight and height of the door, and type of hinge being used. Two hinges are generally sufficient on each door.

BUTT HINGES are available in a variety of sizes. Large sizes are commonly used for swinging doors in homes and other buildings. Smaller sizes are used for doors and boxes in furniture and cabinets. Two decorative butt hinges are shown in Fig. 17-1. Butt hinges can be attached directly to the surface, but they are commonly mounted in recesses called GAINS. Each gain should be deep enough for the thickness of one leaf. See Fig. 17-2.

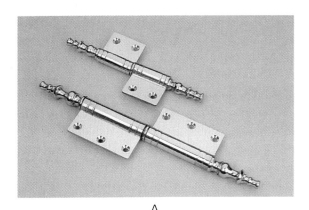

A

B

Fig. 17-1. Butt hinges are mounted flush to the surfaces. A–Solid brass ornamental hinges. B–Brass butler's hinge used for drop-leaf tables.

155

Fig. 17-2. Installing a butt hinge. The gain depth is equal to the thickness of the leaf.

SURFACE HINGES have an "H" or "HL" shape. They can be mounted either flush or offset. They are mounted on the face of the cabinet door and on the frame. See Fig. 17-3.

Only a portion of a SEMICONCEALED HINGE can be seen when the door is closed. The visible part is generally attached to the front of the cabinet, Fig. 17-4. CONCEALED HINGES are designed for doors that completely cover the frame of the cabinet. In some cases, part of the hinge is mortised into the face of the stock. See Fig. 17-5. Other types of hinges are totally concealed when the door is closed; one is called a SOSS HINGE and the other is called a CYLINDER HINGE, Fig. 17-6. Both of these hinges are easy to install. However, the door must be carefully fit to the opening before attaching the hinges.

Fig. 17-5. A concealed hinge. Left. Door open. Right. Door closed.

Fig. 17-3. Surface hinges are mounted on the surface of the adjoining pieces. (American Plywood Association)

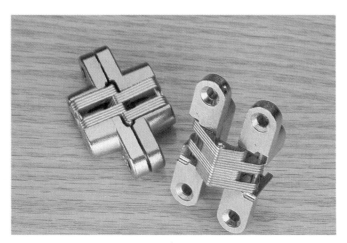

A

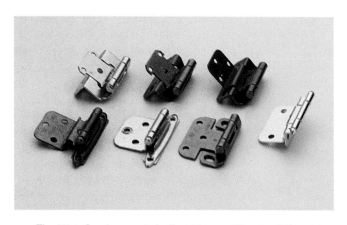

Fig. 17-4. Semiconcealed offset hinges. (Woodcraft Supply)

B

Fig. 17-6. Concealed hinges cannot be seen when the door is closed. A–Soss hinge. B–Cylinder hinge.

Another type of concealed hinge that is used for folding chairs, television stands, and similar products is the ROTARY HINGE, or ROTO HINGE, Fig. 17-7. Holes must be drilled into the stock to accept the hinge.

Fig. 17-7. The rotary hinge rotates on a pivot pin.

New styles of kitchen cabinets have a special hinge that is also totally concealed when the door is closed. This concealed hinge is called a EUROPEAN CABINET HINGE. Part of this hinge is recessed into the surface of one piece, while the other part of the hinge is mounted flush with the surface. See Fig. 17-8.

Fig. 17-8. A European cabinet hinge.

Stereo cabinets sometimes require special-purpose hinges such as those shown in Fig. 17-9. You will note that one part of these hinges is attached to a surface with screws, while the other surface fits onto a glass door or lid.

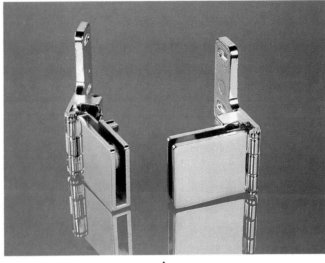

A

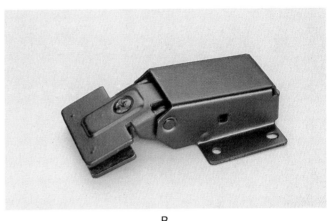

B

Fig. 17-9. Special-purpose hinges. A–Glass door hinge for stereo cabinet. B–Dust cover hinge for a turntable.

PULLS AND KNOBS

Pulls and knobs help you when opening drawers or doors. Pulls and knobs are generally selected to match hinges and other hardware. There are a variety of styles available, Fig. 17-10. Some types of pulls are mounted flush with the surface. These pulls can be used on sliding doors so that adjacent doors can slide past one another. When using a flush-mounted pull, you must first make a recess in the door to fit the pull. The most common types of pulls and knobs are surface mounted. These pulls and knobs are attached with screws from the backs of the doors or drawers. A hole must be drilled through the door or drawer to accept the screw.

CATCHES AND LATCHES

Catches and locks are used to hold furniture and cabinet doors closed. They are available in

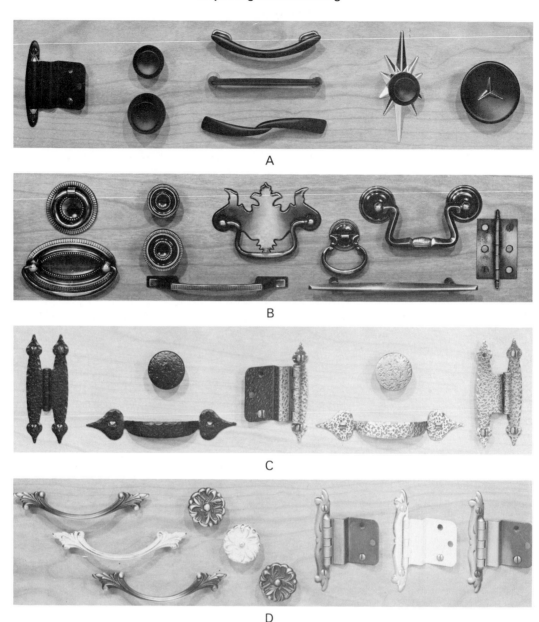

Fig. 17-10. Styles of pulls and knobs. A–Contemporary. B.–Modern and Traditional.
C–Early American. D–French Provincial.

many different styles. Catches hold the doors closed through magnetic or mechanical means. MAGNETIC CATCHES are popular and practical. Keep the catch and magnet free of any type of varnish or paint, since this will reduce the magnetic attraction between the two surfaces. Fig. 17-11 shows three ways to mount a magnetic catch.

Mechanical catches are the most common and inexpensive type of catches. A FRICTION CATCH uses a bent steel catch that holds a head mounted on the door, Fig. 17-12. The catch is generally mounted on the door frame or cabinet shelf, while the strike is usually mounted to the

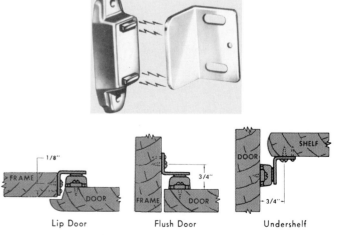

Fig. 17-11. Parts and uses of a magnetic catch.

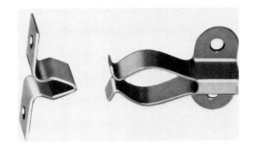

Fig. 17-12. A friction catch.

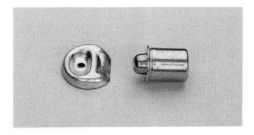

Fig. 17-15. Bullet catches offer little
resistance when being opened.

door. A ROLLER CATCH is a mechanical
catch that relies on a spring-loaded roller to hold
the door closed. Fig. 17-13 illustrates two methods of mounting a single-roller spring catch. Sin-
gle- and double-roller catches are available.
ELBOW CATCHES consist of a spring-action
lever that holds the bent edge of a catch. See Fig.
17-14. The catch is usually fastened to the cabinet door and the strike is attached to the frame
or a shelf in the cabinet. The lever on the catch
must be moved to release the strike.

Fig. 17-13. Single- and double-roller catches.
(Woodcraft and Supply)

Fig. 17-14. Elbow catch.

BULLET CATCHES are inexpensive and
easy to install, Fig. 17-15. This type of catch
does not require a great deal of force to open the
door or drawer. The catch is generally flush

mounted on the frame or face of the cabinet. A
hole is drilled for the strike, and the strike is
fastened into the hole.

A type of catch that is commonly used on stereo cabinets is the TOUCH LATCH, Fig. 17-16.
This type of catch requires a small amount of
space between the door and the latch base.
When the door is pushed, a spring releases the
latch and actually pushes the door open. This is
convenient if someone has their hands full and
needs to get into the cabinet.

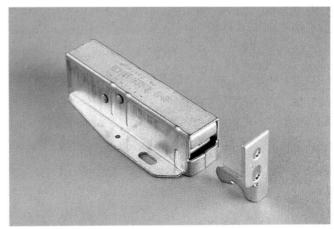

Fig. 17-16. A touch latch is used to automatically open a
cabinet door as you push on the face of it.

LOCKS

Locks are used to protect the contents of a
door or drawer. They can be used on chests of
drawers, rolltop desks, and sliding doors. Three
types of locks are commonly used. When the key
of a BOLT-ACTION LOCK is turned, the bolt
moves in a straight line. When the key of a
CAM-ACTION LOCK is turned, a flat metal
arm rotates into a slot. The lock shown in Fig.
17-17 is a small cam-action lock. A RATCHET-
ACTION LOCK is commonly used on sliding
glass doors. A bent metal strap with teeth along

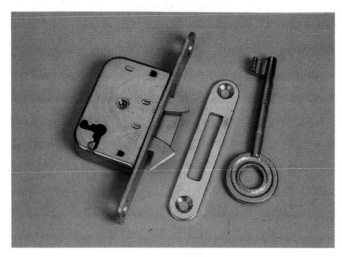

Fig. 17-17. A small chest lock with a key.

one edge is placed perpendicular to the edge of one door. A lock is placed over the strap to secure it into position.

SLIDING TRACKS

Numerous types of sliding mechanisms are available for drawers and doors. The manufacturer's installation instructions should be followed carefully since there is such variety in styles.

The type of sliding mechanism used with a drawer is shown in Fig. 17-18. The drawer is supported and moved on rollers that are attached to each side of the lower drawer rail. A third roller, attached to the drawer front, moves in a metal channel support. The metal channel support is fastened to the rail and to the cabinet back or vertical support. The support guides the drawer as it is moved forward or backward.

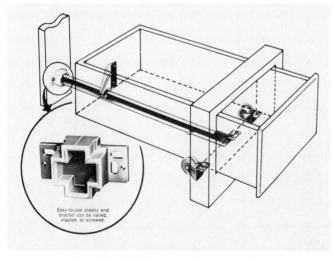

Fig. 17-18. Drawer slide assembly.

TEST YOUR KNOWLEDGE, Unit 17

Please do not write in this text. Place your answers on a separate sheet of paper.

1. Butt hinges are often mounted in mortises or recesses called _____.
2. Surface type hinges are mounted on the face of the cabinet door and on the frame. True or False?
3. The hinge pin of a butt hinge may be either _____ or _____.
4. A hinge in which only a small part of the hinge is shown is called a _____ hinge.
5. _____ and _____ are used to hold furniture and cabinet doors closed.
6. _____ are available for either drawers or doors in a variety of styles.
7. Hardware is available in many styles and qualities. True or False?
8. Most hardware items are very similar in size, shape, and application, and are completely interchangeable. True or False?
9. A hinge is two pieces of metal wrapped around a pin. What are these two pieces of metal called?
10. Large butt hinges are used for swinging doors found in a home. True or False?
11. A hinge that is not visible when the door is closed is called a _____ hinge.
12. List an application for a rotary hinge.
13. It is usually not possible to buy a knob that matches the finish and style of the hinge you have chosen. True or False?
14. Name three different catches discussed in this unit.
15. A bullet catch is easy to install. True or False?
16. Locks for drawers and doors are typically available in three types. What are these types?
17. Sliding mechanisms are available for both doors and drawers. True or False?

ACTIVITIES

1. Carefully look at the hardware found on furniture and cabinets in your home. Do you have any of the following? Where were these hardware items used in your homes?
   A. Butt hinges.
   B. Drawer guides.
   C. Drawer pulls.

D. Offset hinges.

E. Hidden hinges.

F. Touch latches.

G. Bullet catches.

H. Keyed locks.

2. Visit a store that sells hinges, pulls, and other cabinet hardware items. Answer the following questions:

   A. What kind of store did you visit?

   B. Did they have butt hinges? What color were they? Did they have different sizes? Were they the same price? Did they have any butt hinges with loose pins?

   C. Were you able to find any drawer pulls or knobs? Could you match some of the pulls with similar hinges? Were all the pulls the same size? Did you find a pull or a knob you particularly liked?

3. Use two small pieces of pine or other softwood from the scrap bin and a small butt hinge. Mount the hinge on the surface of the board, when on the edge, and try to mortise to inset the hinge. Answer the following questions:

   A. After installing the hinges, did both pieces fold or hinge together evenly?

   B. Of the three methods used to attach the butt hinge, which was the easiest? Which was the most difficult? Which method looked the best? Why?

   C. Did you have problems with the screw fitting smoothly in the hinge recess? What could you do to improve this problem? What type of screw was provided with the hinge?

4. Use the same piece of scrap stock. Install a pull or a knob. Carefully list each step necessary to complete this task.

5. Find a drawer at home or school that uses metal guides to support the drawer. Remove the drawer (not the guide) and answer the following questions:

   A. Was the drawer difficult to remove? If yes, why?

   B. Is the length of the drawer and the length of both pieces of the drawer guide the same? What is each length?

   C. Measure the width of the opening for the drawer and measure the width of the drawer. Are they the same? Why?

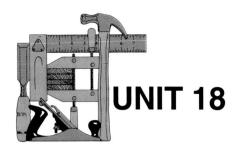

UNIT 18

CARVING

Seldom is it possible to enhance the beauty and worth of a product without a significant expense for materials, supplies, and tools. Caricature carving and chip carving each present such an opportunity. In this unit, you will be introduced to carving by providing the basics for figure carving and chip carving. After reading this unit, you will be able to identify basic tools, grips, design options, and also begin to appreciate the art of carving.

Many of you have observed both simple and complex carvings used to decorate furniture. Perhaps you enjoyed playing with a wooden carved toy figure of a dog or a bird. If you enjoy the outdoors, you may have decoys that have been carved from wood. Woodworkers for many years have used carvings to cause us to focus on certain details. Some people carry a small penknife and piece of wood in their pocket to keep active during their leisure moments throughout the day. Today, thousands of people—both men and women—are spending their leisure time carving. An entire industry has been created to provide special carving tools, accessories, and projects to carve. Hundreds of books have been written and a number of videos have been made to provide instruction and guidance for those interested in carving.

SAFETY

Throughout this unit, safe procedures are presented. You will also be alerted to potential hazards that could lead to injury. The following general suggestions should help you to carve safely:

1. Always keep your knife sharp.
2. Determine your cutting path before beginning your cut.
3. Always be mindful of where other parts of your body are in relationship to the cutting path of the knife.

4. Consider wearing a safety glove, leather thumb guard, or wrapping your fingers and/or your thumb with several layers of adhesive tape. See Fig. 18-1.
5. Never use your arm strength to make a cut.
6. Use masking tape to wrap the knife blade to reduce the length of the exposed blade.

TOOLS

Both chip carving and caricature carving use a very basic knife. Although many folding pocket knives work well, you should use a nonfolding knife (unless the blade locks), Fig. 18-2. The knife handle should be designed so it fits comfortably into your hand. See Fig. 18-3.

Fig. 18-1. A leather thumb guard or woodworker's glove helps to prevent personal injury if the carving knife slips. (Woodcraft Supply)

Fig. 18-2. Use a folding knife only if the blade locks into position. (Woodcraft Supply)

Fig. 18-3. Knife handles should fit comfortably into your hands. The knife at the top is a detail knife, which is used for shaping detail work. The knife at the bottom is a general-purpose carving knife. It is used for roughing out a shape, shaping, and general whittling. (Woodcraft Supply)

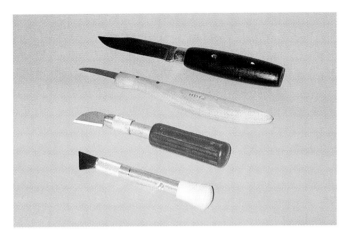

Fig. 18-4. A variety of knives may be used for carving. A sloyd knife is shown at the top. The bottom two knives are X-acto knives, which have been designed for carving. Note the blades and handles of each.

High carbon steel knife blades hold an edge better and longer than stainless steel blades. X-acto® knives may also be used successfully for carving. Fig. 18-4 shows an X-acto knife with a large handle and another that has been modified for a stabbing operation in chip carving. X-acto knife blades may be sharpened several times before they need to be replaced.

FIGURE CARVING

FIGURE CARVING, or CARICATURE CARVING, has provided joy and interest for people for hundreds of years. Often called WHITTLING, the product produced from a scrap of wood and a simple knife is not intended to be functional such as a cabinet or table. Rather, its purpose is fun and enjoyment. No expensive tools or materials are required. Whittling can be done almost anywhere and anytime you have a spare moment.

The wood required for figure carving should be large enough for you to lay out your design and easily hold and/or clamp. The grain structure should be tight and even. Basswood is a good choice for a beginner. If another wood is chosen, first look at the end grain. If you notice light and dark grain, you will find hard and soft areas as you whittle; this piece should be avoided. You should also begin your carving experience with a softwood rather than a hardwood.

When you choose your wood, also pay particular attention to the direction of the face grain. If the figure you are carving has a narrow feature, such as the leg of a horse, make sure the grain runs with the length of the leg.

Technique

Using a sketch that presents at least four views aids in laying out figures. The four minimum views would be front, back, top, and side. A second side and bottom may be helpful if there is a major shape change or detail not represented by the other views. With the design on paper, cut out each of the views and carefully trace them onto the wood block using a pencil. Make sure to orient each view properly–lay out the head on the head end and the tail on the tail end, etc. Also, watch for problems with the grain direction.

The pattern you have just traced is called the SILHOUETTE. Carefully consider all the lines you have drawn on the block of wood. Note any lines that should not be cut because detail or another face may be lost. Now remove as much of the waste wood as possible using a hand coping saw, jig saw, or band saw. This procedure is called ROUGHING OUT.

You may have to temporarily reattach certain pieces of the silhouette you have removed in order to have a flat surface to continue your rough cutting. Masking tape works well for this reattachment. Some traditional figures may be purchased in a roughed-out stage, thus saving you some time (but increasing the cost). After roughing out the figure, lay out your design again to use as a guide for carving.

Depending on size and design, you may be able to clamp your carving in a vise or mount it on a separate board for clamping. When learning to carve, you should consider these clamping options carefully. Many experienced carvers hold their work in their hands or between their knees. Be extremely careful when making cuts that could slip and injure yourself. Plan each of your cuts before making them. Consider where your hand, fingers, legs, knees, etc., are in relation to your planned cut. They should not be in the cutting path of the knife. A good safety rule to follow is to cut away from yourself as much as possible.

When whittling, two different types of cuts are normally utilized. The first is the PARING CUT. The paring cut is made in a manner similar to peeling an apple. The knife is gripped in the dominant hand (right hand for right-handed individuals, left for left-handed individuals) and pulled toward the thumb. The thumb should be well below the cutting path. The hand holding the wood should be clear of the cutting path as well. Only pressure from the hand is applied to the cut. No arm strength should be involved. Adding arm strength reduces accuracy and greatly increases the risk of the knife slipping and possibly causing injury.

The second cut is called a LEVERING CUT. The knife is again held in the dominant hand. The cutting edge of the blade is facing away from you. As the knife edge contacts the wood, the thumb of the opposite hand pushes and guides the blade as the knife is rotated in the hand. This procedure provides a great deal of control and is very safe.

When making roughing cuts with the knife, remove as much wood as possible without splitting the wood in front of the knife's cutting edge. When making finish cuts, the length of the cut should be about 1/4 or 3/8 inch long. Remember to use only hand pressure (no arm pressure) and determine the cutting path before making the cut.

CHIP CARVING

Chip carving is an old method of decorating wood products—the process is simple, fast, and very effective. Several of the products shown in Unit 22 can be enhanced and personalized using chip carving. Most chip carving is completed using a specially designed knife called a CHIP-CARVING KNIFE. Chip-carving knives have evolved to where only about 1 to 1 1/2 inches of the blade is exposed. You can wrap masking tape around a portion of this blade to allow only about 3/8 inch of the point to be exposed for safety. A second knife is utilized for making accents. This second knife is called a STAB KNIFE, Fig. 18-5.

DESIGN LAYOUT

Chip carving patterns may be either geometric designs or freeform designs, Fig. 18-6. Geometrical

Fig. 18-5. The upper knife is called a stab knife. The lower knife is a chip-carving knife. (Woodcraft Supply)

Fig. 18-6. Upper—Geometric design. Lower—Freeform design.

forms are laid out using a pencil, ruler, and a compass. Freeform designs, as the name implies, are created without the use of these tools. Practice making designs first on paper, then transfer your design to the wood. The design you make on paper may be cut out and traced onto the surface of the wood. If you are confident in your abilities, you can directly lay out the design on the wood using a pencil.

WOOD

When choosing a wood for chip carving, it is best to chose a straight, tight-grained wood that is not too dense. Basswood is an excellent wood for chip carving. White pine is also a good carving wood, but it may be a little more difficult for beginners. A slightly higher than normal moisture content in any wood allows for easier carving.

TECHNIQUE

Holding the chip-carving knife properly is essential for a successful design to be completed while also keeping safety in mind. There are two basic methods of holding or grasping the knife. The holding of the knife is also called the GRIP. The first grip is to place your thumb against the side of the handle close to the blade. Then wrap your fingers around the handle with the top of the handle resting in the palm of your hand as shown in Fig. 18-7.

The second grip for the chip-carving knife is simply moving your thumb to the top of the knife (unsharpened edge) called the SPINE, Fig. 18-8. Press down with the thumbprint portion of the knife with your thumb to make the cut. You will notice this second grip basically reversed the cutting angle, allowing you to cut in the opposite direction of the first grip.

With the knife properly positioned, place your workpiece firmly in your lap. Then place the end of your thumb and first knuckle of your index finger on the wood. The cutting edge of the knife should be facing you. Keep your elbow close to your side for better control. Remember that you should cut with your hand, not with your arm. Rotate the tip of the knife into the wood, increasing the depth in relationship to the width. The angle remains at 65 degrees throughout the cut and the inside of the thumb joint along with the index finger always stays in contact with the knife. This procedure allows for control and provides for safe cutting action.

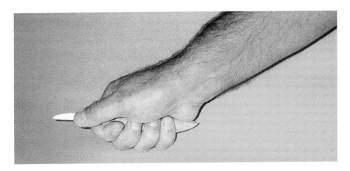

Fig. 18-7. The primary grip for a chip-carving knife. Hold the knife handle firmly.

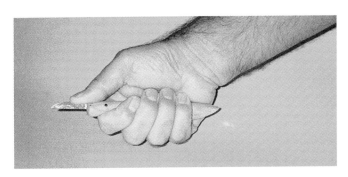

Fig. 18-8. Compare the position of the carver's hand in this photograph with the position of the carver's hand in Fig. 18-7.

While making the cuts, it is essential to maintain the same angle between the blade and the surface of the wood whether using the first grip or the second grip. The depth of the cut will always be determined by the width of the cut. The angle of the sides–whether cutting toward or away from yourself–remains the same. You should visualize where the center of the cut will be below the surface of the wood, and push the knife deeply enough to reach this center and still maintain the angle.

STRAIGHT CHIPS are basically a "V" cut (incised) into the surface of the wood. The first cut is made, then the wood is rotated, and a second cut then completes the "V." This technique is used for curved as well as straight lines. Remember to pull (draw) the knife smoothly with even pressure.

TRIANGULAR CHIPS are made in a similar manner as straight chips except that three separate cuts are required. Normally, the grip is alternated from the first grip to the second grip and then back to the first grip to reduce the rotation of the stock. The recess made by this cut is called a TRIFACETED HOLE.

Whenever possible, new cuts should be completed in a single motion and away from completed cuts.

This technique will make the carving sharper in appearance and avoid damage to the completed work due to a slip of the knife. Since the knife widens away from the point of the blade, it is often necessary to raise the handle to allow for turning a radius. This need may also occur when the grain changes direction. Remember to maintain your thumb and index finger position on the knife and to maintain the 65 degree angle.

The stab knife is held in a "jabbing" grip with the blade being pressed straight into the wood. This knife is used primarily for recesses other than those that can be cut with the chip-carving knife. The stab knife does not remove material, it simply makes recesses in the wood.

SHARPENING

If you notice the edges of your cuts are no longer sharp and crisp, it is probably time to sharpen your knife. Another indication of a dulling knife is that additional pressure is required to make the cut. Remember sharp tools are safer! They require less force, are easier to control, and present less chance of slippage. Sharp tools make crisp, clean cuts.

Seldom is a grinding procedure necessary for a carving tool. Most carving knives may be effectively sharpened using a hone as shown in Fig. 18-9. Several different types of hones are commonly used. The INDIA STONE and the ARKANSAS STONE both require oil as a lubricant to remove the fine pieces of metal removed during sharpening. A third type of stone, the CERAMIC STONE, cuts dry (requires no lubricant) and may not require any stropping.

A STROP is a strip of leather attached to a piece of wood. A fine abrasive such as white jeweler's rouge, aluminum oxide powder, or yellow strop compound is often rubbed onto the leather surface. The knife is then "stropped" back and forth to remove any burr left by the honing process. When honing and stropping a knife, the blade is pulled first in one direction a number of times (ten times, for example) then in the opposite direction the same number of times. This procedure keeps the edge of the blade centered. The angle for sharpening is extremely important. For a chip-carving knife, the blade is nearly flat against the hone or strop producing about a 10 degree angle. For a stab knife, the angle is increased to 30 degrees.

Fig. 18-9. Using a hone to sharpen a carving knife. (Woodcraft Supply)

TEST YOUR KNOWLEDGE, UNIT 18

Please do not write in this text. Place your answers on a separate sheet of paper.

1. A chip-carving design is difficult to lay out on the wood's surface. True or False?
2. List three tools used to lay out a geometric design for chip carving.
3. Name two knives that are used for chip carving.
4. What wood is the best for both figure carving and chip carving?
5. For the beginner, what other woods will work well for figure carving?
6. What is the normal length of the blade exposed from the handle of a chip-carving knife?
7. Define the term "silhouette."
8. Describe how triangular chips are made when wood carving.
9. List three types of stones that can be used to sharpen carving knives.
10. Define the term "strop."

ACTIVITIES

1. Bring into class catalogs, brochures, or magazines containing pictures of carvings used on furniture or figures that have been carved from wood. If you have permission to cut out the pictures, make a poster for display in the classroom.
2. List the characteristics of a good carving wood. Using an outline map of the United States, indicate where these woods may be found.
3. Prepare several sketches of a design that might be used for the top of a jewelry box.

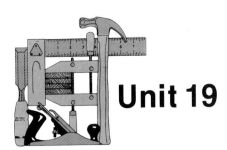

Unit 19

AUTOMATED MANUFACTURING

Many aspects of our everyday lives have become mechanized and automated. Automation allows identical parts to be made with very little input from an operator. After reading this unit, you will be able to trace the history of automated manufacturing. In addition, you will be able to define basic acronyms (words formed with the first letter of a series of words) used in automated manufacturing.

HISTORY OF AUTOMATED MANUFACTURING

Machinery that performs certain procedures repetitively with a minimal amount of input on the part of the operator is referred to as being AUTOMATED. An automated machine can be very simple, performing only one specialized operation, Fig. 19-1. An automated machine can also be very complex, performing several hundred related tasks in a short amount of time.

The first automated machine was developed in 1725 in England for the purpose of knitting. This machine performed simple knitting operations faster and with greater uniformity than could be accomplished by a person. This particular machine was controlled by a card that had holes punched in it. The card was "read" by the machine, instructing it what to perform next.

An automatic loom was developed in the early 1800s by M.J. Jacquard. These looms used a card with a series of holes punched in it to automatically produce a uniform pattern in carpets and fabrics.

Another type of automated machine was developed in 1863 for entertainment purposes.

Fig. 19-1. Multiple spindle drill press creates rows of holes for cabinet construction. (Riviera Cabinets)

The player piano, as it became known, utilized a removable roll of paper with holes punched across its width. When the roll of paper was installed in a modified piano, the piano would sound notes based on where the holes were punched in the tape.

Inventors soon realized the advantages of using an automated manufacturing system. In addition to hiring fewer employees to perform unskilled tasks, the quality of the end product was also much better.

167

At the same time, inventors were also developing jigs and fixtures to help in the manufacturing process. JIGS are devices that hold the part to be machined, and also positions and holds the cutting tool. FIXTURES are devices that position and hold a part, but do not actually guide the cutting tool. See Fig. 19-2.

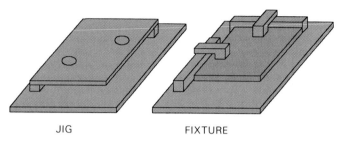

JIG   FIXTURE

Fig. 19-2. Jigs position and hold the part, and also guide the cutting tool. Fixtures position and hold the part, but do not guide the tool.

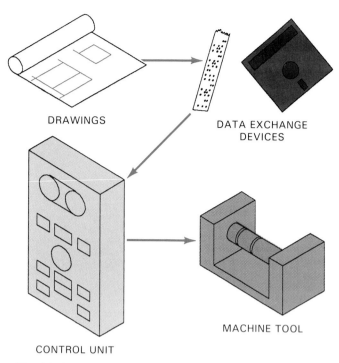

DRAWINGS   DATA EXCHANGE DEVICES

CONTROL UNIT   MACHINE TOOL

Fig. 19-3. A numeral control system includes a data exchange device, control unit, and some type of machine tool.

These jigs and fixtures led to the American system of interchangeable parts. Prior to this time, each part was custom made to fit the product being manufactured. If a new part was required, it would need to be specially made for that product. A product made of interchangeable parts allowed a person to use a "stock" item, rather than having a part custom made.

During World War II, the need for machined parts became so great that skilled machine operators could not meet the demand. Mass production and automated manufacturing allowed companies to produce materials for the war effort in large quantities, and at a minimal cost. At the same time, hydraulic and pneumatic devices were being incorporated into the standard machines to increase productivity. Electric (not electronic) switches and controls were added to increase production even more.

As a result of this demand and the increasing need for precision parts, the Massachusetts Institute of Technology (MIT) began working with the concept of NUMERICAL CONTROL (NC). The result was a machine controlled by a paper tape containing small punched holes or some other means of data communication. See Fig. 19-3. These holes indicated the axial movement of the machine. The first numerically controlled machines were modified hand-operated milling machines. These machines were able to be con-

trolled in three separate directions, or axes, at the same time. Although these machines could perform certain tasks very well, they were very expensive and required specially trained operators and technicians. MIT even developed a special machine language to "talk" to these machines. This language was known as AUTOMATICALLY PROGRAMMED TOOLS, or APT.

Computer development in the 1960s and 1970s allowed engineers to develop a system of controls that directly connected the computer to the machine, eliminating the need for punch tape or cards. This process became known as DIRECT NUMERICAL CONTROL (DNC). The use of the computer allowed for rapid program changes and provided for better storage of previous programs. See Fig. 19-4.

Since the invention and development of the microprocessor (small computer chip), machines now can be controlled with smaller computers. This process is called COMPUTER NUMERICAL CONTROL (CNC). The microprocessor allows for faster programming and increased accuracy. See Fig. 19-5. It has reduced the cost of equipment control, permitting use by even small manufacturing operations. Not only are these CNC machines easy to use, but they can also be adapted to a variety of machines.

Fig. 19-4. A direct numerically controlled lathe.
(Light Machines Corp.)

Today, many cabinet shops have CNC routers that perform complex operations rapidly and accurately, Fig. 19-6. Saws are equipped with CNC controls that quickly determine what cuts are to be made to receive the maximum usable amount of lumber from a board. Lathes equipped with CNC controls can duplicate a variety of different shapes in a short amount of time.

COMPONENTS OF AN AUTOMATED MANUFACTURING SYSTEM

An automated manufacturing system goes far beyond the walls of a shop floor. Tasks, such as bookkeeping, scheduling of materials, design and engineering, and shipping are important parts of an automated manufacturing system.

Each of these areas is interdependent on the other areas. If the scheduling of when the raw materials are to be received is done incorrectly, tasks such as manufacturing and shipping will also be affected. There must be excellent communication between all areas that are involved in the automated manufacturing facility.

One area that has received a great deal of attention in recent years is COMPUTED-AIDED DRAFTING (CAD). A computer system can handle the development of a product, from its inception all the way to engineering changes that might be made in the manufacturing process. A CAD system not only allows for the drawing of a product, but also allows a product to be designed and tested. Critical flaws can be detected before the product is manufactured on the shop floor. In Fig. 19-6, the design generated on the CAD system is input into the control unit. The piece of stock on the bed is then routed based on the design.

The design of a product creates a database of information that is important to many aspects of an automated manufacturing system. An estimator can figure out how much material must be purchased to manufacture the product. An accountant can determine the cost of the product by figuring out the amount of time and capital (money) that is required to manufacture the product. The manufacturing facility can also use this database to determine which machines will be required for production, as well as how the machines should be set up. The machine operators will need to make very few adjustments

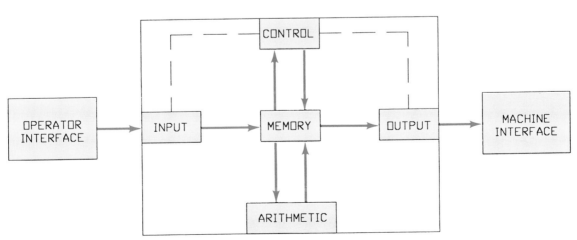

Fig. 19-5. CNC components. The operator interface allows a person to input commands or information to the control unit (the second component). The final component, the machine interface, carries out the commands and performs the functions.

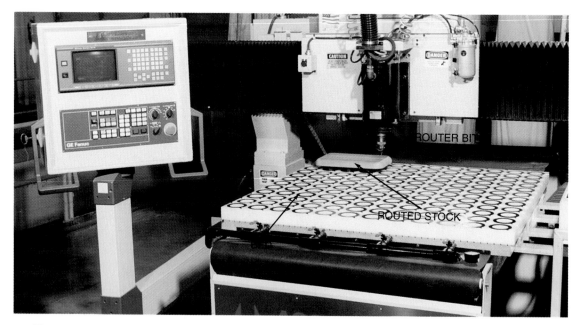

Fig. 19-6. The piece of stock on the bed is routed based on the design developed on a CAD system. (Accu-Router, Inc.)

to the equipment when all of the information has been received and the machines have been initially set up.

The computerized linking of numerically controlled manufacturing systems to computer-aided design equipment is known as CAD/CAM. This term denotes a fully computerized system of design and manufacture. If this computerized system actually controls the production of a product or assembly from design through manufacture, it is often referred to as COMPUTER-INTEGRATED MANUFACTURING (CIM). See Fig. 19-7.

Fig. 19-7. A computer-integrated manufacturing setup. (Accu-Router, Inc.)

IMPORTANCE OF AUTOMATED MANUFACTURING

How important is automated manufacturing? Today, almost every item we use is made using some type of automation. The lack of automation would affect essential items such as housing, furniture, and clothing costs, as well as drastically increase the price of food.

Automation will not eliminate skilled jobs in manufacturing and construction. Many jobs that are done using automation can be done by an individual, but frequently people are not available to do the job or do not want the job due to its mundane nature. Someone must operate the automated machines. The operator must not only be skilled in using the equipment, but also be knowledgeable in the entire CIM process. A person should also have a good knowledge of wood technology and woodworking procedures to create a product that resembles the design.

TEST YOUR KNOWLEDGE, Unit 19

Please do not write in this text. Place your answers on a separate sheet of paper.

1. What task did the earliest automated machine perform?
2. Jigs and fixtures led to the American system of interchangeable parts. Discuss the roles that jigs and fixtures played in the development of automated manufacturing.
3. What is the name of the machine language developed by MIT?
4. The process of controlling machines from a computer is called _____.
5. Numerically controlled machines travel in specified directions called _____.
6. Define the following acronyms:

APT	CAD/CAM
CNC	MIT
NC	DNC
CAD	CIM

ACTIVITIES

1. Look up the terms "automated machines," "automated manufacturing," "numerical control," "computer-aided design," "computer-aided manufacturing," and "computer-integrated manufacturing," at your library. Make a list of five articles or books that are listed for these terms.
   A. Did you find other terms that are similar to these terms? What were they?
   B. What types of equipment were discussed?
   C. Was any of the equipment used for woodworking? Describe these machines.
   D. Did any of the references discuss a language or code system used to communicate with the NC machines? What were these languages or codes?

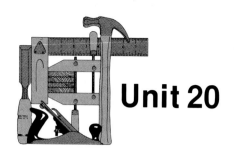

Unit 20

ENTREPRENEURSHIP, MANUFACTURING ENTERPRISE

Each day, you make contact with many different kinds of businesses. Some businesses provide a SERVICE. Businesses involved in the service industry provide a service, such as a hospital caring for people or an auto technician that repairs your car. Other businesses provide a PRODUCT, such as a cabinetmaker that makes and sells cabinets and furniture. Still other businesses provide a SERVICE AND PRODUCT. A restaurant is an example of a business that provides services and products. After studying this unit, you will be able to describe the role of an entrepreneur as he or she manages a business to meet its goals and purposes. In addition, you will be able to recognize the importance of making a profit from meeting a company's objectives, rather than being its sole objective.

Every business enterprise does not exist simply for its own good, but rather to fulfill a suspected need. Businesses must have a goal (purpose) to give the employees some direction. Meeting these goals or purposes means that there will be some type of results. If a business is successful in meeting its goals, it is generally referred to as "making a profit." What exactly is "profit"? PROFIT is not the goal of the business, but rather a result of its goals and purpose. Profit is a type of a test–a test of performance. It tells us about the success of the business enterprise. In addition, profit is a reward for effort and risk.

A person that is concerned with a company's goals by managing resources is called an ENTREPRENEUR. An entrepreneur is more than a boss or an owner. He or she is concerned with careful management of a business' resources. Resources are used by a business to meet its goals, and thereby show a profit.

RESOURCES

What are a company's resources? When you think of resources, you generally think of money. MONEY is an important resource for any business but it is not the only resource. Any business enterprise must also consider the EQUIPMENT or MACHINES, MATERIALS, and PERSONNEL. You must clearly understand these other three resources to have a successful business. When considering equipment, you must understand what tooling is available, as well as the condition and capability of each item. You must ask yourself whether the different pieces of equipment work together or do they need modification to function in a manufacturing cell. Is there an operation that can best be performed on one particular machine? Are there other machines that can perform the same task?

What kinds of material are available? Often materials must be ordered before a manufacturing operation can begin. How long is the period of time from placing an order until you can expect delivery? This is called LEAD TIME. Is there going to be a storage problem when the materials arrive? Do they have to be paid for immediately? What is the expected condition of the raw materials upon arrival?

People are also important when considering resources. What is the work force? Are they skilled or unskilled? Are they consistently available? What is their cost? What types of working conditions must be maintained?

A potential company resource you may have to develop are its customers. You must produce a product that meets a customer's need. You may have an available market population that is ready and waiting for the product, but more often the customers must be created. You have to present your product, along with its features, advantages, and benefits in an effort to convince your customer of the need for your product. Often a small number of products are produced and marketed (sold) to a select group. This process is called TEST MARKETING. If the response is positive, the product sells. Additional products are then manufactured and more customers are sought.

Money in a business is either a resource or the result of successfully meeting the company's goals. As a resource, money can be used to purchase time by buying a portion of the product in its final form, by hiring additional employees or extending their working time, or perhaps even purchasing additional machines and equipment. However, money is also profit–the reward for meeting the businesses' goals and purposes. The real profit (or loss) of an enterprise can only be projected after the enterprise activity ceases. Some companies issue a profit statement even though their activity has not ceased. This profit statement is then based upon a specific time frame within the life of the company. This statement could be issued annually, quarterly, or even weekly. Remember, profit is not the cause of a business enterprise, but rather the result. Most businesses project a profit based upon anticipated sales and costs of resources.

Money is a resource that is a constant consideration of the entrepreneur. If a ready supply of money to pay for supplies, personnel salaries, equipment costs, etc., is not available, a "cash flow" problem may be occurring. Additional money and financing may be necessary.

FINANCING

Financing a business may be accomplished in several different manners. The owner of the business may wish to INVEST his or her own money. This will give the owner all of the profit, but also all of the risk of losing the investment. The owner may wish to borrow additional funds. These funds would then be called a LOAN. A loan requires the person or business borrowing

the money to repay the principle along with a fee for the use of the money for a specific time period. This fee is called INTEREST. The LENDER (person loaning the money) does not receive any of the company's profit, but only the interest on the money loaned. If your business cannot repay the loan on time with the interest, the loan is said to be in DEFAULT. The lender can then legally require payment of the loan and interest. The business may have to sell its products at a loss, dispose of some of its equipment, lay off some of the workforce, etc., to make payment. If the business' resources are less than the money owed, the business may have to go out of business.

Businesses are often financed by the suppliers of the raw materials. If a quantity of lumber is purchased and delivered with payment to be made 30 days after delivery, the business can manufacture and sell its product without making any payment to the supplier for 30 days. Payment must be made after 30 days, however.

The most common method of financing a business is by investors. An investor places a certain amount of money with a business. The investor receives a SHARE of the business for this investment. The investor is then called a SHAREHOLDER. The shareholder "shares" in the profits of the enterprise, and also "shares" in the risks of the business. If the company profits, the shareholder profits. If the company loses, the value of the share is reduced. Normally, shares are offered to interested investors for a specific amount of money per share. This value of the share can increase or decrease as a result of the expected profit or loss of the company.

To be an effective entrepreneur, a person must understand the relationships each of the resources has with one another. Every employee of the company, called the WORKFORCE, has the right to know what his responsibilities are in the manufacturing and sales of the product. Therefore, each job is clearly defined by listing skills, operations, times, and expected pay. A person can then apply for any position that is available.

Likewise, the role of each piece of equipment must be described for the product being manufactured. When the interaction of relationships are graphically shown the graph is called a FLOWCHART. The entrepreneur must the flowchart for the most efficient manufacture of the product.

TEST MARKETING

Products are often test marketed and believed to be a salable product, yet the product is rejected by the customer. When a product is not accepted by a customer the customers' objections must be determined. If it is determined that the quality of the product is less than that of the sample or less than expected, quality control efforts may become necessary to overcome the customer's objection.

Several considerations must be made to successfully test market a product. A sample of the product must be made. The sample should be representative of the finished product. When the product is marketed is extremely important. If a product has a holiday theme, such as a greeting card holder, it should not be marketed during January or February, but rather during October or early November. Determining the potential customer is also important. Friends and relatives will nearly always purchase a product you are manufacturing whether or not they need the item. You must test market the product outside the home and school environment. Some products sell very well when marketing "door to door," but if displayed for sale at a basketball game, no sales would be made.

The individuals in the selling force are extremely important. They must know the product. They should have necessary sales literature, order blanks and receipts readily available. Much of the success in sales are the sellers and their knowledge of the product. A positive appearance and attitude are needed for successful sales. Many salespersons receive most, if not all, of their pay from commissions. A COMMISSION is an amount of money, often a percentage, for the sale of each item. If a salesperson does not sell the product they receive no compensation. Good salespeople practice their sales pitches. The SALES PITCH is the verbal communication the salesperson uses to convince the customers of their need for the product.

The business manager or treasurer are very important people in a successful enterprise. These people control and record all money transactions. The business manager should know if the materials are being billed at the stated price and if the sale price of the completed product is being received. This person can immediately notify the entrepreneur of any problems that may be occurring with the cash flow before they get out of hand.

The entrepreneur must make many decisions regarding money during the business enterprise. One of the most difficult decisions is the purchase of additional tooling. If your business is going to make wooden toys for Christmas gifts, one of the parts will be wheels. There are a number of cutters that will fit in a drill press or a router to accurately and quickly make wheels of different sizes. The entrepreneur must decide whether it is the best use of resources to buy the special cutter or to buy the wheels ready-made. If the entrepreneur buys the cutter, he or she has to train an operator, be concerned with quality control, worry about time, in addition to the cost of the cutter.

MANUFACTURING ACTIVITY

The manufacturing activity discussed in this unit may be changed to meet local conditions and restrictions.

The procedure to follow when setting up a typical business enterprise is as follows:

1. Establish a Company
   A. Determine name
   B. Determine officers to be elected
   C. Specify proposed goals and purposes
   D. State location
   E. Establish time frame
2. Develop a List of Proposed Products
   A. List required resources for each proposed product
   B. Determine the projected market
   C. Estimate cost of manufacture
   D. Establish the projected selling price
3. Finance Enterprise
   A. Sell shares, obtain a loan, etc.
   B. Hire business manager or place funds with the treasurer
   C. Order materials and supplies
   D. Activate sales force
4. Design Manufacturing Sequence
   A. Determine tools

B. Assign tasks to workforce

C. Manufacture product

5. Deliver product

6. Determine actual costs of products and resulting profit

7. Distribute profit to shareholders after payment of all loans and outstanding bills

8. Dissolve company

Decide on Product

At your first meeting (with your instructor serving as advisor) you should decide on the product to be manufactured. Selecting the tested product covered later in this Unit is suggested.

Determine Company Name

The name selected should be appropriate, businesslike, and not too long. Since this is a class activity in which all students are expected to participate, each member of the class should make an effort to come up with a good name for the new company which is being organized.

Each class member should write one or more names on a slip of paper. The slips should be collected, proposed names discussed, and a vote taken to determine which company name is to be used.

Do not include the term "Incorporated," or "Corporation" after the company name. Each of these is a legal term that can be used only in cases where a state charter has been obtained.

Company Officials

If your company is to be successful, it must be operated in an efficient, businesslike manner. This means you will need capable company officials, also capable workers. It is suggested that you elect:

1. General Manager

2. Office Manager

3. Purchasing Agent

4. Sales Manager

5. Safety Director

Duties of the company officials (as described in the following paragraphs) should be discussed before holding an election.

General Manager. Your General Manager will be expected to:

1. Exercise general supervision over entire activity.

2. Train workers; assign workers to jobs.

3. Check on, and be responsible for product quality and manufacturing efficiency.

4. Authorize bills to be paid by Office Manager; authorize purchase orders before making purchases.

5. Prepare and submit reports as required by your Advisor (Instructor).

6. Cooperate with your Advisor, and other company officials.

Office Manager. The Office Manager should:

1. Maintain attendance records. Check absentees for valid excuses.

2. Keep company's financial records (8 1/2 x 11 loose leaf notebook suggested).

3. Keep a record of all money received on RECEIPTS page of record book, Fig. 20-1.

4. All cash receipts should be deposited in a local bank and a checking account should be established.

5. Pay all bills, invoices previously authorized by your General Manager, by writing

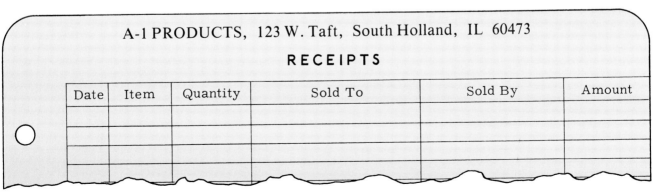

Fig. 20-1. Manufacturing activity records–cash receipts.

checks. Make a complete record in your checkbook, which shows date and amount of money deposited in checking account and checks written. Show balance–amount in bank, after each check is written. See Fig. 20-2. Be sure your figures are accurate because this is the only record your company has of the cash on hand.

6. Keep stock sales and ownership records.
7. Cooperate with your Advisor and other company officials.

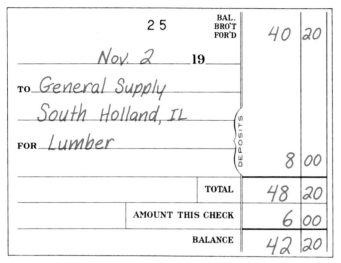

Fig. 20-2. Manufacturing activity records–checkbook record of bills paid.

Purchasing Agent. The Purchasing Agent should:

1. Check with Advisor relative to materials and supplies needed to manufacture product selected.
2. Arrange to have printed, or run off on school duplicator, stock certificates, purchase orders, and other forms needed.
3. Have purchase orders authorized by General Manager before issuing order.
4. Obtain materials required from school stock or purchase from outside source.

5. Cooperate with Advisor and other company officials.

Sales Manager. The Sales Manager should:
1. Help decide on how product is to be packaged, and provide instructions on product use, to include in the package.
2. Plan sales program; help decide on price to charge for product, where and how product is to be sold.
3. Cooperate with Advisor and other company officials.

Safety Director. The Safety Director should:
1. Enforce safety rules.
2. Stop all horseplay and call attention to undesirable conduct.
3. Be alert to hazards.
4. Take steps to eliminate possible accident causes.
5. See to it that equipment and tools are in good operating condition.
6. Check to make sure machine guards are in place and students are using eye protection and protective clothing as specified by Advisor.
7. If someone is injured, even slightly, contact Advisor immediately.
8. Cooperate with Advisor and other company officials.

Raising Capital

In operating your new business, you will need money (capital) to pay bills until you start taking in cash from the sale of your product. Most corporations raise money by selling stock to the public. It is suggested you do the same.

Getting stock certificates printed, and keeping the necessary records, is the responsibility of your Office Manager. See Fig. 20-3.

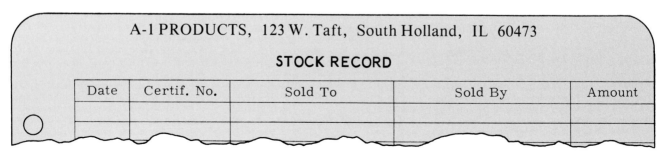

Fig. 20-3. Manufacturing activity–stock ownership record.

STOCK CERTIFICATE

A–1 PRODUCTS
South Holland, IL

One Share

Par Value 50¢

Certificate Number

_____

Redeemable Within
One Year After Issue

Date Issued

_____

This Certifies That (please print)

_____

First Name   Initial   Last Name

_____

Street Address   City   State   Zip

Is the Owner of One Share, Par Value 50¢, of the stock of A–1 Products.

_____   _____
Stockholder's Signature   for A–1 Products

Stockholder by signature, okays operation of Company by Student Officials elected by Student Stockholders.

Fig. 20-4. Stock certificate form suggestions.

Let's assume that you need $40.00. This may be raised by selling 80 shares of stock at $.50 each. See Fig. 20-4 for a suggested Stock Certificate form.

This should be run off on a duplicating machine on two different colors of stock . . . 100 copies of each, yellow and white suggested. Number the certificates 1 to 100.

Each student will be expected to purchase a share of stock at $.50. When starting to sell stock (on your own time) it is a good idea to make your first sale to yourself. Using a ball point pen and carbon paper, fill out the stock certificate form in duplicate, with the white copy on top. On the share you sell to yourself sign in two places, where the stockholder's signature is required, and as a representative of your company. Keep the white copy. Turn in the yellow copy (carbon) and the $.50 to your Office Manager. It is that person's job to keep an accurate record of stock sales, and to see to it that the cash turned in is deposited in the bank. See Fig. 20-5.

It is suggested you limit stock sales to one share per customer. The stock should be divided so that each student has approximately the same

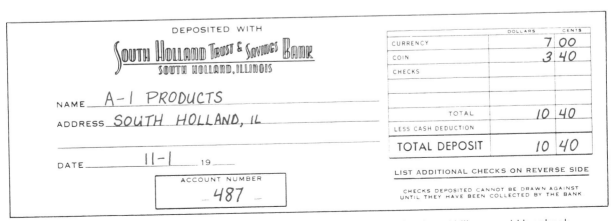

Fig. 20-5. All cash received from product sales is deposited in the bank and bills are paid by check.

177

number of shares to sell. When contacting prospective purchasers–local business men, parents, neighbors, friends, be businesslike. Describe your company and its operations briefly. Be enthusiastic. Try to give your prospect the impression she or he is buying a share in a GOING BUSINESS, and is *not* "donating to charity." Explain that you cannot guarantee results in advance, but that your company expects to operate profitably and when the business is closed out to redeem the stock at full par value ($.50 per share) and pay a small dividend.

After a share of stock has been sold, fill out the stock certificate as was described. Be sure to print. Ask your purchaser to read the certificate to make sure everything is understood and is agreeable, then ask the buyer to sign. Hand the top (white) copy to your purchaser. As you leave don't forget to say "thank you" (like you really mean it.)

Establishing a Projected Selling Price

In establishing a selling price for your product, it is suggested you determine the total cost per item, then add to this about 25%. The extra 25% is to cover the cost of material wasted, and to pay a dividend to stockholders when the business is closed out.

Each student participating in the project (all are stockholders) is expected to help sell the company's product. If the product selected is small, such as the item described in this unit, you will probably find it advisable to make up the products in advance so you can provide "on the spot" delivery.

Keep an accurate record of all sales–quantity sold, name of customer, and amount collected. Turn these records and the cash collected over to your Office Manager for handling.

Manufacturing in the Woods Laboratory

One project for mass production with proven student interest and sales is the candy dispenser, Fig. 20-6.

Mass Producing the Candy Dispenser

Each candy dispenser is made from one piece of 3/4-inch white pine measuring 8-inches wide and 14-inches long, and a one-pint canning jar with a lid band. This product can be made either

Fig. 20-6. Candy dispensers used for the manufacturing enterprise.

using hand tools (as with the square example), or with power tools (as with the round example). It can be naturally finished, stained, or painted. The dispenser slide can be adapted to fit a variety of candy pieces less than 1/2-inch diameter. The working drawing for the square candy dispenser is shown in Fig. 20-7.

Hand Tool Method

1. Lay out 14-inch (1′-2″) lengths of the 1 x 8 white pine using a rule and square. Use a hand saw to cut the pine, using care in cutting these pieces square.
2. Lay out a one-inch wide piece along one side of the 14-inch board. Cut this piece from the 1 x 8 using a rip saw, being careful to follow the line. Fig. 20-8 shows a stock cutting list layout for this product.
5. Lay out the 5, 4, and 3 1/2 inch marks carefully on the remaining stock. Square these measurements off.
6. Use the back saw to cut each of the pieces in step 3 to size.
7. Use a hand plane (jack or smooth plane for the edges and block plane for the ends) to square each piece according to plan. One piece is 5-inches square, another is 4-inches square, and the last is 3 1/2-inches square. The 1 x 12 should also be carefully smoothed.
8. Use the marking gauge to lay out a 1/4-inch chamfer around the perimeter of the 4- and 5-inch pieces. Use a hand plane to accurately cut the chamfer. (This step can be omitted if the edges are to be routed.)

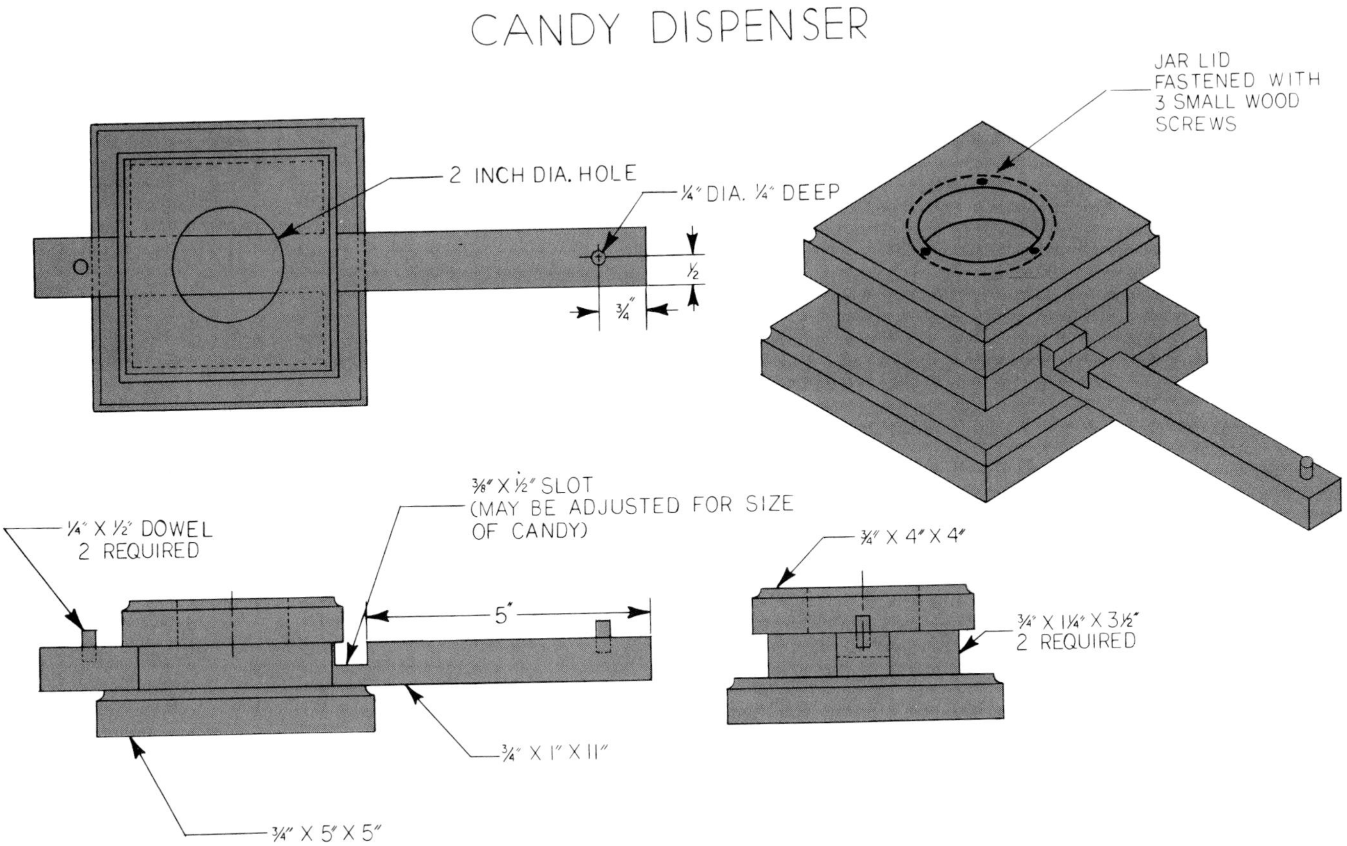

CANDY DISPENSER

2 INCH DIA. HOLE

¼″ DIA. ¼″ DEEP

½

¾″

JAR LID
FASTENED WITH
3 SMALL WOOD
SCREWS

⅜″ X ½″ SLOT
(MAY BE ADJUSTED FOR SIZE
OF CANDY)

¼″ X ½″ DOWEL
2 REQUIRED

5″

¾″ X 1″ X 11″

¾″ X 5″ X 5″

¾″ X 4″ X 4″

¾″ X 1¼″ X 3½″
2 REQUIRED

Fig. 20-7. Working drawings for the square-design candy dispenser.

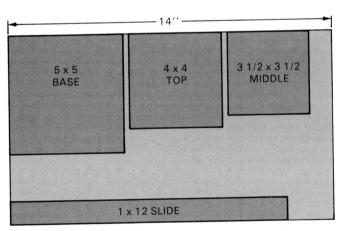

14″

5 x 5
BASE

4 x 4
TOP

3 1/2 x 3 1/2
MIDDLE

1 x 12 SLIDE

Fig. 20-8. Stock cutting layout for use with the candy dispenser.

Fig. 20-9. Mark the center of the 4-inch part.

9. Lay out and cut the 3 1/2-inch piece into three separate pieces. The two outside pieces should be 1 1/4-inches wide. This cut should be a ripping cut, not a crosscut. The center piece can be discarded.

10. Lay out and mark the center of the 4-inch part. Mark the center with an awl, Fig. 20-9. Use an expansive bit mounted in a bit brace to bore a two-inch diameter hole through it using the center marked by the awl.

11. If a router is to be used, select a router design for the edges of the 4-inch and 5-inch parts. Mount the pieces in a vise or on the table top, and rout the edges. (This step can be omitted if the edges are chamfered.)

Assembly

1. Lay the 5-inch part on the bench. Place the 1 x 12-inch piece across this part, approximately

centered. Use the hot glue gun to attach the two 1 1/4 x 3 1/2 inch pieces to the 5-inch piece, using the 1 x 12 as a guide.

2. Leave the 1 x 12 in place and attach the 4-inch square piece to the two 1 1/2 x 3 1/2 inch pieces using adhesive. Keep the 1 x 12 with this assembly as other 1 x 12 pieces may not fit.

3. Cut two pieces of 1/4-inch diameter dowel about 3/4-inch long. Sand one end of each

piece to remove the burrs. Glue the dowels into place using white glue.

Finishing

1. Identify each assembly and its slide with a different number or letter. This should be done lightly in a location that will not show after final assembly.

2. Use 80 to 120 grit abrasive paper to custom fit the slide to the assembly. Allow enough

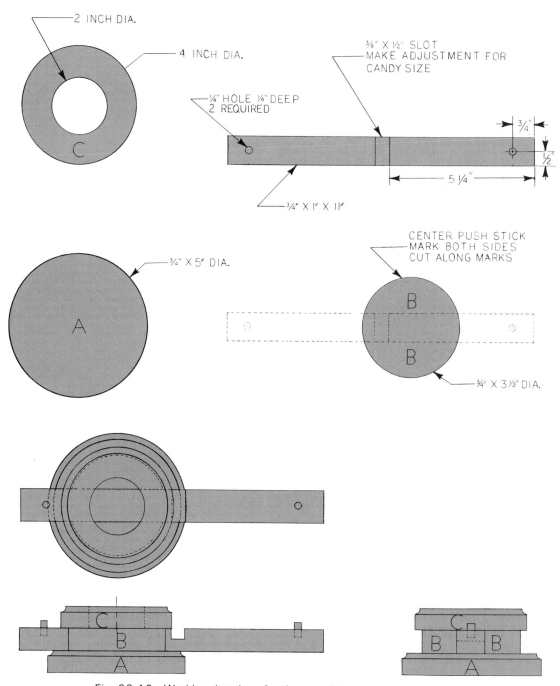

Fig. 20-10. Working drawings for the round-design candy dispenser.

clearance for the chosen finish to be applied.
3. Sand the entire project with progressively finer paper starting with 120 grit and ending with 180 grit.
4. Wipe the saw dust from assembly and slide using a tack rag.
5. Apply desired finish, making sure it is not a lead-based finish.

Attaching the Jar
1. Place the jar lid band on top of the 4-inch piece carefully spacing it around the 2-inch hole. Use an awl to punch three holes equally spaced through the lid band into the top of the assembly.
2. Use three 3/8 inch x No. 4 wood screws to attach the lid band to the assembly.
3. Mount the jar onto the assembly. Test the slide using the desired candy.

Power Tool Method
The square-design candy dispenser can also be made using power tools. However, a round design, as shown in Fig. 20-10, will be utilized when using power tools to construct it. The procedure for making the square-design candy dispenser is different than the one used for making the round design.

1. Lay out 14-inch (1'-2") lengths of the 1 x 8 white pine using a rule and square. Use a table saw or radial arm saw to cut the pine, using care in cutting these pieces square.
2. Lay out a one-inch wide piece along one side of the 14-inch board. Cut this piece from the 1 x 8 using the table saw. See Fig. 20-8 for the stock cutting layout.
3. Lay out a dado in the 1 x 12 to accept the desired candy size. Cut a dado across the center slightly larger than the candy size.
4. Lay out the 1/4-inch diameter holes at each end of the 1 x 12 piece. Use the depth guide on the drill bit. Drill the holes 1/4-inch deep using the drill press.
5. Lay out the 5, 4, and 3 1/2 inch marks carefully on the remaining stock. Square these measurements off.
6. Use the band saw or jigsaw to cut the top, base, and middle pieces in step 3 to size.
7. Lay out the center of each of the pieces, as shown in Fig. 20-11. Mark this center using

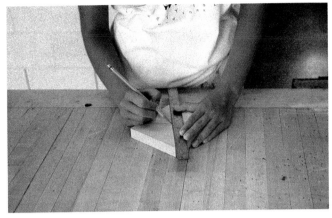

Fig. 20-11. Lay out the center of each of the pieces.

an awl. Make sure the indentation is deep enough to accept the pivot point in step 9.
8. Construct a simple circle-cutting jig mounted to the miter gauge groove of the band saw. See Fig. 20-12.

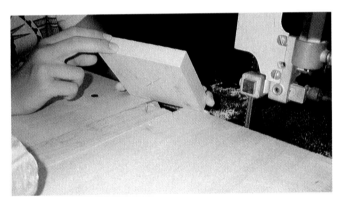

Fig. 20-12. Construct a simple circle-cutting jig.

9. Place the mark made by the awl on top of the pivot point of the circle-cutting jig and cut out a circle from each piece. See Fig. 20-13. Make sure the stock is flush with the

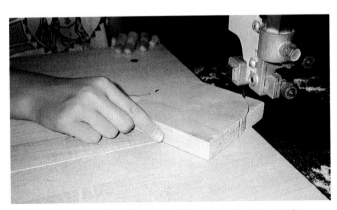

Fig. 20-13. Cut the round pieces using the circle-cutting jig.

table. If it is "wobbling" on the table, make the pivot indentation deeper. The 5-inch piece should yield a 5-inch diameter circle, the 4-inch piece should yield a 4-inch diameter circle, and the 3 1/2-inch piece should yield a 3 1/2-inch diameter circle.

10. When all of the circles have been cut, move the circle-cutting jig to the disk sander and sand all the circles using the awl mark as a guide. See Fig. 20-14.

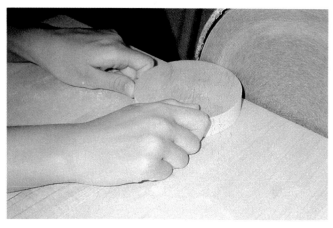

Fig. 20-14. Use the circle-cutting jig to sand the edges.

11. Design a jig similar to the one shown in Fig. 20-15 to cut the 3 1/2-inch diameter circles into half moons. These will form the center section of the main assembly. The jig shown will work on either the radial arm saw or the table saw with slight modification.

12. Select a router bit and set up the router to cut the desired design on the 5- and 4-inch pieces. The pieces can be held in place on plastic laminate using a spot of hot glue, Fig. 20-16. Rout each piece, moving the

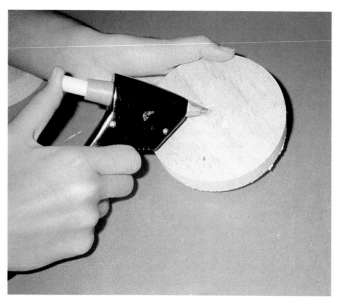

Fig. 20-16. Use hot melt glue to attach the parts to plastic laminate.

router in a counterclockwise direction. Keep the router moving to reduce burning and eliminate most of the sanding. See Fig. 20-17.

13. Use a screwdriver to carefully pry off the parts from the laminated plastic, Fig. 20-18.

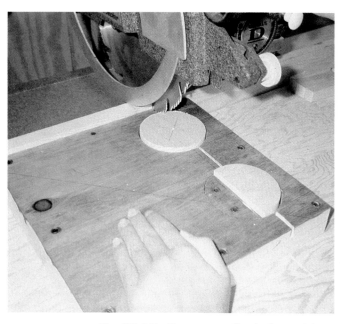

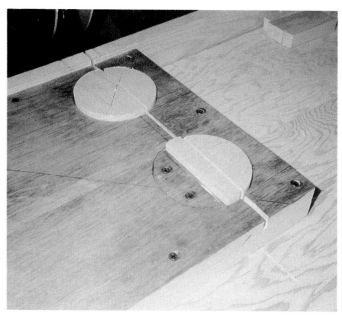

Fig. 20-15. Construct a jig similar to this one to cut the 3 1/2-inch pieces into half moons.

Fig. 20-17. Move the router counterclockwise around the parts.

Fig. 20-18. Pry the parts off the laminate.

Finishing

1. Identify each assembly and its slide with a different number or letter. This should be done lightly in a location that will not show after final assembly.
2. Use 80 to 120 grit abrasive paper to custom fit the slide to the assembly. Allow enough clearance for the chosen finish to be applied.
3. Sand the entire project with progressively finer paper starting with 120 grit and ending with 180 grit. Use a finish sander for the 120 grit paper, and complete sanding using hand sanding methods.
4. Wipe the saw dust from assembly and slide using a tack rag.
5. Apply desired finish, making sure it is not a lead-based finish.

Attaching the Jar

1. Place the jar lid band on top of the 4-inch piece carefully spacing it around the 2-inch hole. Use an awl to punch three holes equally spaced through the lid band into the top of the assembly.
2. Use three 3/8 inch x No. 4 wood screws to attach the lid band to the assembly.
3. Mount the jar onto the assembly. Test the slide using the desired candy.

TEST YOUR KNOWLEDGE

Please do not write in this text. Place your answers on a separate sheet of paper.

1. List three resources.
2. Profit is the main goal or purpose of any business enterprise. True or False?
3. The fee paid to a lender to borrow money is called _____.
4. A person who manages a business enterprise's resources to accomplish its goals is called a(n) _____ _____.
5. Taking a chance when investing in a company is called the _____.
6. The flowchart shows the relationships of the various resources as a product is being manufactured. True or False?
7. Marketing a product includes sales. List two other activities that are included with marketing.

ACTIVITIES

1. Go to the library and look up the term "corporation." Prepare a brief report to the class about corporations and what benefit it would be to incorporate your business enterprise.
2. Go to the library and look up the term "bankruptcy." Prepare a report to the class discussing the kinds of bankruptcy and the effects upon a person or business.
3. Prepare a chart of potential officers for a business enterprise. Clearly define the role of each office. Which offices are necessary for a class operated business activity?
4. Divide the class into small groups of three or four. Have each group submit a potential product for manufacturer in the class. Make sure to carefully note equipment required, personnel skills, costs, potential market, etc.
5. After each class has made its presentation decide on one or two products for test marketing. Make a market sample. Test the sample and report back to the shareholders with a recommendation.

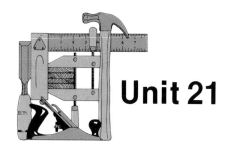

Unit 21

CAREERS IN WOODWORKING INDUSTRIES

The woodworking field offers many opportunities for employment. New and improved uses of forest products are developed each year. Production, service, and maintenance of forest products requires a variety of professional, skilled, and semiskilled workers. After reading this unit, you will be able to identify several careers involved in the woodworking industry. In addition, you will be able to describe some of the tasks involved in each career.

Our forest products industry ranks high among American industries, in the number of full-time employees and total salaries and wages paid. Professional positions in the woodworking industry may require a college education, or an equivalent, with some types of positions requiring a master's degree. Skilled and semiskilled jobs in the industry usually require specialized training and experience.

FORESTRY

New foresters are needed in the industry every year. Foresters perform many types of duties, both indoors and outdoors. They are concerned with growing and protecting trees, planting seedlings, building fire roads, fighting timber fires, and controlling insects that may damage the trees. In addition, foresters help to decide when trees are ready to be harvested, and also make provisions for the next crop of timber. See Fig. 21-1.

FOREST SERVICE MANAGEMENT

The Forest Service is a division of the U.S. Department of Agriculture. It is dedicated to the best use, development, and conservation of our

Fig. 21-1. A forester planting Douglas fir trees. (John Walker)

nation's forest lands. Foresters are specialists in environmental problems. They are concerned with maintaining the best managed forests available. Their concerns are not limited to trees, however. They are also concerned with soil conservation, clean water, and the protection and preservation of native wildlife. The career opportunities with the Forest Service are almost endless. See Fig. 21-2.

A

B

Fig. 21-2. Forestry involves growing trees, as well as harvesting mature trees. A—Tree farm nursery. (Weyerhauser) B—Harvesting trees using a skidder. (Southern Forest Products Assoc.)

BUILDING CONSTRUCTION

The construction industry is the largest consumer of wood and wood by-products. Over 80 percent of the new homes built in this country use wood for their structural framework. See Fig. 21-3. The average home contains about 10,000 board feet of lumber. Employment in the construction industry is not limited to residential construction, but also includes commercial construction, such as concrete formwork, etc. A variety of employment opportunities are available in the construction industry.

INDUSTRIAL WOODWORKER

The cabinet and furniture manufacturing industries offer rewarding futures to professional,

Fig. 21-3. Carpenters build new homes. A wide range of wood products are used for structural framework. How many different wood products can you find in this photograph?

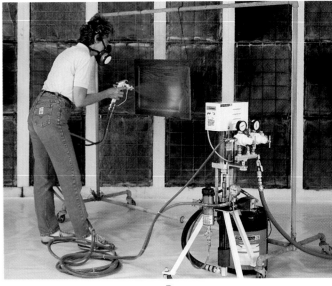

Fig. 21-4. Industrial woodworkers may be involved with the raw materials or the finished product. A—Stacking flat sliced veneer. (Capital Machine Co., Inc.) B—Finishing doors before attaching them to the cabinet. (DeVilbiss)

skilled, and semiskilled workers. These positions require people to perform a variety of duties, ranging from tool repair to actual manufacturing of products. See Fig. 21-4.

OTHER PROFESSIONS

PATTERNMAKERS produce patterns that are used for metal casting. These people must be able to shape wood to exacting dimensions. RESEARCH TECHNICIANS perform a variety of tasks needed in the analysis and testing of forest products. TECHNOLOGY EDUCATION TEACHERS provide students with the opportunity to work with a variety of tools, materials, and processes used in industry. ENGINEERS are needed to analyze and test forest products, and also to explore and develop new products through research.

TEST YOUR KNOWLEDGE, Unit 21

Please do not write in this text. Place your answers on a separate sheet of paper.

1. List four activities performed by a forester.
2. The Forest Service is a division of what U.S. department?

3. List two items that a forester is concerned about other than trees.
4. The average house contains how many board feet of lumber?
5. List three professions, other than foresters or carpenters, that use wood during an average work day.

ACTIVITIES

1. Choose a profession in the woodworking industry. Visit your library to prepare a report on it. Be sure to include how many people are employed in the profession, the employment outlook, the type of training necessary, working conditions, and any other pertinent information.
2. Carefully list as many different parts, items, furniture, equipment, etc., found in your house as possible. Possible examples include floor joists, stairs, carpet, kitchen sink, etc. Underline those items that are wood or a wood by-product.
3. Interview someone who works in the woodworking industry. Prepare a list of questions to ask before the interview. Report your findings to the class.

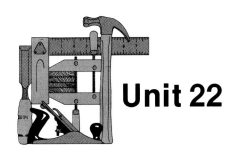

Unit 22

WOODWORKING PRODUCTS

Designing and constructing products will allow you to *think* and *plan*. You will need to experiment, do research with different materials, and learn to solve numerous problems when you are planning a product.

There are several steps involved in planning and constructing a product. These steps are covered in detail in unit 2, but are also outlined here for your reference. Remember, when planning your product, there are several methods that can be used to perform a given task. For example, you can cut an inside opening in a piece of stock using either a coping saw or an electric jigsaw.

Design Considerations
    Function or Usefulness
    Kind of Wood
    Size of the Product
    Proportion or Durability
Steps in Planning a Product
    Identify the Problem
    Sketch the Product
    Determine the Available Resources
    Determine Required Tools and Equipment
    Prepare a Working Drawing
        Compute Lumber Measure
        Prepare Bill of Materials
        Make a Stock Cutting List
Steps in Constructing a Product
    Prepare a Plan of Procedure
    Construct the Product
    Determine Your Overall Success

SELECTING A PRODUCT

Your products should be something that you are interested in making. Many of the decisions that you make about your product will be based on the tools you have available, the cost of the materials, and your ability. In addition, you should consider the time allotted to construct the product, and is the product worth the time and effort that will be needed.

Be sure to use your imagination freely. Carefully plan the details of your product. Create the drawings that will be needed to construct the product, develop a plan of procedure, and get your instructor's approval before beginning work on your product.

WOODWORKING PRODUCTS

A variety of products have been included on the following pages. Some of the products require more experience than others. Use these product designs as ideas only. Use your imagination to modify and personalize these designs to your own liking.

The first few products include suggestions for the type of wood and other materials to be used, the tools required, and a possible plan of procedure. Remember that these items are only suggestions; there may be alternative methods that can be used to construct the products.

The remainder of the product designs include only the drawings. It is up to you to develop alternative designs, create a stock cutting list, select the wood and other materials to be used, and determine which tools and equipment to use. Draw on the information included in this book, and the experiences that you have had throughout this course to design, plan, and construct a product that you will enjoy for years to come.

Letter or Napkin Holder

A letter or napkin holder is a useful product that can be made easily. It consists of three parts, and is assembled with four flat head wood screws.

Irregular shapes, such as the ones shown for this product, are best reproduced on graph paper. Use graph paper that has 1/2 inch squares for best results. The alternate design suggestions can be enlarged and reproduced on graph paper.

The shape of the back piece can be changed, or another piece matching the front piece could be used. If you want to allow more room for letters or napkins, move the front piece toward the front of the base piece. The width of the base piece could also be increased so there is more room between the front and the back.

Stock List

Quantity	Part	Size (Inches) S2S
1	Back	1/2 x 5 3/4 x 6 1/2
1	Base	1/2 x 3 1/4 x 6
1	Front	1/2 x 5 3/4 x 6 1/2

Wood to Use
Willow, white pine, poplar, or redwood.

Other Materials

Quantity	Description	Size
4	Flat head wood screws	No. 6 x 1 in.
	Abrasive paper	60, 100, and 150 grits
	Finish	
	Felt or flock	

Tools Required
Coping saw, try square, compass, crosscut saw, ripsaw, files, hand drill and bit, countersink, screwdriver, pencil, marker, and woodburning kit.

Plan of Procedure
1. Prepare stock cutting list.
2. Create a full-size template. Use rubber cement to bond the paper design onto cardboard, and then cut it out with scissors.
3. Select your stock, being careful to use the grain direction affording the greatest strength.
4. Lay out stock to rough dimensions.
5. Saw stock to rough dimensions with crosscut saw and ripsaw.
6. Transfer the desired shape of the front piece to the stock by placing the template on the stock and tracing around it.
7. Cut out the shape using a coping saw or jigsaw.
8. Use a wood straightedge as a guide to cut the straight edges to finished size.
9. File all edges to remove saw marks.
10. Sand edges and surfaces with 60, 100, and 150 grit abrasive paper.
11. Add the detail lines using a woodburning kit or marker.
12. Lay out, drill, and countersink for No. 6 x 1 in. flat head wood screws.
13. Assemble the parts using wood screws and a screwdriver.
14. Apply the desired finish.
15. Attach felt or spray on flock to the bottom surface of the base to provide protection to the furniture.

LETTER OR NAPKIN HOLDER

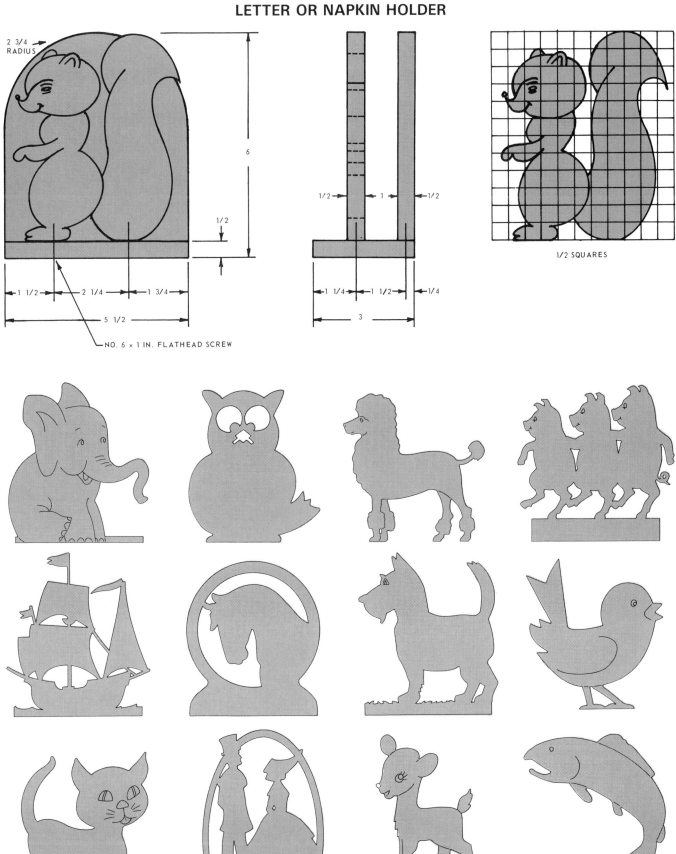

2 3/4 RADIUS

6

1/2

1 1/2 — 2 1/4 — 1 3/4

5 1/2

NO. 6 x 1 IN. FLATHEAD SCREW

1/2 — 1 — 1/2

1 1/4 — 1 1/2 — 1/4

3

1/2 SQUARES

Alternative design suggestions for the letter or napkin holder. Try to create your own designs. Place 1/4 inch graph paper over the designs and transfer them to 1/2 inch graph paper.

189

Jigsaw Cut-Outs

Jigsaw cut-outs are easy products to create. They require a minimal amount of time, effort, and tools to construct. Jigsaw cut-outs can be used for wall hangings or children's toys. Be sure to use a lead-free finish if you plan to use these cut-outs for children.

Stock List

Dependent on the size of the final product. Allow about 1/2″ waste on all sides when planning the cut-out.

Wood to Use

Sugar pine, white pine, mahogany, willow, or redwood for beginners. Hardwoods, such as oak or walnut, can be used by experienced woodworkers.

Other Materials

Description   *Size*
Abrasive paper   60, 100, and 150 grits
Finish

Tools Required

Coping saw or jigsaw, scissors, and pencil. A crosscut saw or ripsaw may be required to cut the stock to rough length and width.

Plan of Procedure

1. Transfer the outline of the design onto tracing paper.
2. Create a full-size template. Use rubber cement to bond the paper design onto cardboard, and then cut it out with scissors.
3. Select your stock, being careful to use the grain direction affording the greatest strength.
4. Lay out stock to rough dimensions.
5. Saw stock to rough dimensions with crosscut saw and ripsaw.
6. Transfer the desired shape of the front piece to the stock by placing the template on the stock and tracing around it.
7. Cut out the shape using a coping saw or jigsaw.
8. File all edges to remove saw marks.
9. Sand edges and surfaces with 60, 100, and 150 grit abrasive paper.
10. Apply finish to the cut-out as desired.

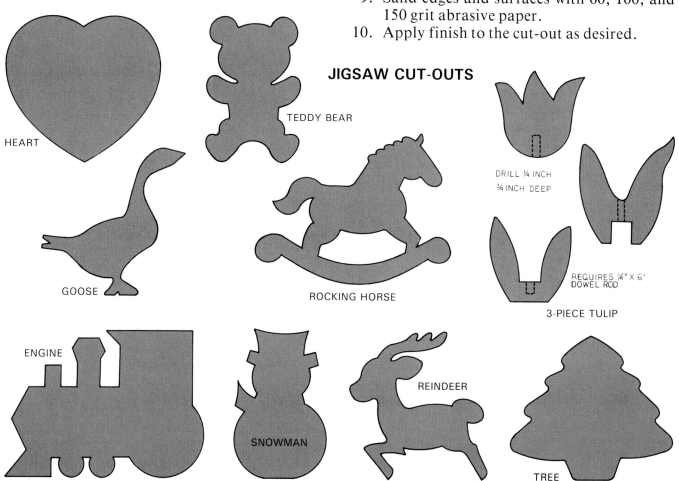

JIGSAW CUT-OUTS

HEART

TEDDY BEAR

GOOSE

ROCKING HORSE

DRILL ¼ INCH
¾ INCH DEEP

REQUIRES ¼″ X 6″ DOWEL ROD

3-PIECE TULIP

ENGINE

SNOWMAN

REINDEER

TREE

Alternative design suggestions for the jigsaw cut-outs. Try to create your own designs. Place 1/4 inch graph paper over the designs and then enlarge them to the size you desire.

nimal Caricatures

Creating animal caricatures with carving ·ols is an interesting hobby. The caricatures mphasize the distinguishing characteristics of ie animal. You can enjoy this hobby without :ing an expert, or without spending a great deal ? money for tools and equipment.

tock List

Dependent on the size of the final product. llow about 1/2″ waste on all sides when plan-ng the caricature.

/ood to Use

Straight-grained wood, especially sugar pine, hite pine, basswood, poplar, and cottonwood, ·r beginners. Walnut, mahogany, and sweet ım can be used for experienced wood carvers.

ther Materials

escription	Size
brasive paper	60, 100, and 150 grits
nish	

ools Required

Coping saw or jigsaw, scissors, pencil, and ıarp knife, such as a sloyd knife, art knife with terchangeable blades, or ordinary pocket knife.

Plan of Procedure

1. Transfer the outline of the design onto trac-ing paper.
2. Cut around the outer edges of the design with scissors. Bond this pattern to the wood using rubber cement. Make sure that the grain of the wood runs parallel with the thinnest portion of the design.
3. Cut out the profile of the design with a cop-ing saw or jigsaw.
4. Use a pencil to draw the front, top, and end views on the wood.
5. Cut away the excess stock using a coping saw wherever possible.
6. Whittle with a series of short cuts. The rough appearance adds character to the carving.
7. Observe the drawing of the completed cari-cature. Try to shape your carving as shown. Make several light cuts rather than one heavy cut. Rotate the wood as you carve.
8. Lightly sand your carving as you complete the carving.
9. Apply a natural finish using a thin coat of shellac or wax. If color is desired, a flat fin-ish is preferable. Use a flat enamel or water color.

ANIMAL CARICATURES

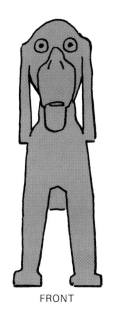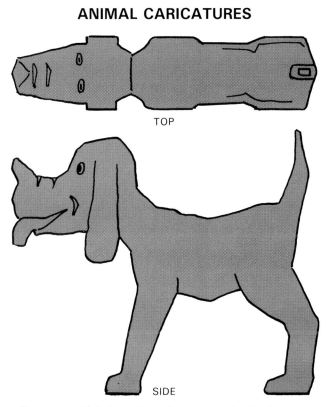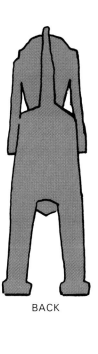

Sketches and full-size patterns for carving animal caricatures.

Use beads for eyes

Roughed out block

Roughed out foot detail

Alternative design suggestions for animal caricatures.

Additional Woodworking Products

The following pages contain additional product ideas. In some cases, the dimensions are indicated through the use of a standard grid. When determining the values of dimensions, multiply the number of grids by the value of each. This measurement will be the finished size. Always add additional stock along the ends and edges to allow for waste.

CHILD'S STEP STOOL

All stock is 3/4-inch #2 pine. Dowels shown are
7/16 inch; 1/2- or 9/16-inch dowels will also work.

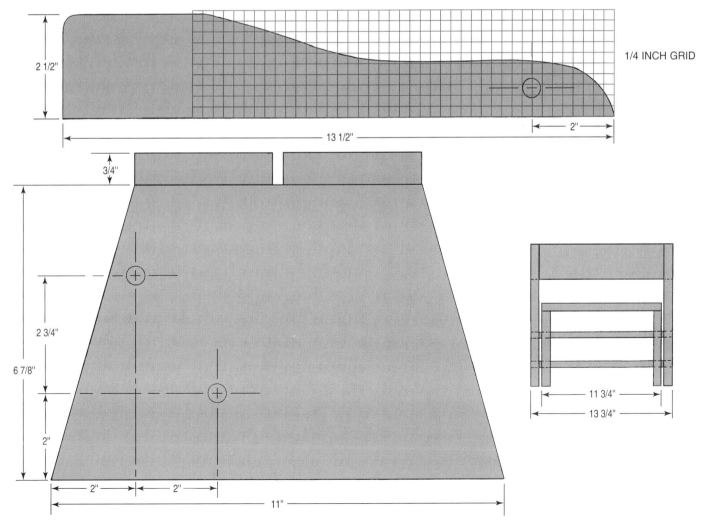

1/4 INCH GRID

2 1/2"

13 1/2"

2"

3/4"

2 3/4"

6 7/8"

2"

2"

2"

11"

11 3/4"

13 3/4"

QUILT RACK

Stock is "off-the-shelf" #2 pine—1 × 12 is shown, but 1 × 10 will also work. Horizontal pieces are #2 pine 1 × 2 with edges rounded over. Outside edges of sides also are rounded over. A heart template can be used for heart layout. All edges are rounded over. This heart serves as a hand grip to pick up rack. Overall width and height may be adjusted as desired.

1/4 INCH GRID

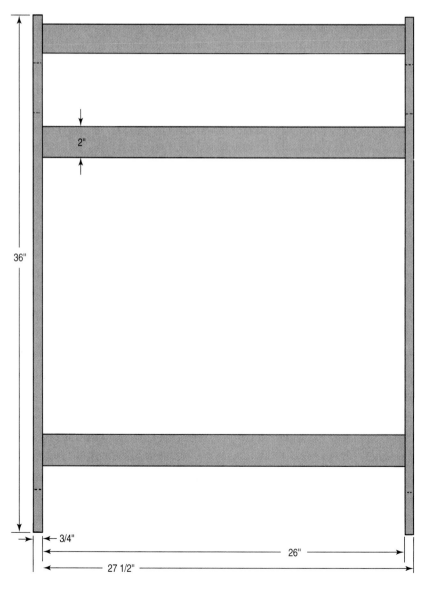

MEDIA RACK

1 × 2 mounting strips are essential if dowels are used or if the rack will be set on a carpeted floor or an uneven floor. Positioning can be varied so that the media is not interfered with. Dowel diameter should be 5/8 inch or 3/4 inch unless the width has been reduced to 18" or less. The two forward dowels may be replaced by a 1 × 2. The rear dowel is necessary for the keeper. Spacing is 6 inches O.C.

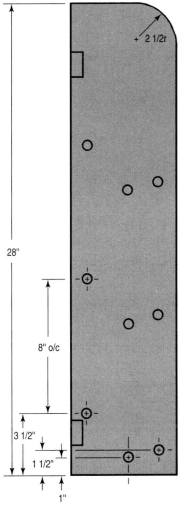

NAPKIN HOLDER

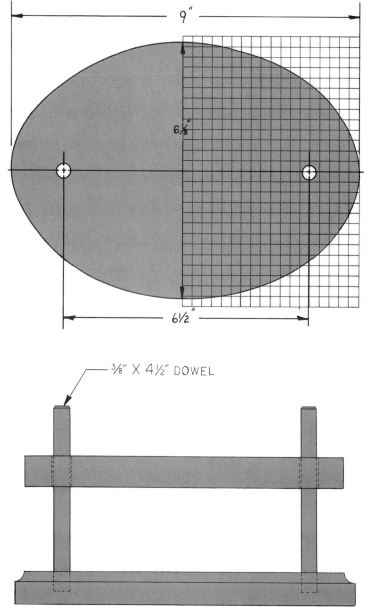

9"

1/4 INCH GRID

6⅛"

6½"

⅜" X 4½" DOWEL

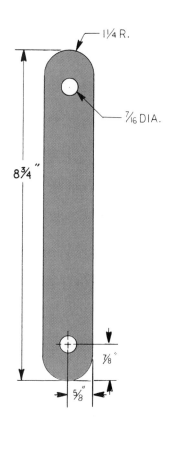

1¼ R.

7⁄16 DIA.

8¾"

7⁄8"

5⁄8"

SCONCE

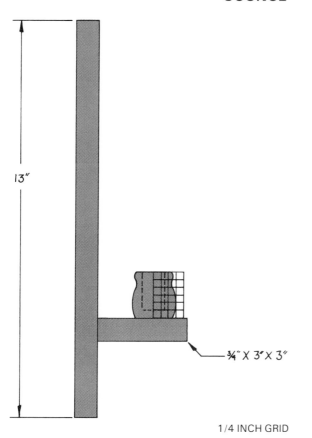

13"

¾" X 3" X 3"

1/4 INCH GRID

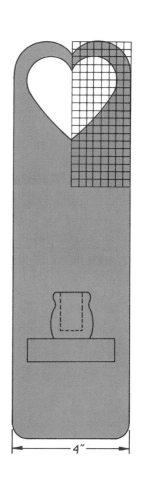

4"

COAT RACK

WELCOME

1/4 INCH GRID

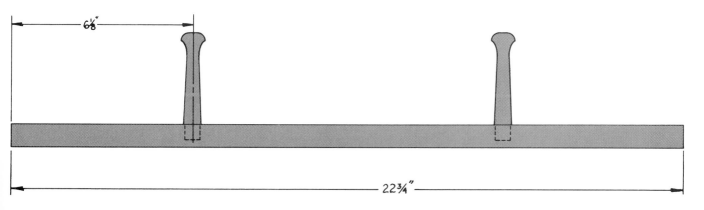

6⅛"

4½"

22¾"

COLONIAL TABLE OR PLANT STAND

Turning is from 2 × 2. Balance is 3/4-inch stock. Grain direction is critical to prevent the leg from breaking. Upper portion of the leg is cupped to fit radius of spindle. Options to this design would be to cut the flats at attachment points of spindle or use a sliding dovetail. The sliding dovetail changes the turning design below the leg attachment point.

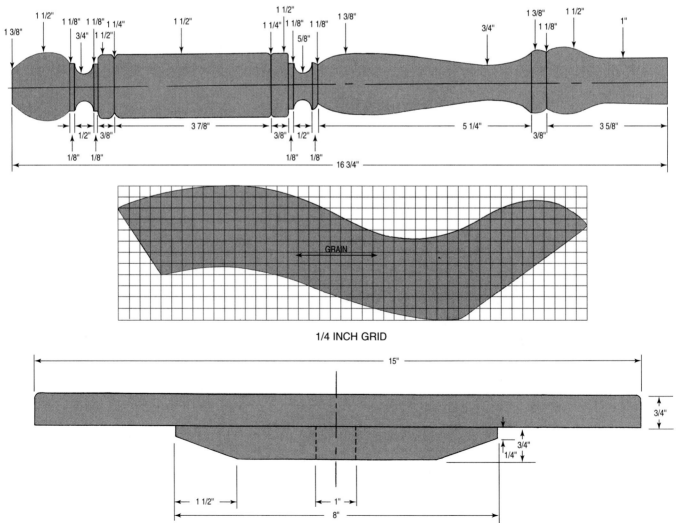

1/4 INCH GRID

CUTTING BOARDS

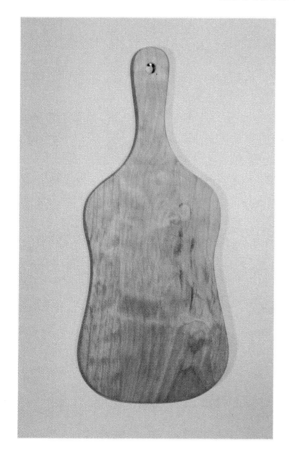

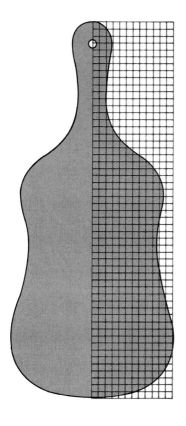

1/4 INCH GRID

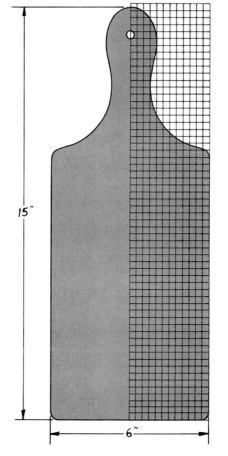

15"

6"

CANDLE SCONCE

The stock is 3/4-inch pine. 1/4-inch OGEE or 1/4-inch round over is recommended for top edges of the back. Top edges of the candle bracket have been eased using a portion of a 3/4-inch round over bit.

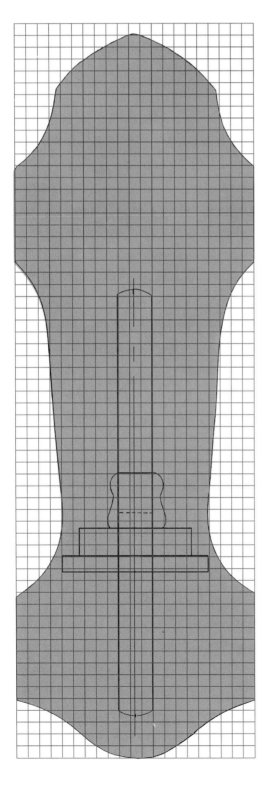

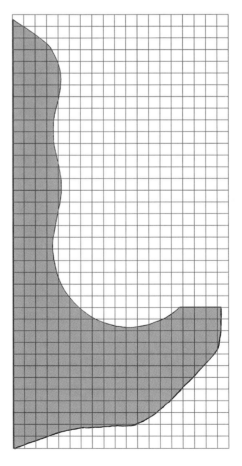

1/4 INCH GRID

HIGH-BACK STOOL

All stock should be 3/4 inch #2 pine. Heart hand hold can be replaced with other design.

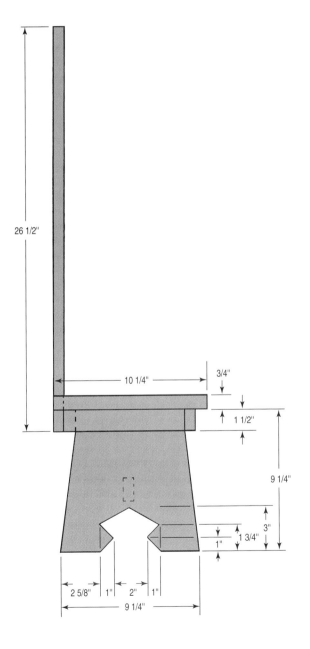

26 1/2"

10 1/4"   3/4"

1 1/2"

9 1/4"

3"

1 3/4"

1"

2 5/8"   1"   2"   1"

9 1/4"

2 1/2"

5 1/2"

1/4 INCH GRID

1 1/2"

3 1/2"

7 1/2"

10 1/2"

12"

SALAD CUTTING BOARD

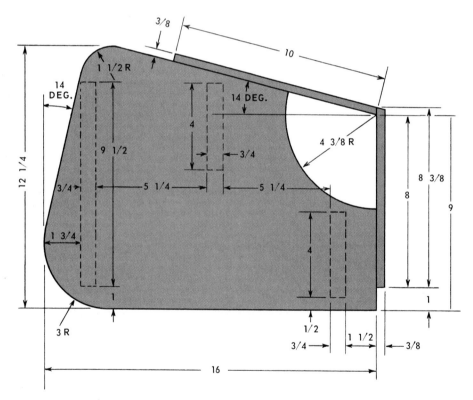

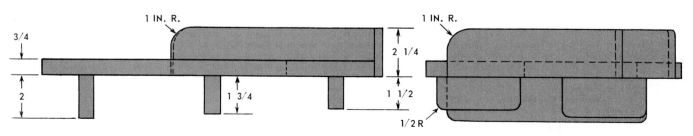

Working drawing for salad cutting board.

CORNER SHELF

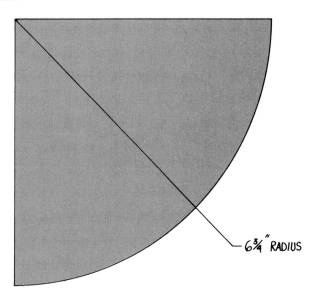

6¾" RADIUS

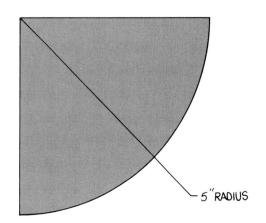

5" RADIUS

1/4 INCH GRID

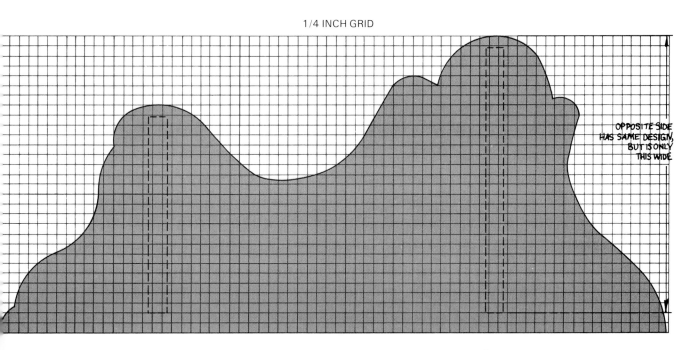

OPPOSITE SIDE
HAS SAME DESIGN,
BUT IS ONLY
THIS WIDE

CORNER SHELF—FRETWORK

All stock should be 3/8-inch solid. Shelf radius is
9 inches. This radius can be adjusted as necessary.

1/4 INCH GRID

STANDING/CORNER SHELF

All stock is 1/4-inch solid. Shelves are 2 3/4-,
3 3/4-, and 5-inch radii. These radii may be adjusted.

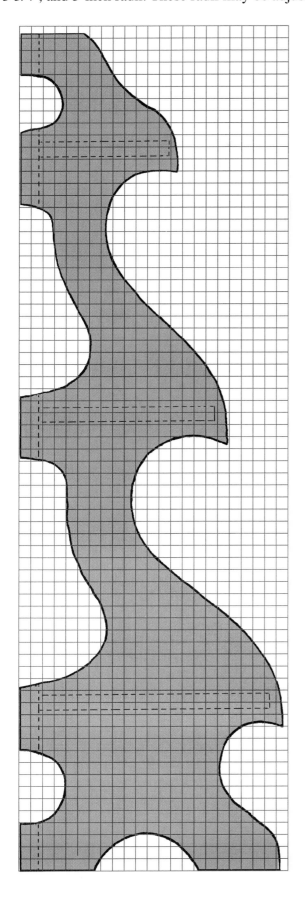

1/4 INCH GRID

Bird Feeder

The bird feeder shown is designed with a hopper so that the bin below is kept full using gravity. The top is easily removed for filling. A piece of clear plastic is used so you can observe the food supply. If desired, you can design and make a wire hanger to hold suet, and attach it to the side of the feeder.

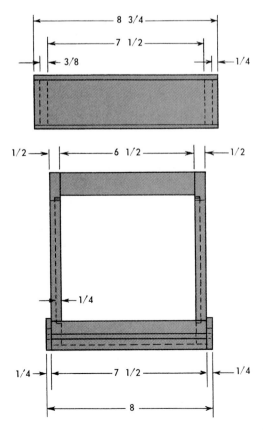
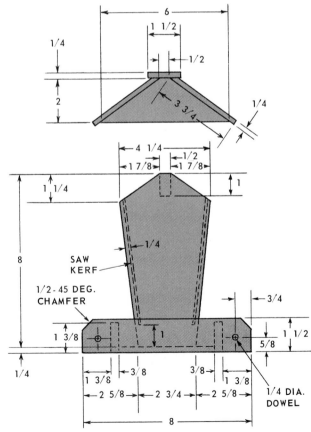

Working drawing for the bird feeder.

BIRD FEEDERS

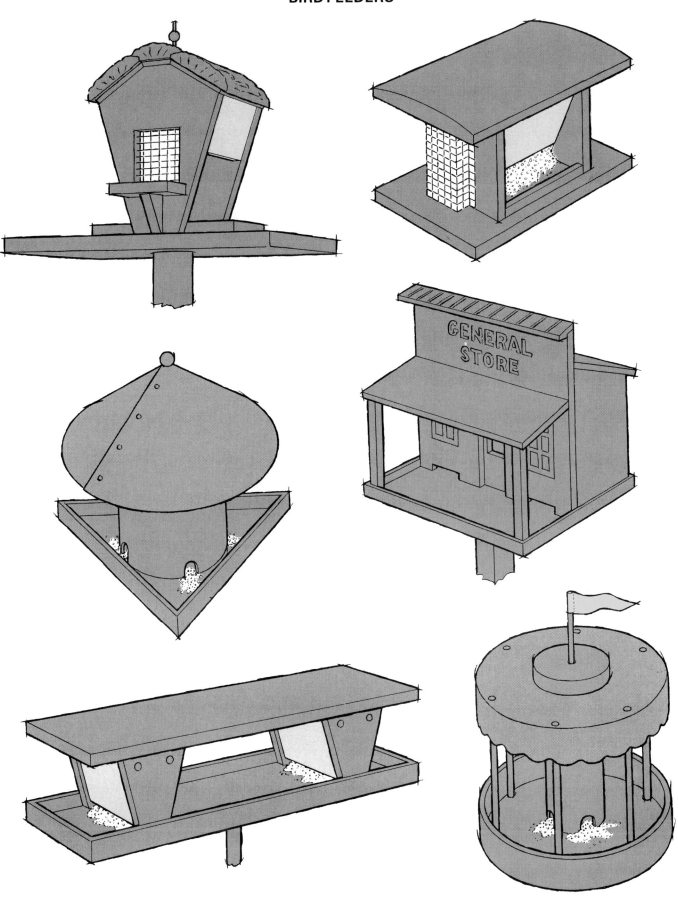

Alternative design suggestions for the bird feeder.

WALL SHELF

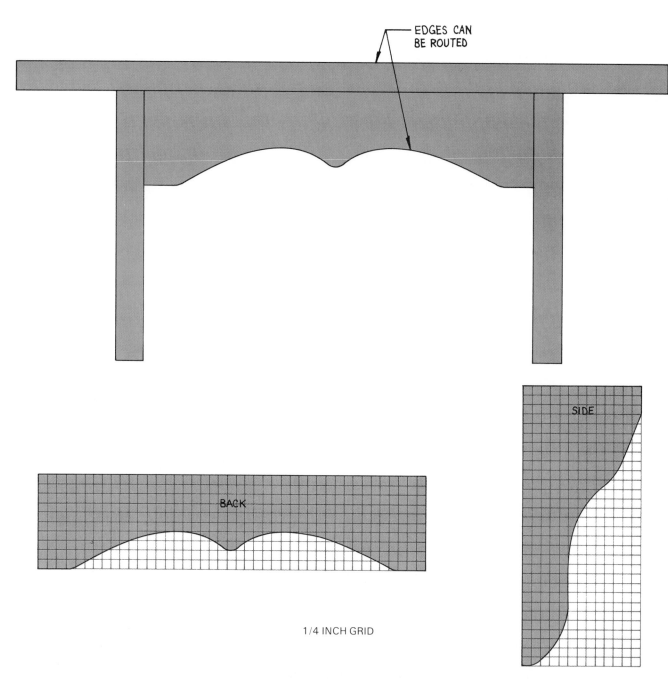

EDGES CAN
BE ROUTED

SIDE

BACK

1/4 INCH GRID

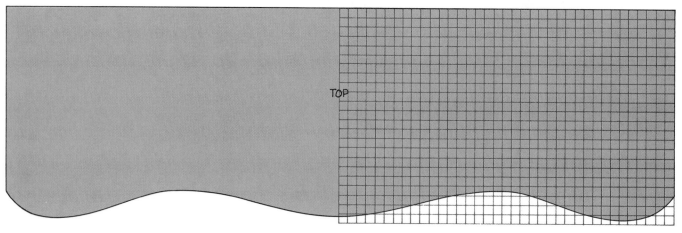

TOP

POOL CUE RACK

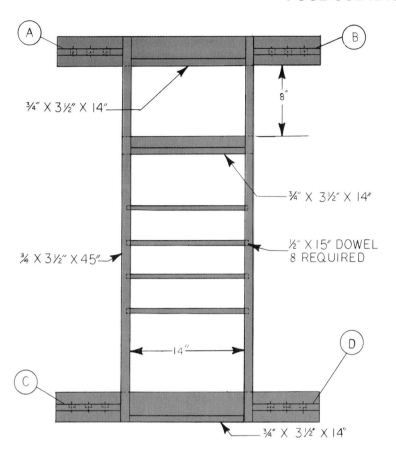

(A)
(B)

¾" X 3½" X 14"

8"

¾" X 3½" X 14"

½" X 15" DOWEL
8 REQUIRED

¾ X 3½" X 45"

14"

(D)

(C)

¾" X 3½" X 14"

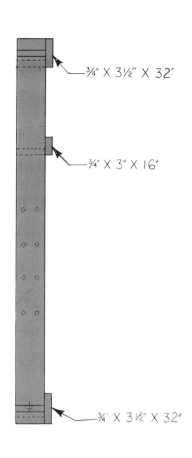

¾" X 3½" X 32"

¾" X 3" X 16'

¾" X 3½" X 32"

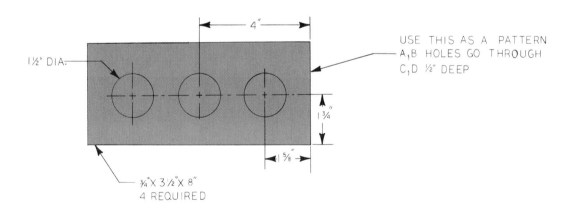

4"

1½" DIA.

USE THIS AS A PATTERN
A,B HOLES GO THROUGH
C,D ½" DEEP

1¾"

1⅝"

¾" X 3½" X 8"
4 REQUIRED

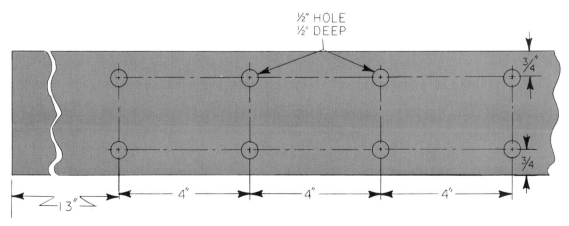

½" HOLE
½" DEEP

¾"

¾

3"

4"

4"

4"

ROLLTOP BREAD BOX

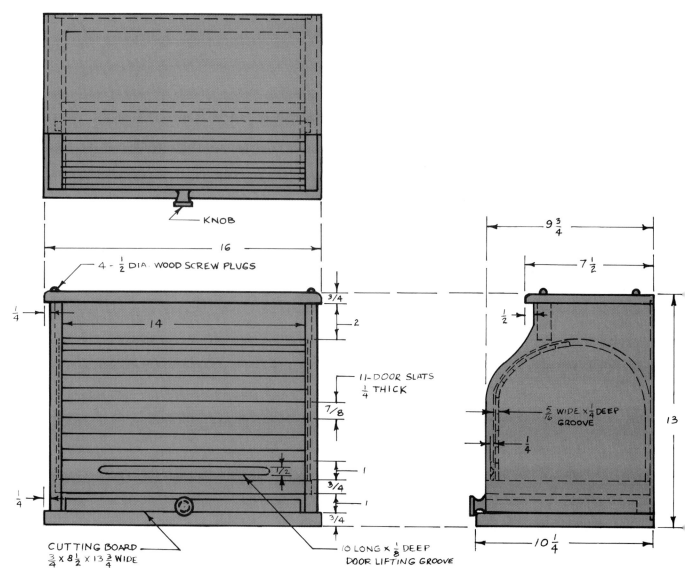

KNOB

16

4 - ½ DIA. WOOD SCREW PLUGS

¼

14

¾

2

11-DOOR SLATS
¼ THICK

7/8

½

1

¾

1

¼

CUTTING BOARD
¾ X 8½ X 13¾ WIDE

10 LONG X ⅛ DEEP
DOOR LIFTING GROOVE

9¾

7½

½

5/16 WIDE X ¼ DEEP
GROOVE

¼

13

10¼

CHILDREN'S PICNIC TABLE

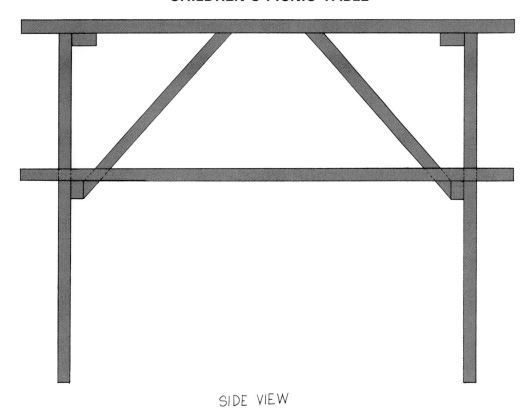

SIDE VIEW

NOTE: NOT DRAWN
TO SCALE

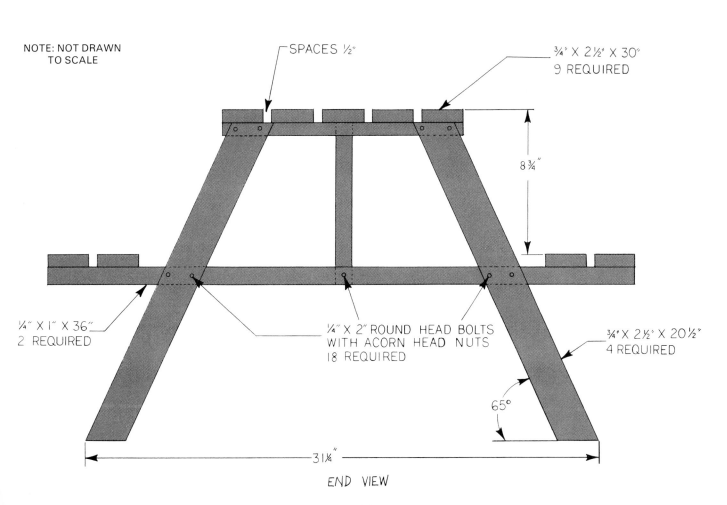

SPACES ½"

¾" X 2½" X 30"
9 REQUIRED

8 ¾"

¼" X 1" X 36"
2 REQUIRED

¼" X 2" ROUND HEAD BOLTS
WITH ACORN HEAD NUTS
18 REQUIRED

¾" X 2½" X 20½"
4 REQUIRED

65°

31¼"

END VIEW

CHILD'S CHAIR

All stock is 3/4-inch #2 pine. Hand hold can be replaced with other design, such as a heart.

1/4 INCH GRID

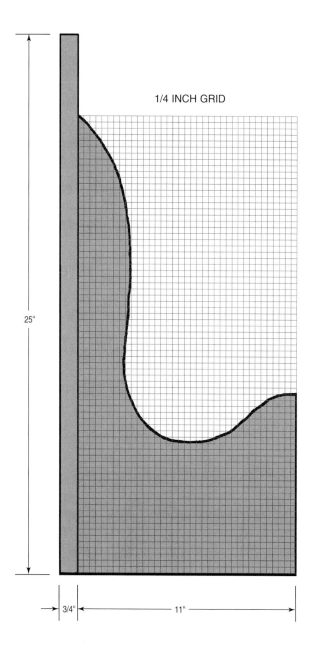

25"

3/4"

11"

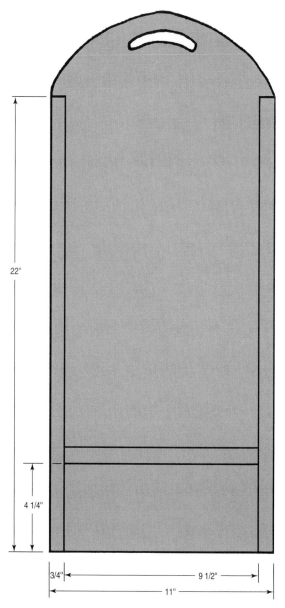

22"

4 1/4"

3/4"

9 1/2"

11"

DOLL CRADLE OR MAGAZINE RACK

All stock is 3/4-inch #2 pine. The ends are from 1 × 12.

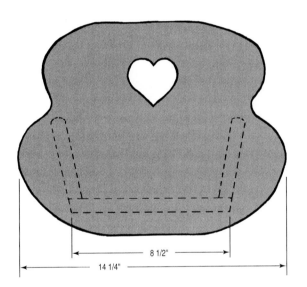

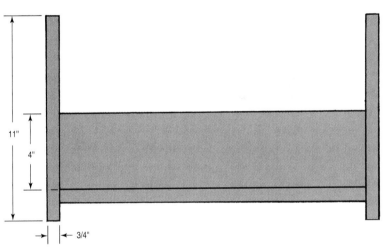

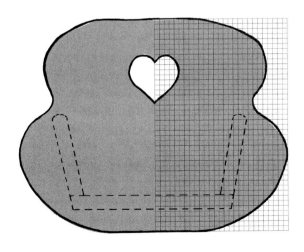

1/4 INCH GRID

MAGAZINE RACK

Ends and bottom are 3/4-inch stock. Sides and center are 3/8-inch plywood.

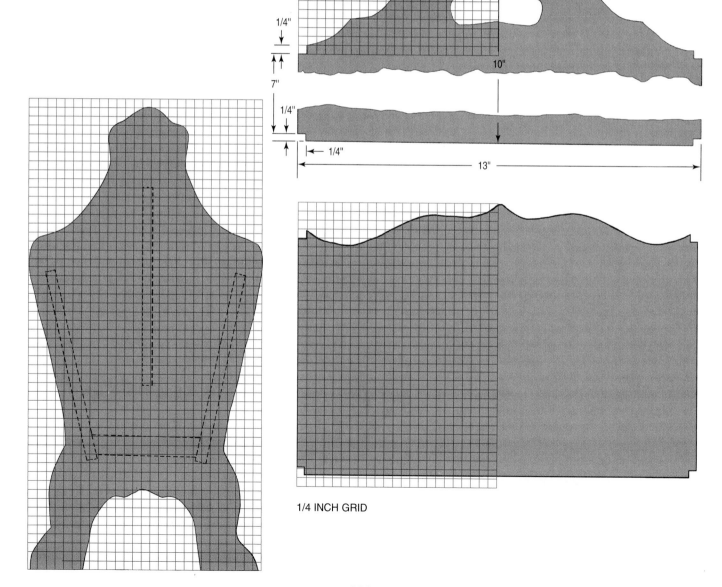

1/4 INCH GRID

ADJUSTABLE BOOK RACK

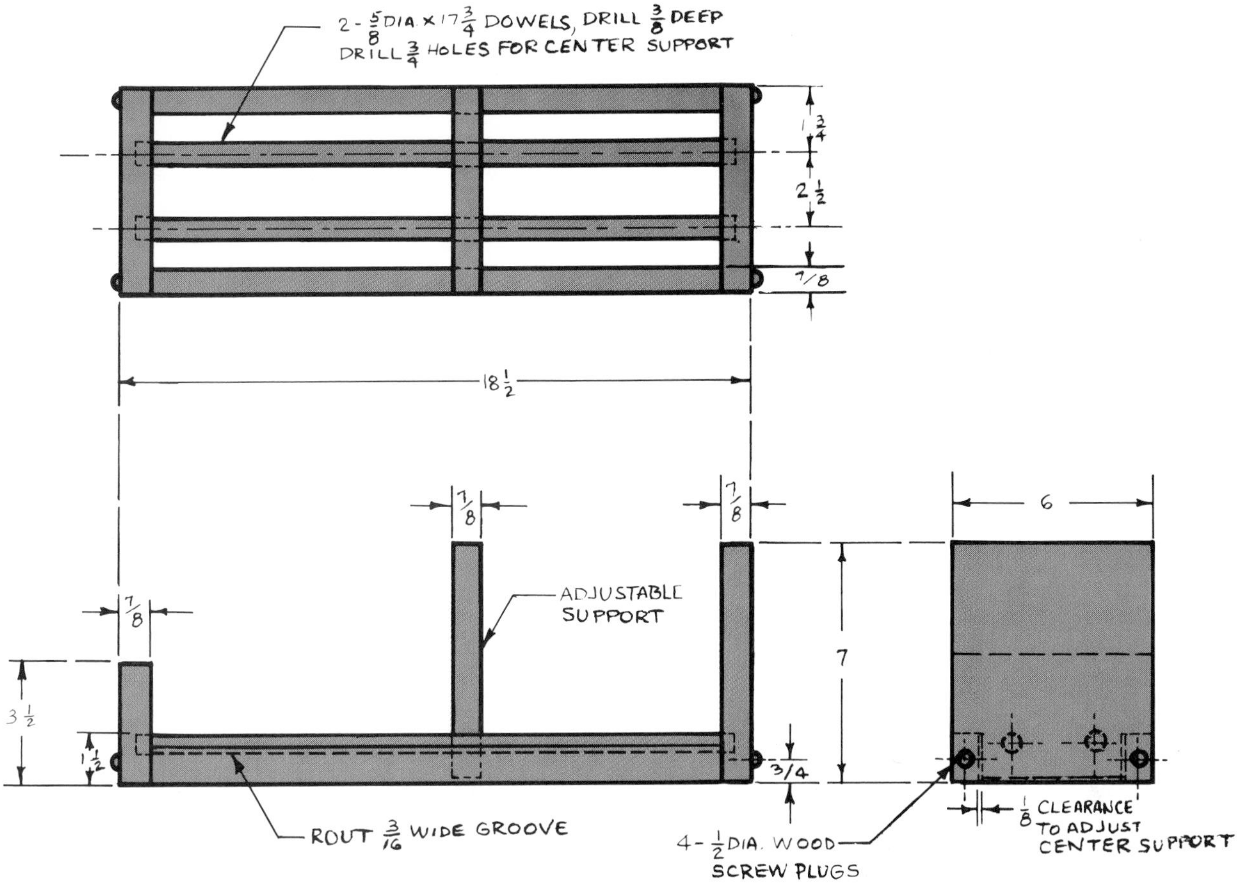
2 - 5/8 DIA. X 17 3/4 DOWELS, DRILL 3/8 DEEP
DRILL 3/4 HOLES FOR CENTER SUPPORT
1 3/4
2 1/2
7/8
18 1/2
7/8
7/8
7/8
ADJUSTABLE SUPPORT
3 1/2
1 1/2
3/4
7
6
ROUT 3/16 WIDE GROOVE
4 - 1/2 DIA. WOOD SCREW PLUGS
1/8 CLEARANCE TO ADJUST CENTER SUPPORT

COLONIAL WALL SHELF WITH DRAWER

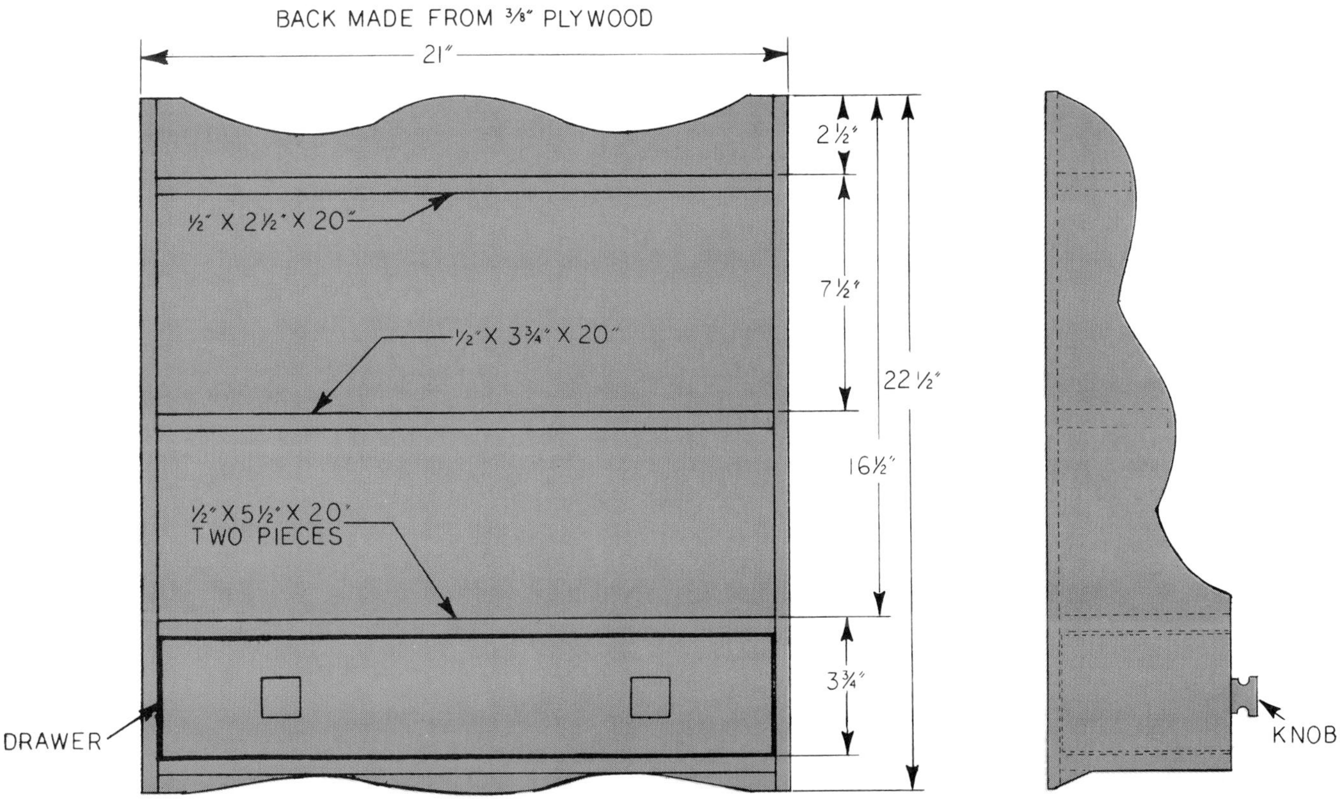
BACK MADE FROM 3/8" PLYWOOD
21"
2½"
½" X 2½" X 20"
7½"
½" X 3¾" X 20"
22½"
16½"
½" X 5½" X 20"
TWO PIECES
3¾"
DRAWER
KNOB

COLONIAL WALL SHELF WITH DRAWER (Continued)

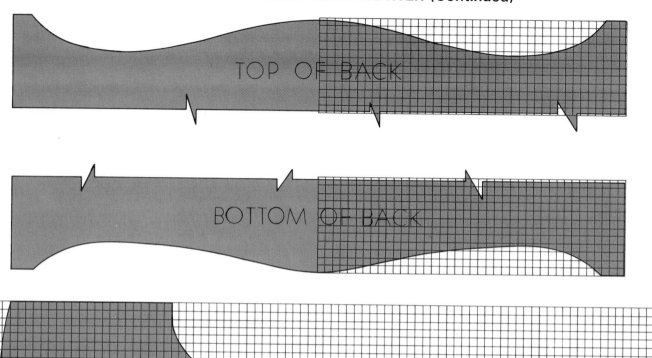

TOP OF BACK

BOTTOM OF BACK

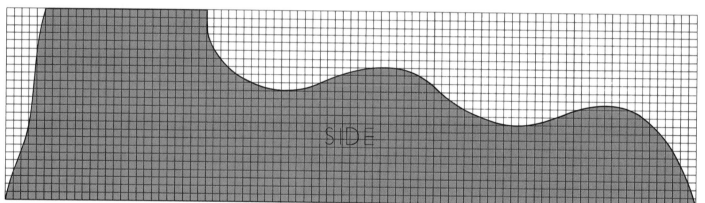

SIDE

1/4 INCH GRID

DRAWER

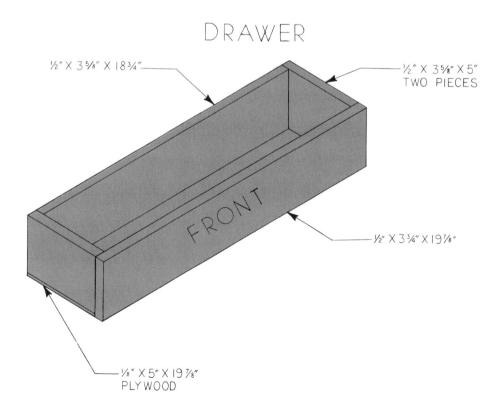

½" X 3⅝" X 18¾"

½" X 3⅝" X 5"
TWO PIECES

FRONT

½" X 3¾" X 19⅞"

⅛" X 5" X 19⅞"
PLYWOOD

GLOSSARY

A

ABRASIVE: Material used to smooth stock surfaces and polish wood finishes.

ACROSS THE GRAIN: Perpendicular to the length of a piece of stock and its fibers.

ADHESIVE: Tacky substance used to bond materials together. Pastes, cements, and glues are types of adhesives.

AGAINST THE GRAIN: Opposite to the grain direction of wood fibers.

AIR-DRYING: Seasoning of lumber by natural means. Lumber is stacked in layers that are separated with stickers (cross strips) to allow free passage of air.

ALKYD RESIN: Synthetic material widely used as a vehicle in paints and enamels to increase durability.

ALLIGATORING: Cracks formed in a finished surface resulting in a mottled pattern similar to the skin on the back of an alligator. Caused by unequal expansion and contraction of separate coats of finish.

ALUMINUM OXIDE: Abrasive made by fusing bauxite ore in an electric furnace. It is used to make abrasive paper, abrasive cloth, and grinding wheels.

AMERICAN TREE FARM SYSTEM: Organization sponsored by woodworking industries. A national system of forest management allowing better production and use of our forest resources, and assuring a future supply of timber.

ANILINE DYES: Oily, synthetic coloring agents produced chemically. Used in making permanent-type wood stain.

ARBOR: Spindle, shaft, or axle on which another revolving part or a cutting tool may be mounted.

ANNUAL RING: Growth ring of a tree formed in a single year. Formed by springwood and summerwood.

ARKANSAS STONE: Hone that requires oil as a lubricant to remove the fine pieces of metal removed during sharpening.

ARRIS: Sharp edge formed by the meeting of two surfaces, such as along the edge of a piece of stock.

ATTACHMENT PLATE: Metal plate designed for fastening a leg to a table with a hanger bolt.

ATOMIZATION: Process of reducing paint or other liquids to minute particles forming a fine mist for spraying.

B

BARE-FACED TENON: Tenon having only one shoulder, exposing one side.

BATTEN: Thin strip of wood used to seal or strengthen the edge joint assembly of two adjacent sheets, pieces of stock, or panels.

BEAD: Projecting band or rim formed on an edge, cylinder, or molding.

BEVEL: Angle that one surface or line makes with another. The angle formed is either greater to or less than 90 degrees.

BILL OF MATERIALS: Detailed list of the items needed to construct a project.

BISCUIT: Thin, football-shaped wood reinforcement set in grooves made with a plate joiner.

BLEACHING: Chemical solution applied to wood to make it lighter in color or to remove water stains. Normally oxalic acid is used, but household bleach will work.

BLEEDING: Transfer of color from one finish coat to another. For example, varnish applied over an unsealed penetrating oil stain dissolves part of its color, resulting in discoloration of the varnish coat.

BLEMISH: Any imperfection or small defect that detracts from the appearance of a surface.

BLIND DADO: Dado that is cut only part of the way across a surface. This makes it invisible from one or both sides.

BLUE STAIN: Discoloration caused by a fungus growth in unseasoned lumber.

BLUSHING: Clouded appearance on a finished mounted surface, often formed by clear spraying lacquer, which dries too fast as it is applied. Humidity in the air is condensed and trapped with the finish, particularly on humid days. A retarding thinner may be added to lacquer to prevent blushing.

BOARD FOOT MEASURE: Standard unit of measurement for most lumber. One board foot is the equivalent to a piece of stock measuring $1'' \times 12'' \times 12''$.

BOILED LINSEED OIL: Certain metallic driers are added to raw linseed oil. The oil is then heat treated and aged for use in the manufacture of varnish and enamel.

BULL-CHAIN: Conveyer for pulling logs lengthwise into the sawmill. Also called ladder-jack.

BURL: Protruding lump on a tree, which when sliced, produces veneer with highly figured grain.

BURLAP: Coarse cloth, usually woven from jute or hemp fibers.

C

CALIPER: Tool used to measure cylindrical stock.

CAMBIUM LAYER: Growth area near the bark of a tree where new cells are formed. The inside of this layer forms new wood cells and the outside forms new bark cells.

CANT: Log that has been slabbed (cut flat) on two or four sides, ready for further processing into lumber or veneer.

CATALYST: Substance that starts and aids in the control of chemical action between two other substances. Commonly used in epoxy cements.

CATCHES: Devices used to hold furniture and cabinet doors closed.

CERAMIC STONE. Hone that cuts dry (requires no lubricant) and may not require any stropping.

CHALKING: Decomposition of paint film that leaves loose powder on the surface.

CHAMFER: Surface formed by planing or sawing at an angle across one arris of a square edge.

CHECKS: Cracks along the grain at the end of a piece of stock and at right angles to the annual rings.

CHIP-CARVING KNIFE: Specially designed knife where only about 1 to 1 1/2 inches of the blade is exposed. Masking tape is usually wrapped around a portion of this blade to allow only about 3/8 inch of the point to be exposed for safety. Most chip carving is completed using this type of knife.

CHUCK: Work-holding device attached to a rotating headstock of a lathe or other machine.

CLEARANCE BLOCK: Piece of stock used to prevent binding when cutting duplicate parts.

CLINCH: Bending over the protruding ends of driven nails.

CLOSE-GRAIN: Wood that has fine fibers that are held closely together.

COLLAR: Ring or flange fastened under the nut on an arbor or spindle as an aid in securing a cutting tool.

COLONIAL FURNITURE: Kind of furniture made during the period of American colonization.

COMMON GRADE: Lumber ranging in grade, from No. 1 to No. 5. Grades depend on size, shape, and condition of knots. Common grade lumber is often used for structural purposes. Also called utility grade.

COMPATIBILITY: Denotes the ability of finishes to mix together without harmful chemical reactions.

CONIFER: Cone-bearing tree. Lumber from conifers is designated as softwood.

CONTEMPORARY FURNITURE: Modern-day furniture made with characteristic smooth, trim lines, and simple construction. Also called modern furniture.

CORE: Center layer of plywood consisting of solid wood, hardboard, particleboard, or veneer.

COTTON MATT: Soft layer of combed cotton used over rubberized hair or other upholstery materials to produce a cushioning effect.

COUNTERBORING: To enlarge part of a hole by boring, using the same center as the original hole. This allows the head of the screw or bolt to be positioned below the surface of the stock.

COUNTERSINKING: To form a cone-shaped recess for receiving the head of a flat head screw or bolt. This allows the top of the head to be flush with the surface.

COVE: Inside curve, or concave shape, formed on an edge, surface, cylinder, or molding.

CRACK: Narrow break or opening along the grain in the surface or at the end of a piece of stock. Also called split.

CROOK: Warped edge of a piece of stock that is curved lengthwise.

CROTCH: Area formed by two adjacent branches in a tree. Crotch lumber is prized for its highly figured grain.

CRYSTALLINE FINISH: Specialty finish, which when dry, forms a mass of wrinkles or crystals.

CUP: Warped surface of a piece of stock that is curved across the grain.

CUP CENTER: Tailstock center for a wood lathe.

D

DADO: Groove with square corners cut across the grain of a piece of stock.

DECAY: Disintegration (breakdown) of wood caused by the action of fungi.

DECIDUOUS: Hardwood (broad-leaf) trees that lose their leaves after each season of growth.

DEFECTS: Imperfections in lumber such as knots, splits, decay, and warp, that lessen its usefulness or value.

DENATURED ALCOHOL: Combination of wood and grain alcohol.

DENSITY: Weight or arrangement of wood fibers in a piece of stock.

DESIGN: Scheme or plan in which ideas and thinking are incorporated as direction for creating with materials and tools.

DIMENSIONAL LUMBER: Lumber that has been cut and surfaced to specific width and thickness. Generally, softwood that has been graded primarily for framing of buildings, in sizes from 2- to 5-inches thick and up to 12 inches wide.

DOVETAIL JOINT: Strong and attractive wood joint consisting of wedge-shaped projections (pins) that fit into matching recesses (sockets).

DOWEL: Cylindrical piece of stock, usually birch, manufactured in a variety of diameters and a standard length of 36 inches. Dowels are often used to strengthen wood joints.

DOWEL PEG: Short dowel made especially for strengthening wood joints when gluing.

DOWEL POINT: Metal cylinder with a flange and a sharp center point. It is used to mark the location of a mating hole for a dowel joint.

DRIER: Catalyst added to a finishing material to speed its curing and drying time.

E

EARLY AMERICAN FURNITURE: Type of furniture made as industry developed during the period of the American Revolution.

EARTH PIGMENTS: Coloring matter, such as ochre, sienna, and umber, used in wood finishes. These pigments are mined from the earth.

ECCENTRIC: Circular piece having an off center rotation of axis. It is used to transform a circular motion to a straight motion.

EMULSION: Suspension of minute particles of one liquid, such as oil, in another, such as water.

EMULSION PAINT: Oil, resin, varnish, or lacquer that is emulsified so that it can be mixed with water.

ENAMEL: Finishing material creating a hard, durable, waterproof finish. It is made by adding pigments to varnish to give it color and opacity.

EQUILIBRIUM MOISTURE CONTENT: Point at which wood reaches a balance in moisture content with the surrounding air.

ESCUTCHEON: Decorative plate fastened around hinges and locks.

EVAPORATION: Conversion of a liquid to a gas. A paint thinner evaporates from the paint solids, leaving a paint film.

EXTENDER: Material used as a filler in paint or glue to provide body and increase its coverage.

F

FACE SURFACE: First surface of a piece of stock that is planed to remove warp. The result is a flat, true surface. It becomes the reference surface for surfacing the remaining edges and surfaces. Also called true, or working surface.

FACTORY LUMBER: Lumber that is prepared especially for windows, doors, interior trim, or other trim components. Also called shop lumber.

FEATHER: Reinforcing strip installed in a groove across the corner into both edges of a miter joint. Also called a key.

FEATHERBOARD: Safety device used in ripping, planing, and shaping operations. This can be made by cutting one end of a board at an angle of from 20 to 40 degrees, then ripping a series of kerfs about 4- to 6-inches long into that end to make it flexible.

FELLING: Process of cutting down a tree.

FENCE: Adjustable bar or strip attached to the table of a machine to guide stock as it is processed. Used extensively in ripping processes.

FIBER: Single cell in wood.

FIGURE: Design yielded in a wood surface by the nature and arrangement of its fibers, its growth rings, wood rays, and knots, and the manner in which a log is sawed.

FIGURE CARVING: Producing a product from a scrap of wood using a simple knife. It is not intended to be functional. Also called caricature carving or whittling.

FINISH GRADE: Ranges from A through D, the best grade being B or Better in softwood. In white pine,

C or D Select applies to lumber 4-inches wide or more with a medium stain covering one-third of the face being permissible. Also called Select grade.

FIRST AND SECONDS (FAS): Best grade of hardwood lumber. Minimum widths of 6 inches and lengths of 8 feet. At least 83 1/3 percent of face is clear stock. No more than 10 percent of an order can be of minimum dimension.

FIXTURE: Device that positions and holds a part, but does not actually guide the cutting tool.

FLATTING AGENT: Substance used in paints, lacquers, and varnishes to reduce its gloss and give it a rubbed appearance.

FLEXIBILITY: Characteristic or quality of a material that permits it to be bent.

FLITCH: Semicircular slab cut from a log. It is further processed into lumber or veneer.

FLOCK: Pulverized or fibrous strands of rayon, plastic, or wool that are blown onto a surface freshly coated with adhesive or paint. Produces a velvet-like finish.

FLOW: Quality of a material that allows it to spread or move evenly into a uniform and level coating.

FLUTING: Rounded, parallel grooves formed in a wood surface.

FOAM RUBBER: Soft, cellular, and highly resilient (capable of returning to its original shape after being deformed) material providing a cushioning effect. Used extensively in upholstery.

FORESTRY: Profession concerned with the conservation, care, development, management, and production of forest lands.

FOREST SERVICE MANAGEMENT: Federal agency dedicated to the best use, development, and conservation of our nation's forest lands. This includes wildlife protection, water and soil conservation, recreation, and research.

FRENCH POLISH: Type of wood finish produced with white shellac, boiled linseed oil, and denatured alcohol.

FRENCH PROVINCIAL FURNITURE: Furniture built during the reigns of Louis XIV–XVI. It has simple, curved lines, and has no ornate carvings.

FURRING: Narrow strips attached to a ceiling, wall, or floor used as a nailing base for other material such as paneling. Also used to level a surface, or form an air space between two surfaces.

G

G1S: Good one side. Refers to plywood having one good side.

G2S: Good two sides. Refers to plywood having both faces good.

GAIN: Notch or mortise made to receive a hinge or other hardware, or another structural member.

GLAZING: Process of installing glass in an opening such as a window. Also means the application of transparent or translucent coatings over another finishing medium to obtain a blended effect.

GLOSS: Finished surface with a high luster and good light-reflecting quality.

GLUE BLOCKS: Small triangular- or rectangular-shaped pieces glued into place to reinforce joints.

GRAIN: Arrangement, direction, quality, appearance, and size of the fibers in wood.

GRIP: The holding of the knife.

GROOVE: Square-cornered channel cut along the grain of a piece of stock.

GUARD: Part of a tool or machine designed to protect its operator from a cutting edge or moving part.

GUSSET: Reinforcing wood or metal member, often a panel or bracket, attached to the corners and intersections of a frame.

H

HANGER BOLT: Threaded fastener used to attach a leg to a table.

HARDBOARD: Composition board made by compressing shredded wood chips to form flat sheets. Lignin, a natural resin, is used to hold the rearranged fibers together.

HARDWOOD: Classification of lumber that comes from broad-leaf (deciduous) trees.

HARDWOOD PLYWOOD: Plywood with the outer veneer being a hardwood.

HARMONY: Design term implying that characteristics of parts in an object are in conformity or form a pleasing arrangement.

HEADSAW: First saw in a sawmill. It cuts logs into slabs, cants, or flitches.

HEARTWOOD: Wood between the pith and the sapwood in a tree or log.

HINGE: Piece of hardware that allows one part to rotate around a pivot point attached to another point.

HOLLOW-CORE CONSTRUCTION: Method of lightweight door construction. Plywood, hardboard, or other sheet material is fastened to a frame of solid wood.

HOLLOW-GROUND: A concave, sharpened edge on a cutting tool left by the circular shape of a grinding wheel.

HOLLOW-WALL SCREW ANCHOR: Fastener used to attach an object to a hollow wall. As it is assembled, the part inside the wall spreads and the fastener tightens.

HONE: Final or finish sharpening of a cutting tool on a whetting stone.

HOOK TOOTH: Saw blade, usually bandsaw, made with extra space between its teeth. Also called skip tooth.

HYGROSCOPIC: Characteristic of wood that causes it to expand as it absorbs moisture and to shrink as it dries.

I

INDIA STONE: Hone that requires oil as a lubricate to remove the fine pieces of metal removed during sharpening.

INLAY: Ornamental decoration fitted into a recess and finished flush with a surface.

INSERT PLATE: Access plate used around the cutting tool of a machine. Also called throat plate.

INSPECTION: Critical examination of workpieces and assemblies to detect errors in fabrication.

INTERCHANGEABILITY: Parts or devices made to dimensions of close tolerances, often by mass production, that will fit into more than one assembly.

J

JIG: Device that holds the part to be machined, and also positions and holds the cutting tool.

K

KERF: Thickness of the cut made in material by the teeth of a saw blade.

KILN: Enclosure with controlled heat and humidity for drying lumber, veneer, and other wood products.

KILN-DRYING: Seasoning of lumber, veneer, and other wood products in a kiln.

KNOT: Hard, circular area, revealing the cross section of a limb or branch embedded in wood during the growth of the tree.

L

LAC: Resinous substance formed by an insect. Used to make shellac.

LACQUER: Hard, durable finishing material made of nitro-cellulose. Drying occurs by evaporation of its solvents.

LAG SCREW: Heavy, round shank wood screw with a square or hex head.

LAMINATE: Product made by bonding thin layers (laminations) of material together with an adhesive.

LEAD SCREW ANCHOR: Anchor made from lead. It is tapped into a hole in a wall and used to hold an object with a screw.

LEVELING: Formation of a smooth film, free of brush marks, on a finished surface.

LEVERING CUT: One of the two whittling cuts. The knife is held in the dominant hand (right hand for right-handed people, left for left-handed people). The cutting edge of the blade is facing away from you. As the knife edge contacts the wood, the thumb of the opposite hand pushes and guides the blade as the knife is rotated in the hand.

LIGNIN: Essential compound in wood that acts as a bonding agent and holds the fibers together.

LINEAR: Measurement in one direction, along a length.

LINSEED OIL: Valuable oil obtained by pressing flax seeds. This oil, in its boiled form, is used alone as a wood finish. It is also extensively used in oil-base paints and finishes.

LUMBER: Boards and planks cut from logs.

LUMBER-CORE PLYWOOD: Plywood made with a core of solid lumber.

M

MACHINE: Assembly of parts designed to apply power with tools in modifying materials by sawing, planing, shaping, turning, drilling, or sanding.

MANDREL: Arbor or spindle on which work can be mounted for rotation.

MARQUETRY: Ornamental decoration consisting of a variety of veneers, forming a design or picture.

MASONRY NAIL: Spiral-fluted steel nail with high tensile strength, which can be driven into masonry. Since this nail is very brittle (caused by heat treating), safety glasses must be worn.

MASS PRODUCTION: Production of parts or products in quantity. Interchangeability plays a major role in this process.

MATERIAL: Supplies needed to construct a part or product, such as lumber, plywood, nails, etc.

MEDULLARY RAY: Rows of cells that run perpendicular to the annual rings toward the pith. Also called wood ray.

MESH: Openings formed by the crossing or weaving of a series of parallel threads or wires, as in a sieve.

MILLWORK: Parts or products made in a manufacturing plant (mill) using wood materials. Examples are moldings, door frames, doors, sashes, and window units.

MINERAL SPIRITS: Petroleum product used as a solvent in oil-base paint and varnish as a substitute for turpentine.

MITER: Joint formed by two members with equal angles.

MOISTURE CONTENT (M.C.): Weight of moisture contained in the wood stated as a percentage of the weight of the wood when kiln dried.

$$M. C. (\%) = \frac{\text{Wet Weight} - \text{Dry Weight}}{\text{Dry Weight}} \times 100$$

MOLDING: Piece of wood cut to a special shape or pattern.

MORTISE: Recess (usually rectangular) cut into a surface to receive another part, such as a tenon.

MULLION: Vertical dividing strip in a window used to separate window units.

MUNTIN: Dividing strip used to separate panes of glass in a window, or panels in panel construction.

N

NAPTHA: Volatile petroleum solvent used as a thinner to reduce enamel, oil-base paint, and varnish.

NATURAL RESINS: Gums and resins that are derived from trees. Used in finishes.

NOMINAL SIZE: Dimension of a piece of lumber before it is surfaced and dried. The term is generally applied to softwoods. Size is normally given to the next full inch in width and thickness. Also called rough size.

O

OIL STAIN: Stain having an oil base.

ON CENTER (O.C.): Layout method used to indicate spacing of members from the center of one to the center of the next.

OPEN-GRAINED: Wood having fibers with holes or pores that are visible without magnification.

OXIDIZE: Chemical reaction caused by materials combining with oxygen. This is part of the curing and drying process of such finishes as varnish, enamel, and oil-base paint.

P

PAINT: Term commonly referring to all protective coatings. Specifically, it is a mixture containing pigment and a vehicle, which can be spread in a thin film on surfaces.

PARING CUT: One of the two whittling cuts. It is made in a manner similar to peeling an apple. The knife is gripped in the dominant hand (right hand for right-handed people, left for left-handed people) and pulled toward the thumb. The thumb should be well below the cutting path. The hand holding the wood should be clear of the cutting path as well.

PARTICLEBOARD: Manufactured lumber product composed of wood particles and shavings bonded together with a synthetic resin.

PASTE WOOD FILLER: Material used to fill open-grained wood in preparation for other finish. It consists of ground silicon (silex), linseed oil, thinner, drier and coloring.

PENNY: Term referring to nail size, abbreviated by the letter "d".

PICTORIAL SKETCH: Method of sketching, resulting in a view of an object that appears approximately as it would by the eye.

PIGMENT: Fine, solid particles in paint that are insoluble in the liquid portion.

PITCH POCKET: Opening in lumber, along its annual rings, that holds or has held a resinous material.

PITH: The center of the cross section of a log or tree.

PLAIN-SAWED LUMBER (FLAT SAWED): Lumber made by sawing the entire log from end to end into lumber. Also called flatsawed lumber.

PLAN OF PROCEDURE: Operations for making a product, listed in a logical sequence.

PLANING MILL: Machine used to smooth the surfaces of rough lumber.

PLANK: Thick piece of stock that is 2- to 4-inches thick and 8-inches or more wide.

PLASTIC WOOD™: Manufactured material used to repair cracks, holes, and defects in wood.

PLUMB: Perpendicular to a level plane, or exactly vertical.

PLY: Term applied to plywood indicating the number of layers used in its manufacture.

PLYWOOD: Manufactured product made with crossbanded layers (plies) of veneer or solid center (core) bonded together with glue. An odd number of plies is always present in plywood.

PNEUMATIC: Related to or operated with air pressure.

POINTS PER INCH: Number of teeth (points) per inch for a saw or saw blade.

POLYMERIZATION: Chemical action in which molecules combine to form larger molecules. Part of the curing and drying process of certain finishing materials.

PROCESS: Planned operation performed in the development or fabrication of a problem or product.

PROPORTION: Ratio of the dimensions of a piece.

PULL: Device used as a handle to open a drawer or a door.

PUMICE: Organic substance made by pulverizing lava rock. Used as a fine abrasive to smooth final coats of certain finishes.

Q

QUARTER ROUND: Trim molding with one square corner and a cross section which forms one-fourth of a cylinder.

QUARTER-SAWN: Log is first cut into quarters and then each quarter is sawed into boards. This process exposes the medullary rays. It also shrinks and cups less.

QUARTER SLICED: Method of cutting layers of veneer from a log.

QUILL: Hollow sleeve on a drill press that rotates, carrying the spindle or mandrel.

R

RABBET: L-shaped recess cut at the end or along the edge of a piece of stock.

RAISED GRAIN: Swelled and loosened fibers on a wood surface caused by moisture.

RANDOM WIDTHS AND LENGTHS: Term used in selling hardwoods when specific lengths and widths may not be specified.

RATCHET: Mechanical device that allows a hand tool, such as a brace or screwdriver, to impart motion in close quarters. The teeth of a gear engage in a pawl to effect motion in one direction only.

REDUCE: To lower the viscosity (thickness) of a finishing material with a thinner or solvent.

REFORESTATION: Process of replanting small seedling trees as the mature trees are harvested.

RELATIVE HUMIDITY: Ratio of water vapor present in the air related to the maximum quantity of water vapor the air can hold at a given temperature.

RELIEF CUT: Cut made to allow a saw blade to cut around a sharp curve without binding.

RESAWING: Ripping a piece of stock to reduce its thickness or to make two thinner pieces.

RESILIENCE: Capability of wood placed under stress to return to its original shape.

RESPIRATOR: Breathing apparatus used to filter harmful particles from the air.

RETARDER: Substance added to a finishing material to prolong its curing and drying time.

ROTARY CUT: Method of cutting veneer by turning a log in a huge lathe against a broad knife with a continuous cut.

ROTTENSTONE: Rubbing and polishing compound made from finely pulverized limestone. It is used to smooth the final coat of certain finishes. Also called tripoli.

ROUGH: Unsurfaced lumber.

ROUGHING OUT: Removing as much of the waste wood from a product as possible. Usually done with a hand coping saw, jig saw, or band saw.

ROUT: To cut recesses into the surfaces or edges of wood including dados, rabbets, veins, coves, and mortises.

RUBBERIZED HAIR MATT: A cushioning material used in upholstering and carpeting.

RUNS: Abnormal flow of finishing material usually caused by excess application.

S

S2S: Surfaced on two sides. Lumber that has been surfaced on two sides.

S4S: Surfaced on four sides. Lumber that has been surfaced on four sides.

SAPWOOD: Outer portion of a log or tree that contains active cells. This is located between the heartwood and cambium layer.

SET: Term referring to amount that the teeth of a saw blade are bent to the side. Used to provide for clearance of the blade when sawing.

SCRAPING CUT: Cut made with the tool cutting edge held at approximately 90 degrees to the material.

SEALER: Finishing material used to seal the pores of close-grained wood. This is also used over stain or filler to prevent bleeding.

SEALER STAIN: Wood finish that combines sealer and stain.

SHAKE: Defect in wood that runs parallel to the annual rings of a board or log.

SHELLAC: Natural finishing material made by dissolving refined lac in denatured alcohol.

SHEARING CUT: Cut in which fibers are severed directly with a sharp cutting edge.

SILHOUETTE: A pattern that is traced on wood stock.

SILICON CARBIDE: Synthetic compound (bluish-black in color) made by fusing coke and silica at high temperatures. It is an extremely hard material used on tools where sharp, durable, cutting edges are needed. It is also crushed and used for abrasive paper and grinding wheels.

SLIPSTONE: Small whetstone having a cross section like a wedge. It is used in sharpening gouges and other cutting tools.

SLOYD KNIFE: Single-blade woodworker's knife used for laying out, carving, trimming, and slicing. Originated in the Scandinavian countries.

SOCKET CHISEL: Chisel with a tapered, hollow tang to receive a handle.

SOFFIT: Lowered section of a ceiling, or the underside of a cornice, beam, or arch.

SOFTWOOD: Wood that comes from conifers, or cone-bearing trees.

SOFTWOOD PLYWOOD: Plywood made entirely of softwood. There are about thirty species of softwoods used in the manufacture of plywood.

SOLIDS: Material remaining in a paint after its liquids have evaporated. In a paint formula, solids are usually indicated by a percentage of weight.

SPIKE: Large common nail, 16d to 60d.

SPINDLE: Shaft, arbor, or axle on which another revolving part or cutting tool can be mounted.

SPINE: The top of the knife (unsharpened edge).

SPIRIT STAIN: Aniline dye mixed with denatured alcohol, used to color wood.

SPLAYED: Pertains to the leg of a chair or table that angles outward in two directions from its seat or top.

SPLINE: Thin, wood reinforcing strip set in grooves cut in adjacent edges of a joint.

SPRAY GUN: Device that atomizes (forms a fine mist) finishing material so it can be applied by spraying in thin, uniform coats.

SPRINGWOOD: Part of the growth of wood in a tree that occurs early during the growing season.

SPUR CENTER: Headstock center that fits into the headstock spindle of a wood lathe.

STAB KNIFE: A chip carving knife utilized for making accents.

STAGGER: To place alternately (offset) from one side to the other of a line.

STAPLE: U-shaped fastener used in a stapler to attach such materials as roofing, tile, and insulation. Commonly used in upholstery.

STARVED JOINT: Wood joint that lacks a sufficient amount of glue to make a strong bond.

STICKERS: Strips of wood used between layers in a pile of lumber to allow air to circulate around each board.

STICK LACQUER OR SHELLAC: Lacquer or shellac in stick form. Used to fill imperfections around knots and other defects. It is available in a variety of colors.

STOCK CUTTING LIST: Pieces of lumber given in the bill of material, which have similar dimensions, are grouped together in larger pieces. This saves time and material when the pieces are cut to finish dimensions.

STRAIGHT CHIPS: A "V" cut (incised) into the surface of the wood. The first cut is made, then the wood is rotated and a second cut then completes the "V." This technique is used for curved as well as straight lines. Remember to pull (draw) the knife smoothly with even pressure.

STRAIGHTEDGE: Wood or metal strip with at least one true edge. It is used to lay out and check parts being processed.

STRESSED WOOD: Wood that is artificially stained and marked to make it appear to be old.

STRETCHER: Horizontal piece used as a tie in a framed structure to reinforce the legs of a table, chair, or desk.

STROP: A strip of leather attached to a piece of wood used to remove any burr left by the honing process. A fine abrasive such as white jeweler's rouge, aluminum oxide powder, or yellow strop compound is often rubbed onto the leather surface.

STRUCTURAL LUMBER: Similar to yard lumber, but it is over 5 inches in thickness and width.

SUMMERWOOD: Part of the growth of wood in a tree that occurs late during the growing season.

SURFACING: Machining a piece of stock using a power planer or hand plane to smooth the surface and to obtain the desired thickness.

SWING: Diameter of the largest piece that can be turned, or the largest circle that can be made by a tool or machine part.

T

TANG CHISEL: Chisel having a solid, tapered tang that is fitted into a handle.

TAPER: Gradual and uniform narrowing in size from one end toward the other of a hole, cylinder, or rectangular piece.

TEMPLATE: Piece of cardboard, metal, hardboard, or other material used as a guide to cut work, transfer a pattern, or check the accuracy of work.

TENON: Protruding part of a mortise and tenon joint.

TENSILE STRENGTH: Resistance of a piece of stock or other material to longitudinal stress (pulling).

THERMOPLASTIC: Resin that softens and becomes flexible each time it is heated.

TEXTURE: General physical appearance and feeling of wood.

THERMOSETTING: Resin that cures, sets, and becomes hard when subjected to heat. Once hardened, it will not resoften when exposed to heat.

THINNER: Liquid for reducing the consistency of a finishing material such as paint.

TIMBERS: Construction lumber with a large cross-sectional area. Generally timbers measure 5 inches or more in thickness and width.

TOENAILING: Attaching the end of a vertical piece to the surface of a horizontal piece with nails driven at an angle.

TONGUE: Protruding part of a tongue and groove joint.

TOOL: Device or instrument used to perform or aid in the performance of a manual or machine process.

TOOL REST: Mechanism for holding or positioning tools to perform cutting operations, such as a lathe tool rest.

TRACKING: Alignment of a blade on the wheels of a bandsaw or the belt on the drums of a belt sander.

TRADITIONAL FURNITURE: Furniture created in Europe, particularly during the 18th and 19th centuries. It is named for the rulers who ordered it built or for the craftsmen who originated it. Typical decorations include gilt, fretwork, carvings, claw and ball feet, and extravagant fabrics.

TRIAL ASSEMBLY: Dry (without glue) assembly of parts to check accuracy and function before final assembly.

TRIANGULAR CHIPS: Made in a similar manner as straight chips, except that three separate cuts are required. Normally, the grip is alternated from the first grip to the second grip and then back to the first grip to reduce the rotation of the stock.

TRIFACETED HOLE: The recess made by the cut of triangular chips.

TRIM: General term referring to a variety of decorative moldings and strips used to finish door and window openings, corners, edges along walls, ceilings, or floors.

TRUE EDGE: Edge that is straight, accurate, and forms a 90 degree angle to the working face. Also called working edge.

TUNG OIL: Drying oil used in water-resistant paints and varnishes. It is obtained from the nut of the Tung tree.

TURNING: Term referring to the use of cutting and shaping tools on the wood lathe. Also refers to the product produced on the lathe.

TURPENTINE: Volatile solvent used to reduce varnish, enamel, and oil-base paints. It is made by distilling gum obtained from certain types of pine trees.

TWIST: Warpage in a piece of lumber when both surfaces and edges are curved lengthwise. Also called wind.

U

UPHOLSTERY: Materials and hardware used to make a soft covering, commonly over a wood frame.

V

VARNISH: Durable, water-resistant finishing material composed of gums or synthetic resins, a vehicle (usually linseed oil or tung oil), and a thinner (such as turpentine).

VARNISH STAIN: Varnish with pigments added so that both stain and varnish are applied at one time.

VEHICLE: Portion of wood finish that is liquid.

VENEER: Thin sheet of wood often laminated to core stock to make plywood or paneling. It is cut, sliced, or sawn from a log, cant, or flitch. When combined with other veneers in plywood, it is sometimes referred to as a ply.

VENEER-CORE PLYWOOD: Plywood made by bonding crossbands of veneers, each band being at right angles to the adjacent bands.

VOLATILE LIQUID: Liquid that evaporates.

W

WANE: Defect in wood characterized by bark or lack of wood along an edge or at a corner of a piece of stock.

WARP: Any variation of shape in lumber from a true surface or edge. This includes cup, bow, wind (twist), and crook.

WASH COAT: Thin coat of sealer, usually shellac or lacquer sealer, applied over stain or paste wood filler.

WATER PUTTY: Dry powder that is mixed with water to form a paste. Used to fill defects in wood surfaces.

WATER STAIN: Wood stain made by dissolving water-soluble colored pigments in water.

WEBBING: Thin, woven strap used to form the support for a stool, chair, or other upholstered seat.

WELT: Cloth covered cord used to form edges in upholstery.

WITH THE GRAIN: Toward the direction or growth pattern of wood fibers.

WORKING DRAWING: Scaled, orthographic drawing usually with two or more views.

Y

YARD LUMBER: Lumber usually available at retail lumber yards consisting of select (finish) grades and common (utility) grades.

INDEX

Casing, 125
Common, 125
Driving, 126
Escutcheon, 125
Finish, 125
Pulling, 126
Ring-shank, 126
Rubber headed, 129
Spiral-shank, 125
Wire nails, 125
Non-grain raising stains, 148
Number 1 common, 15
Numerical control, 168

O

Office manager, 175
Oil, linseed, 152
Oil stain, 147
  Pigments, 147
  Vehicle, 147
Open-grained, 9
Outfeed stand, 60
Outfeed table, 90
Oval head wood screw, 127
Overarm (pin) router, 112
Overcut, 76
Oxalic acid, 146

P

Paint, 151
Panels, manufactured, 18
Paring out, 164
Particleboard, 18
Paste wood fillers, 148
Patternmakers, 186
Pencils, awls, sloyd knives, 40
Pigments, 147
Pilot hole, 128
Pin router, 112
Pitch pocket, 13
Pith, 8
Plan of procedure, 31
Plane, block, 81
Plane iron, 81
Plane iron cap, 81
Planer, 93
Planer or surfacer, 93
  Chip breaker, 93
  Cutterhead, 93
  Lower infeed roller, 93
  Planing stock, 94
  Pressure bar, 93
  Safety and care, 94
  Upper infeed roller, 93

Plane iron cap, 81
Planes, 81–95
  Block plane, 81
  Care and adjustment, 82
  Jack planes and smooth, 81
  Jointer planes and fore, 81
  Portable power, 92
  Router planes and rabbet, 81
Planing, hand, 81–88
  Power, 89–95
Planning, 24–32
Plastic resin glue, 132
Plastic Wood, 145
Plastics cement, 132
Plate, 104–105
  Attachment, 129
Plate joiner, 105
  Safety and care, 105
Plate joinery, 104–105
Plies, 17
Plunge cut, 51
Plycore, 16
Plywood, 16
Plywood, and veneer, 15
Plywood, composition core, 17
  Hardwood plywood, 17
  Lumber core, 17
  Mineral core, 17
  Plycore, 16
  Softwood, 17
Pocket, pitch, 13
Point, fiber saturation, 12
Points, dividers, compass, and trammel, 41
Points, dowel, 98
Points, trammel, 41
Polishing compounds, 138
  FF, FFF, 138
  Pumice, 138
  Rottenstone, 138
Polyurethane, 151
Pores, 9
Position ring guard, 115
Power miter saw, 62
Power planing, 89–95
Pressure bar, 93
Profit, 172
Proportion, 24
Pulls and knobs, 157
Pumice, 138
Purchasing agent, 176
Push drill, 70
Putty, wood putty and water, 145
Putty sticks, 145

Q

Quarter sawing, 11
Quarter slicing, 16